LANDMARKS IN
RUSSIAN LITERATURE

Maurice Baring did more than any other
critic of his time to spread the appreciation
of Russian letters among English-speaking
people.

This paperback edition of his book has an
extra chapter on Russian poetry—a subject
that was largely ignored in the original
work. This chapter is a reprint of Maurice
Baring's introduction to *The Oxford Book
of Russian Verse*.

UNIVERSITY PAPERBACKS

U.P. 7

LANDMARKS
IN RUSSIAN LITERATURE

by

MAURICE BARING

UNIVERSITY PAPERBACKS

METHUEN : LONDON
BARNES & NOBLE : NEW YORK

First published by Methuen & Co Ltd in
March 1910, and reprinted twice
First published in this series in 1960
Printed in Great Britain by
Cox & Wyman Ltd
London, Fakenham and Reading
Catalogue No. (Methuen) 2/6757/27

University Paperbacks are published
by METHUEN & CO LTD
36 Essex Street, Strand, London WC2
and BARNES & NOBLE INC
105 Fifth Avenue, New York 3

Contents

Publisher's Note

The author says little in this book about Russian poetry. We have therefore, with the kind permission of the Oxford University Press, included at the end the Introduction which Maurice Baring wrote for *The Oxford Book of Russian Verse*.

The reader should remember that except for Chapter VIII Maurice Baring wrote *Landmarks in Russian Literature* in 1910. We have left his text almost entirely unchanged.

Preface

THE CHAPTERS IN this book on Tolstoy and Tourgeniev, and those on Chekov and Gogol have appeared before. That on Tolstoy and Tourgeniev in *The Quarterly Review*; those on Chekov and Gogol in *The New Quarterly*; my thanks are due to the Editors and Proprietors concerned for their kindness in allowing me to reprint these chapters here.

The chapter on Russian Characteristics appeared in *St. George's Magazine*; the rest of the book is new. In writing it I consulted, besides many books and articles in the Russian language, the following:

The Works of Turgeniev. Translated by Constance Garnett. Fifteen vols. London: Heinemann, 1906.

The Complete Works of Count Tolstoy. Translated and edited by Leo Wiener. Twenty-four vols. London: Dent, 1904–5.

La Roman Russe. By the Vicomte E. M. de Vogüé. Paris: Plon, 1897.

Tolstoy as Man and Artist: with an Essay on Dostoievski. By Dimitri Merejkowski. London: Constable, 1902.[1]

Ivan Turgeniev: la Vie et l'Œuvre. By Émile Haumant. Paris: Armand Colin, 1906.

The Life of Tolstoy. First Fifty Years. By Aylmer Maude. London: Constable, 1908.

A Literary History of Russia. By Prof. A. Brückner. Edited by Ellis H. Minns. Translated by H. Havelock. London and Leipsig: Fisher Unwin, 1908.

Realities and Ideals of Russian Literature. By Prince Kropotkin.

[1] This is an abridgement of a larger book by the author.

Russian Poetry and Progress. By Mrs. Newmarch. John Lane.

By far the best estimate of Tolstoy's work I have come across in England in the last few years was a brilliant article published in the Literary Supplement of *The Times*, I think in 1907, which, it is to be hoped, will be republished.

Introduction

A BOOK DEALING with the literature of a foreign country appeals to a double audience: the narrow circle of people who are intimately familiar with that literature in its original tongue, and the large public which is imperfectly acquainted even with translations of some of its books. One of these audiences must necessarily be sacrificed. For if you address yourself exclusively to the specialists, the larger public will be but faintly interested; while if you have the larger public in view alone, the narrower circle of those who are familiar with the language will hear nothing from you which they do not already know too well. In the case of a literature such as Russian, it is obvious which audience has the claim to the greater consideration; but while this book is addressed to those who are interested in but not intimately familiar with Russian literature, I entertain the hope that these essays may not prove entirely uninteresting to the closer students of Russian. I have tried to make a compromise, and while especially addressing myself to the majority, not to lose sight of the minority altogether.

The standpoint from which I approach Russian literature is less that of the scholar than of an admiring and sympathetic friend. I have tried to understand what the Russians themselves think about their own literature, and in some manner to reflect their point of view as it struck me either in their books or in conversation with many men and women of many classes throughout several years.

It has always seemed to me that there are two ways of writing about a foreign literature: from the outside and from the inside. Take a language like French, for instance, and the study of French poetry in particular. Many English students of

French poetry seem to me to start from the point of view that although much French verse has many excellent qualities, those qualities which are peculiarly French and which the French themselves admire most are not worth admiring. Thus it is that we have had many excellent critics telling us that although the French poetry of the Renaissance is admirable and the French Romantic epoch produced men of astounding genius, yet the poets of another sort, whom the French set up on a permanent pinnacle as models of classic perfection, such as Racine or La Fontaine, are not poets at all. Some critics have even gone further, and have maintained that admirable as the French language is as an instrument for writing prose, it cannot properly be used as a vehicle for writing poetry, and that French poetry cannot be considered as being in the same category or on the same footing as the verse of other nations. This is what I call the outside view, and I am not only not persuaded of its truth, but I am convinced that it is false, for two reasons:

First, because I cannot help thinking that the natives of a country must be the best judges of their own tongue and of its literature, and that foreign critics, however acute, may fail to appreciate certain shades of meaning and sound which particularly appeal to the native—for instance, I am sure it is more difficult for a foreigner to appreciate the music of Milton's diction than for an Englishman. Secondly, since I learnt French at the same time as I learnt English, and became familiar with French verse long before I was introduced to the works of English poets, from my childhood up to the present day French poetry has seemed to me to be just as beautiful as the poetry of any other country, and the verse of Racine as musical as that of Milton. I have, moreover, sometimes suspected that the severe sentences I have seen passed on the French classics by English critics were perhaps due to imperfect familiarity with the language in question, and that it even seemed possible that in condemning French verse they were ignorant of the French laws of metre and scansion; such ignorance would certainly prove a serious obstacle to proper appreciation.

This digression is to make clear what I mean when I say that I have tried to approach my subject from the inside; that is to say, I have tried to put myself into the skin of a Russian, and to look at the literature of Russia with his eyes, and then to explain to my fellow-countrymen as clearly as possible what I have seen. I do not say I have succeeded, but I have been greatly encouraged in the task by having received appreciative thanks for my former efforts in this direction from Russians who are, in my opinion, the only critics competent to judge whether what I have written about their people and their books hits the mark or not.

One of the great difficulties in writing studies of various Russian writers is the paradoxical thread that runs through the Russian character. Russia is the land of paradoxes. The Russian character and temperament are baffling, owing to the paradoxical elements which are found united in them. It is for this reason that a series of studies dealing with different aspects of the Russian character often have the appearance of being a series of contradictory statements. I have therefore in the first chapter of this book stated what I consider to be the chief paradoxical elements of the Russian character. It is the conflicting nature of these elements which accounts for the seemingly contradictory qualities that we meet with in Russian literature. For instance, there is a passive element in the Russian nature; there is also something unbridled, a spirit which breaks all bounds of self-control and runs riot; and there is also a stubborn element, a tough obstinacy. The result is that at one moment one is pointing out the matter-of-fact side of the Russian genius which clings to the earth and abhors extravagance; and at another time one is discoursing on the passion certain Russian novelists have for making their characters wallow in abstract discussions; or, again, the cheerfulness of Gogol has to be reconciled with the 'inspissated gloom' of certain other writers. All this makes it easy for a critic to bring the charge of inconsistency against a student whose object is to provide certain sidelights on certain striking examples, rather than a comprehensive view of the whole, a task which is beyond the scope and powers of the present writer.

The student of Russian literature who wishes for a comprehensive view of the whole of Russian literature and of its historic significance and development, cannot do better than read Professor Brückner's solid and brilliant *Literary History of Russia*, which is admirably translated into English.

The object of my book is to interest the reader in Russia and Russian literature, and to enable him to make up his mind as to whether he wishes to seek after a more intimate knowledge of the subject.

The authors whose work forms the subject of this book belong to the period which began in the fifties and ended before the Russo-Japanese War. The work of Tchekov represents the close of that epoch which began with Gogol. After Tchekov the dawn of a new era was marked by the startling advent of Maxim Gorky into Russian literature. Then came the war, and with it a torrent of new writers, of new thoughts, of new schools, of new theories of art. The most remarkable of these writers is no doubt Andreev; but in order to discuss his work as well as that of other writers who followed in his train, it would be necessary to write another book. The student of Russian literature will notice that I have omitted many Russian authors who are well known in the epoch which I have chosen. I have omitted them for reasons which I have already stated at the beginning of this Introduction, namely, that there is not in England a large enough circle of readers interested in Russian literature to the extent of wishing to read about its less well-known writers. I think the authors I have chosen are typical of the generations they represent, and I hope that this book may have the effect of leading readers from books *about* Russia and Russian literature, to the country itself and its books, so that they may be able to see with their own eyes and to correct the impressions which they have received secondhand.

CHAPTER I

Russian Characteristics

THE DIFFICULTY IN explaining anything to do with Russia to an English public is that confusion is likely to arise owing to the terms used being misunderstood. For instance, if one describes a Russian officer, a Russian bureaucrat, a Russian public servant, or a Russian schoolmaster, the reader involuntarily makes a mental comparison with corresponding people in his own country, or in other European countries where he has travelled. He necessarily fails to remember that there are certain vital differences between Russians and people of other countries, which affect the whole question, and which make the Russian totally different from the corresponding Englishman. I wish before approaching the work of Russian writers, to sketch a few of the main characteristics which lie at the root of the Russian temperament by which Russian literature is profoundly affected.

The principal fact which has struck me with regard to the Russian character, is a characteristic which was once summed up by Professor Milioukov thus: 'A Russian,' he said, 'lacks the cement of hypocrisy.' This cement, which plays so important a part in English public and private life, is totally lacking in the Russian character. The Russian character is plastic; the Russian can understand everything. You can mould him any way you please. He is like wet clay, yielding and malleable; he is passive; he bows his head and gives in before the decrees of Fate and of Providence. At the same time, it would be a mistake to say that this is altogether a sign of weakness. There is a kind of toughness in the Russian character, an irreducible obstinacy which makes for strength; otherwise the Russian Empire would not exist. But where the want of the cement of hypocrisy is most noticeable, is in the personal relations of

Russians towards their fellow-creatures. They do not in the least mind openly confessing things of which people in other countries are ashamed; they do not mind admitting to dishonesty, immorality, or cowardice, if they happen to feel that they are saturated with these defects; and they feel that their fellow-creatures will not think the worse of them on this account, because they know that their fellow-creatures will understand. The astounding indulgence of the Russians arises out of this infinite capacity for understanding.

Another point: This absence of hypocrisy causes them to have an impatience of cant and of convention. They will constantly say: 'Why not?' They will not recognize the necessity of drawing the line somewhere, they will not accept as something binding the conventional morality and the artificial rules of conduct which knit together our society with a bond of steel. They may admit the expediency of social laws, but they will never prate of the laws of any society being divine; they will merely admit that they are convenient. Therefore, if we go to the root of this matter, it comes to this: that the Russians are more broadly and widely human than the people of other European or Eastern countries, and, being more human, their capacity of understanding is greater, for their extraordinary quickness of apprehension comes from the heart rather than from the head. They are the most humane and the most naturally kind of all the peoples of Europe, or, to put it differently and perhaps more accurately, I should say that there is more humanity and more kindness in Russia than in any other European country. This may startle the reader; he may think of the lurid accounts in the newspapers of massacres, brutal treatment of prisoners, and various things of this kind, and be inclined to doubt my statement. As long as the world exists there will always be a certain amount of cruelty in the conduct of human beings. My point is this: that there is less in Russia than in other countries, but the trouble up to the last two years has been that all excesses of any kind on the part of officials were unchecked and uncontrolled. Therefore, if any man who had any authority over any other man happened to be brutal, his brutality had a far wider scope and far richer opportunities than that of a corresponding overseer in another country.

During the last three years Russia has been undergoing a violent evolutionary process of change, what in other countries has been called a revolution; but compared with similar phases in other countries, and taking into consideration the size of the Russian Empire, and the various nationalities which it contains, I maintain that the proportion of excesses has been comparatively less. There are other factors in the question which should also be borne in mind; firstly, that politically Russia is about a century behind other European countries, and the second is that Russians accept the fact that a man who does wrong deserves punishment, with a kind of Oriental fatality, although the pity which is inherent in them causes them to have a horror of capital punishment.

Now, let us take the first question, and just imagine for a moment what the treatment of the poor would be in England were there no such thing as a *habeas corpus*. Imagine what the position of the police would be, if it held a position of arbitrary dominion; if nobody were responsible; if any policeman could do what he chose, with no further responsibility than that towards his superior officers. I do not hesitate to say that were such a state of things to exist in England, the position of the poor would be intolerable. Now, the position of the poor in Russia is not intolerable; it is bad, owing to the evils inseparable from poverty, drink, and the want of control enjoyed by public servants. But it is not intolerable. Were it intolerable, the whole of the Russian poor, who number ninety millions, would have long ago risen to a man. They have not done so because their position is not intolerable; and the reason of this is, that the evils to which I have alluded are to a certain extent mitigated by the good-nature and kindness inherent in the Russian temperament, instead of being aggravated by an innate brutality and cruelty such as we meet with in Latin and other races.

Again, closely connected with any political system which is backward, you will always find in any country a certain brutality in the matter of punishments. Perhaps the cause of this—which is the reason why torture was employed in the Middle Ages, and why it is employed in China at the present day—is that only a small percentage of the criminal classes are ever arrested; therefore when a criminal is caught, his treatment is often unduly severe. If you read, for instance, the sentences of corporal punishment, etc., which were passed in England in the eighteenth century by county judges, or of the punishments which were the rule in the Duke of Wellington's army in the Peninsular War, they will make your hair stand on end by their incredible brutality; and England in the eighteenth century was politically more advanced than Russia is at the present day.

With regard to the second point, the attitude of Russians towards the question of punishments displays a curious blend of opinion. While they are more indulgent than any other people when certain vices and defects are concerned, they are ruthless in enforcing and accepting the necessity of punishment in the case of certain other criminal offences. For instance, they are completely indulgent with regard to any moral delinquencies, but unswervingly stern in certain other matters; and although they would often be inclined to let off a criminal, saying: 'Why should he be punished?' at the same time if he is punished, and severely punished, they will accept the matter as a part of the inevitable system that governs the world. On the other hand, they are indulgent and tolerant where moral delinquencies which affect the man himself and not the community are concerned; that is to say, they will not mind how often or how violently a man gets drunk, because the matter affects only himself; but they will bitterly resent a man stealing horses, because thereby the whole community is affected.

This attitude of mind is reflected in the Russian Code of Laws. The Russian Penal Code, as M. Leroy-Beaulieu points out in his classic book on Russia, is the most lenient in Europe. But the trouble is, as the Liberal members of the Duma are constantly repeating, not that the laws in Russia are bad, but that they are overridden by the arbitrary conduct of individual officials. However, I do not wish in this article to dwell on the causes of political discontent in Russia, or on the evils of the bureaucratic régime. My object is simply to point out certain characteristics of the Russian race, and one of these characteristics is the leniency of the punishment laid down by law for offences which in other countries are dealt with drastically and severely; murder, for instance. Capital punishment was abolished in Russia as long ago as 1753 by the Empress Elizabeth; corporal punishment subsisted only among the peasants, administered by themselves (and not by a magistrate) according to their own local administration, until it was abolished by the present Emperor in 1904. So that until the revolutionary movement began, cases of capital punishment, which only occurred in virtue of martial law, were rare, and from 1866 to 1903 only 114 men suffered the penalty of death throughout the whole of the Russian Empire, including the outlying districts such as Caucasus, Transbaikalia, and Turkestan;[1] and even at the present moment, when the country is still practically governed by martial law, which was established in order to cope with the revolutionary movement, you can in Russia kill a man and only receive a few years' imprisonment. It is the contrast of the lenient treatment meted out to non-political prisoners with the severity exercised towards political offenders which strikes the Russian politician today, and it is of this contradiction that he so bitterly complains. The fact, nevertheless, remains—in spite of the cases, however numerous, which arose out of the extraordinary situation created by the revolutionary movement, that the sentence of death, meted out by the judicial court, is in itself abhorrent to the Russian character.

I will now give a few minor instances illustrating the indulgent attitude of the Russian character towards certain moral delinquencies. In a regiment which I came across in Manchuria during the war there were two men; one was conscientious, brave to the verge of heroism, self-sacrificing, punctilious in the performance of his duty, and exacting in the demands he made on others as to the fulfilment of theirs, untiringly energetic, competent in every way, but severe and uncompromising. There was another man who was incurably lax

[1] See Tagantseff, *Russian Criminal Law*.

in the performance of his duty, not scrupulously honest where the Government money was concerned, incompetent, but as kind as a human being can be. I once heard a Russian doctor who was attached to this regiment discussing and comparing the characters of the two men, and, after weighing the pros and cons, he concluded that as a man the latter was superior. Dishonestly in dealings with the public money seemed to him an absolutely trifling fault. The unswerving performance of duty, and all the great military qualities which he noted in the former, did not seem to him to count in the balance against the great kindness of heart possessed by the latter; and most of the officers agreed with him. It never seemed to occur to these men that any one set of qualities, such as efficiency, conscientious-ness, or honesty, were more indispensable, or in any way superior to any other set of qualities. They just noticed the absence of them in others, or, as often happened, in themselves, and thought they were amply compensated for by the presence of other qualities, such as good-nature or amiability. And one notices in Russian literature that authors such as Dostoievsky are not content with showing us the redeeming points of a merely bad character, that is to say, of a man fundamentally good, but who indulges in vice or in crime; but they will take pleasure in showing you the redeeming points of a character which at first sight appears to be radically mean and utterly despicable. The aim of these authors seems to be to insist that, just as nobody is indispensable, so nobody is superfluous. There is no such thing as a superfluous man; and any man, however worthless, miserable, despicable and mean he may seem to be, has just as much right to be understood as any one else; and they show that, when he is understood, he is not, taking him as a whole, any worse than his fellow-creatures.

Another characteristic which strikes one in Russian litera-ture, and still more in Russian life, especially if one has mingled in the lower classes, is the very deeply rooted sense of pity which the Russians possess. An Englishman who is lame, and whom I met in Russia, told me that he had experienced there a treatment such as he had never met before in any other country. The people, and especially the poor, noticed his lameness, and, guessing what would be difficult for him to do, came to his aid and helped him.

In the streets of Moscow and St Petersburg you rarely see beggars beg in vain; and I have observed, travelling third class in trains and in steamers, that when the poor came to beg bread for food off the poor, they were never sent empty away. During the war I always found the soldiers ready to give me food, however little they had for themselves, in circumstances when they would have been quite justified in sending me about my business as a pestilential nuisance and camp-follower. It is impossible for a man to starve in Russia. He is perfectly certain to find some one who will give him food for the asking. In Siberia the peasants in the villages put bread on their window-sills, in case any fugitive prisoners should be passing by. This fundamental goodness of heart is the most important fact in the Russian nature; it, and the expression of it in their literature, is the greatest contribution which they have made to the history of the world. It is probably the cause of all their weakness. For the defects indispensable to such qualities are slackness, and the impossibility of conceiving self-discipline to be a necessity, or of recognizing the conventional rules and prejudices which make for solidity, and which are, as Professor Milioukov said, as cement is to a building.

The result of the absence of this hard and binding cement of prejudice and discipline is that it is very difficult to attain a standard of efficiency in matters where efficiency is indispensable. For instance, in war. In a regiment with which I lived for a time during the war there was a young officer who absolutely insisted on the maintenance of a high standard of efficiency. He insisted on his orders being carried out to the letter; his fellow-officers thought he was rather mad. One day we had arrived in a village, and one of the younger officers had ordered the horses to be put up in the yard facing the house in which we were to live. Presently the officer to whom I have alluded arrived, and ordered the horses to be taken out and put into a separate yard, as he considered the arrangement which he found on his arrival to be insanitary—which it was. He went away, and the younger officer did not dream of carrying out his order.

'What is the use?' he said, 'the horses may just as well stay where they are.'

They considered this man to be indulging in an unnecessary pose, but he was not, according to our ideas, in the least a formalist or a lover of red tape; he merely insisted on what he considered to be an irreducible minimum of discipline, the result being that he was a square peg in a round hole. Moreover, when people committed, or commit (and this is true in any department of public life in Russia), a glaring offence, or leave undone an important part of their duty, it is very rare that they are dealt with drastically; they are generally threatened with punishment which ends in platonic censure. And this fact, combined with a bureaucratic system, has dangerous results, for the official often steps beyond the limits of his duty and takes upon himself to commit lawless acts, and to exercise unlawful and arbitrary functions, knowing perfectly well that he can do so with impunity, and that he will not be punished. And one of the proofs that a new era is now beginning in Russia is a series of phenomena never before witnessed, and which have occurred not long ago—namely, the punishment and dismissal of guilty officials, such as, for instance, that of Gurko, who was dismissed from his post in the Government for having been responsible for certain dishonest dealings in the matter of the Famine Relief.

Of course such indulgence, or rather the slackness resulting from it, is not universal. Otherwise the whole country would go to pieces. And yet so far from going to pieces, even through a revolution things jogged on somehow or other. For against every square yard of slackness there is generally a square inch of exceptional capacity, and a square foot of dogged efficiency, and thus the balance is restored. The incompetency of a Stoessel, and a host of others, is counterbalanced not only by the brilliant energy of a Kondratenko, but by the hard work of thousands of unknown men. And this is true throughout all public life in Russia. At the same time, the happy-go-lucky element, the feeling of 'What does it matter?' of what they call *nichevo*, is the preponderating quality; and it is only so far counterbalanced by sterner qualities as to make the machine go on. This accounts also for the apparent weakness of the revolutionary element in Russia. The ranks of these people, which at one moment appear to be so formidable, at the next moment seem to have scattered to the four winds of heaven. They appear to give in and to accept, to submit and be resigned to fate. But there is nevertheless an undying passive resistance; and at the bottom of the Russian character, whether that character be employed in revolutionary or in other channels, there is an obstinate grit of resistance. Again, one is met in Russian history, from the days of Peter the Great down to the present day, with isolated instances of exceptional energy and of powers of organization, such as Souvorov, Skobelieff, Todteleben, Kondratenko, Kilkov, and, to take a less known instance, Kroustalieff (who played a leading part in organizing the working classes during the great strike in 1905).

The way in which troops were poured into Manchuria during the war across a single line, which was due to the brilliant organization of Prince Kilkov, is in itself a signal instance of organization and energy in the face of great material difficulties. The station at Liaoyang was during the war under the command of a man whose name I have forgotten, but who showed the same qualities of energy and resource. On the day Liaoyang was evacuated, and while the station was being shelled, he managed to get off every train safely, and to leave nothing behind. There were many such instances which are at present little known, to be set against the incompetence and mismanagement of which one hears so much.

It is perhaps this blend of opposite qualities, this mixture of softness and slackness and happy-go-lucky *insouciance* (all of which qualities make a thing as pliant as putty and as yielding as dough) with the infinite capacity for taking pains, and the inspiring energy and undefeated patience in the face of seemingly insuperable obstacles, which makes the Russian character difficult to understand. You have, on the one hand, the man who bows his head before an obstacle and says that it does not after all matter very much; and, on the other hand, the man who with a few straws succeeds in making a great palace of bricks. Peter the Great was just such a man, and Souvorov and Kondratenko were the same in kind, although less in degree. And again, you have the third type, the man who, though utterly defeated, and apparently completely submissive, persists in resisting—the passive resister whose obstinacy is unlimited, and whose influence in matters such as the revolutionary propaganda is incalculable.

It has been constantly said that Russia is the land of paradoxes, and there is perhaps no greater paradox than the mixture in the Russian character of obstinacy and weakness, and the fact that the Russian is sometimes inclined to throw up the sponge instantly, while at others he becomes himself a tough sponge, which, although pulled this way and that, is never pulled to pieces. He is undefeated and indefatigable in spite of enormous odds, and thus we are confronted in Russian history with men as energetic as Peter the Great, and as slack as Alexeieff the Viceroy.

People talk of the waste of Providence in never making a ruby without a flaw, but is it not rather the result of an admirable economy, which never deals out a portion of coffee without a certain admixture of chicory?

CHAPTER II

Realism of Russian Literature

THE MOMENT A writer nowadays mentions the word 'realism' he risks the danger of being told that he is a disciple of a particular school, and that he is bent on propagating a peculiar and exclusive theory of art. If, however, Russian literature is to be discussed at all, the word 'realism' cannot be avoided. So it will be as well to explain immediately and clearly what I mean when I assert that the main feature of both Russian prose and Russian verse is its closeness to nature, its love of reality, which for want of a better word one can only call realism. When the word 'realism' is employed with regard to literature, it gives rise to two quite separate misunderstandings: this is unavoidable, because the word has been used to denote special schools and theories of art which have made a great deal of noise both in France and England and elsewhere.

The first misunderstanding arises from the use of the word by a certain French school of novelists who aimed at writing scientific novels in which the reader should be given slices of raw life; and these novelists strove by an accumulation of detail to produce the effect of absolute reality. The best known writers of this French school did not succeed in doing this, although they achieved striking results of a different character. For instance, Emile Zola was successful when he wrote epic panoramas on subjects such as life in a mine, life in a huge shop, or life during a great war; that is to say, he was poetically successful when he painted with a broad brush and set great crowds in motion. He produced striking pictures, but the effect of them at their best was a poetic, romantic effect. When he tried to be realistic, and scientifically realistic, when he endeavoured to say everything by piling detail on detail, he merely succeeded in being tedious and disgusting. And so far from telling the whole truth, he produced an effect of distorted exaggeration such as one receives from certain kinds of magnifying and distorting mirrors.

The second misunderstanding with regard to the word 'realism' is this. Certain people think that if you say an author strives to attain an effect of truth and reality in his writings, you must necessarily mean that he is without either the wish or the power to select, and that his work is therefore chaotic. Not long ago, in a book of short sketches, I included a very short and inadequate paper on certain aspects of the Russian stage; and in mentioning Tchekov, the Russian dramatist, I made the following statement: 'The Russian stage simply aims at one thing: to depict everyday life, not exclusively the brutality of everyday life, nor the tremendous catastrophes befalling human beings, nor to devise intricate problems and far-fetched cases of conscience in which human beings might possibly be entangled. It simply aims at presenting glimpses of human beings as they really are, and by means of such glimpses it opens out avenues and vistas into their lives.' I added further that I considered such plays would be successful in any country.

A reviewer, commenting on this in an interesting article, said that these remarks revealed the depth of my error with regard to realism. 'As if the making of such plays,' wrote the reviewer, 'were not the perpetual aim of dramatists! But a dramatist would be putting chaos and not real life on the stage if he presented imitations of unselected people doing unselected things at unselected moments. The idea which binds the drama together, an idea derived by reason from experience of life at large, is the most real and lifelike part in it, if the drama is a good one.'

Now I am as well aware as this reviewer, or as any one else, that it is the perpetual aim of dramatists to make such plays. But it is an aim which they often fail to achieve. For instance, we have had, during the last thirty years in England and France, many successful and striking plays in which the behaviour of the characters although effective from a theatrical point of view, is totally unlike the behaviour of men and women in real life. Again, when I wrote of the Russian stage, I never for a moment suggested that the Russian dramatist did, or that any dramatist should, present imitations of unselected people doing unselected things at unselected moments. As my sketch was a short one, I was not able to go into the question in full detail, but I should have thought that if one said that a play was true to life, and at the same time theatrically and dramatically successful, that is to say, interesting to a large audience, an ordinary reader would have taken for granted (as many of my readers did take for granted) that in the work of such dramatists there must necessarily have been selection.

Later on in this book I shall deal at some length with the plays of Anton Tchekov, and in discussing that writer, I hope to make it clear that his work, so far from presenting imitations of unselected people doing unselected things at unselected moments, are imitations of selected but real people, doing selected but probable things at selected but interesting moments. But the difference between Tchekov and most English and French dramatists (save those of the quite modern school) is, that the moments which Tchekov selects appear at first sight to be trivial. His genius consists in the power of revealing the dramatic significance of the seemingly trivial. It stands to reason, as I shall try to point out later on, that the more realistic your play, the more it is true to life; the less obvious action there is in it, the greater must be the skill of the dramatist; the surer his art, the more certain his power of construction, the nicer his power of selection.

Mr Max Beerbohm once pointed this out by an apt illustration. 'The dramatist,' he said, 'who deals in heroes, villains, buffoons, queer people who are either doing or suffering either tremendous or funny things, has a very valuable advantage over the playwright who deals merely in humdrum you and me. The dramatist has his material as a springboard. The adramatist must leap as best he can on the hard high road, the adramatist must be very much an athlete.'

That is just it: many of the modern (and ancient) Russian playwriters are adramatists. But they are extremely athletic; and so far from their work being chaotic, they sometimes give evidence, as in the case of Tchekov, of a supreme mastery over the construction and architectonics of drama, as well as of an unerring instinct for what will be telling behind footlights, although at first sight their choice does not seem to be obviously dramatic.

Therefore, everything I have said so far can be summed up in two statements: Firstly, that Russian literature, because it deals with realism, has nothing in common with the work of certain French 'Naturalists,' by whose work the word 'realism' has achieved so wide a notoriety, secondly, Russian literature, although it is realistic, is not necessarily chaotic, and contains many supreme achievements in the art of selection. But I wish to discuss the peculiar quality of Russian realism, because it appears to me that it is this quality which differentiates Russian literature from the literature of other countries.

I have not dealt in this book with Russian poets, firstly, because the number of readers who are familiar with Russian poetry in its original tongue is limited; and, secondly, because it appears to me impossible to discuss Russian poetry, if one is forced to deal in translations, since no translation, however good, can give the reader an idea either of the music, the atmosphere, or the charm of the original. But it is in Russian poetry that the quality of Russian realism is perhaps most clearly made manifest. Any reader familiar with German literature will, I think, agree that if one compares French or English poetry with German poetry, and French and English Romanticism with German Romanticism, one is conscious, when one approaches the work of the Germans, of entering into a more sober and more quiet dominion; one leaves behind one the exuberance of England: 'the purple patches' of a Shakespeare, the glowing richness of a Keats, the soaring rainbow fancies of a Shelley, the wizard horizons of a Coleridge. One also leaves behind one the splendid rhetoric and glitter of France: the clarions of Corneille, the harps and flutes of Racine, the great many-piped organ of Victor Hugo, the stormy pageants of Musset, the gorgeous lyricism of Flaubert, the jewelled dreams of Gautier, and all the colour and the pomp of the Parnassians. One leaves all these things behind, and one steps into a world of quiet skies, rustling leaves, peaceful meadows, and calm woods, where the birds twitter cheerfully and are answered by the plaintive notes of pipe or reed, or interrupted by the homely melody, sometimes cheerful and sometimes sad, of the wandering fiddler.

In this country, it is true, we have visions and vistas of distant hills and great brooding waters, of starlit nights and magical twilights; in this country, it is also true that we hear the echoes of magic horns, the footfall of the fairies, the tinkling hammers of the sedulous Kobolds, and the champing and the neighing of the steeds of Chivalry. But there is nothing wildly fantastic, nor portentously exuberant, nor gorgeously dazzling; nothing tempestuous, unbridled, or extreme. When the Germans have wished to express such things, they have done so in their music; they certainly have not done so in their poetry. What they have done in their poetry, and what they have done better than any one else, is to express in the simplest of all words the simplest of all thoughts and feelings. They have spoken of first love, of spring and the flowers, the smiles and tears of children, the dreams of youth and the musings of old age—with a simplicity, a homeliness no writers of any other country have ever excelled. And when they deal with the super-natural, with ghosts, fairies, legends, deeds of prowess or phantom lovers, there is a quaint homeliness about the recital of such things, as though they were being told by the fireside in a cottage, or being sung on the village green to the accompaniment of a hurdy-gurdy. To many Germans the phantasy of a Shelley or of a Victor Hugo is essentially alien and unpalatable. They feel as though they were listening to men who are talking too loud and too wildly, and they merely wish to get away or to stop their ears. Again, poets like Keats or Gautier often produce on them the impression that they are listening to sensuous and meaningless echoes.

Now Russian poetry is a step farther on in this same direction. The reader who enters the kingdom of Russian poetry, after having visited those of France and England, experiences what he feels in entering the German region, but still more so. The region of Russian poetry is still more earthly. Even the mysticism of certain German Romantic writers is alien to it. The German poetic country is quiet and sober, it is true; but in its German forests you hear, as I have said, the noise of those hoofs which are bearing riders to the unknown country. Also you have in German literature, allegory and pantheistic dreams which are foreign to the Russian poetic temperament, and therefore unreflected in Russian poetry.

The Russian poetical temperament, and, consequently, Russian poetry, does not only closely cling to the solid earth, but it is based on and saturated with sound common sense, with a curious matter-of-fact quality. And this common sense with which the greatest Russian poet, Pushkin, is so thoroughly impregnated, is as foreign to German *Schwärmerei* as it is to French rhetoric, or the imaginative exuberance of England. In Russian poetry of the early part of the nineteenth century, in spite of the enthusiasm kindled in certain Russian poets by the romantic scenery of the Caucasus, there is very little feeling for nature. Nature, in the poetry of Pushkin, is more or less conventional: almost the only flower mentioned is the rose, almost the only bird the nightingale. And although certain Russian poets adopted the paraphernalia and the machinery of Romanticism (largely owing to the influence of Byron), their true nature, their fundamental sense, keeps on breaking out. Moreover, there is an element in Russian Romanticism of passive obedience, of submission to authority, which arises partly from the passive quality in all Russians, and partly from the atmosphere of the age and the political régime of the beginning of the nineteenth century. Thus it is that no Russian Romantic poet would have ever tried to reach the dim pinnacles of Shelley's speculative cities, and no Russian Romantic poet would have uttered a wild cry of revolt such as Musset's 'Rolla'. But what the Russian poets did do, and what they did in a manner which gives them an unique place in the history of the world's literature, was to extract poetry from the daily life they saw round them, and to express it in forms of incomparable beauty. Russian poetry, like the Russian nature, is plastic. Plasticity, adaptability, comprehensiveness, are the great qualities of Pushkin. His verse is 'simple, sensuous and

REALISM OF RUSSIAN LITERATURE

impassioned'; there is nothing indistinct about it, no vague outline and no blurred detail; it is perfectly balanced, and it is this sense of balance and proportion blent with a rooted common sense, which reminds the reader when he reads Pushkin of Greek art, and gives one the impression that the poet is a classic, however much he may have employed the stock-in-trade of Romanticism.

Meredith says somewhere that the poetry of mortals is their daily prose. It is precisely this kind of poetry, the poetry arising from the incidents of everyday life, which the Russian poets have been successful in transmuting into verse. There is a quality of matter-of-factness in Russian poetry which is unique; the same quality exists in Russian folk-lore and fairy tales; even Russian ghosts, and certainly the Russian devil, have an element of matter-of-factness about them; and the most Romantic of all Russian poets, Lermontov, has certain qualities which remind one more of Thackeray than of Byron or Shelley, who undoubtedly influenced him.

I will quote as an example of this one of his most famous poems. It is called 'The Testament', and it is the utterance of a man who has been mortally wounded in battle.

> '*I want to be alone with you,*[1]
> *A moment quite alone.*
> *The minutes left to me are few,*
> *They say I'll soon be gone.*
> *And you'll be going home on leave,*
> *Then tell . . . but why? I do believe*
> *There's not a soul, who'll greatly care*
> *To hear about me over there.*
>
> *And yet if some one asks you, well,*
> *Let us suppose they do—*
> *A bullet hit me here, you'll tell,—*
> *The chest,—and it went through.*
> *And say I died and for the Tsar,*
> *And say what fools the doctors are;—*

[1] This translation is in the metre of the original. It is lateral; but hopelessly inadequate.

And that I shook you by the hand,
And thought about my native land.

My father and my mother, there!
   They may be dead by now;
To tell the truth, I wouldn't care
   To grieve them anyhow.
If one of them is living, say
I'm bad at writing home, and they
Have sent us to the front, you see,—
And that they needn't wait for me.

They've got a neighbour, as you know,
   And you remember I
And she . . . How very long ago
   It is we said good-bye!
She won't ask after me, nor care,
But tell her ev'rything, don't spare
Her empty heart: and let her cry;—
To her it doesn't signify.'

The words of this poem are the words of familiar conversation; they are exactly what the soldier would say in such circumstances. There is not a single literary or poetical expression used. And yet the effect in the original is one of poignant poetical feeling and consummate poetic art. I know of no other language where the thing is possible; because if you translate the Russian by the true literary equivalents, you would have to say: 'I would like a word alone with you, old fellow,' or 'old chap,'[1] or something of that kind; and I know of no English poet who has ever been able to deal successfully (in poetry) with the speech of everyday life without the help of slang or dialect. What is needed for this are the Russian temperament and the Russian language.

I will give another instance of what I mean. There is a Russian poet called Krilov, who wrote fables such as those of La Fontaine, based for the greater part on those of Æsop. He

---

[1] In the Russian, although every word of the poem is familiar, not a word of slang is used.

wrote a version of what is perhaps La Fontaine's masterpiece, 'Les Deux Pigeons,' which begins thus:

> *'Two pigeons, like two brothers, lived together.*
> *They shared their all in fair and wintry weather.*
> *Where the one was the other would be near,*
> *And every joy they shared and every tear.*
> *They noticed not Time's flight. Sadness they knew:*
> *But weary of each other never grew.'*

This last line, translated literally, runs: 'They were sometimes sad, they were never bored.' It is one of the most poetical in the whole range of Russian literature; and yet how absolutely untranslatable!—not only into English, but into any other language. How can one convey the word 'boring' so that it shall be poetical, in English or in French? In Russian one can, simply from the fact that the word which means boring, 'skouchno', is just as fit for poetic use as the word 'groustno', which means sad. And this proves that it is easier for Russians to make poetry out of the language of everyday than it is for Englishmen.

The matter-of-fact quality of the Russian poetical temperament—its dislike of exaggeration and extravagance—is likewise clearly visible in the manner in which Russian poets write of nature. I have already said that the poets of the early part of the nineteenth century reveal (compared with their European contemporaries) only a mild sentiment for the humbler aspects of nature; but let us take a poet of a later epoch, Alexis Tolstoy, who wrote in the fifties, and who may not unfairly be called a Russian Tennyson. In the work of Tolstoy the love of nature reveals itself on almost every page. His work brings before our eyes the landscape of the South of Russia, and expresses the charm and the quality of that country in the same way as Tennyson's 'In Memoriam' evokes for us the sight of England. Yet if one compares the two, the work of the Russian poet is nearer to the earth, familiar and simple in a fashion which is beyond the reach of other languages. Here, for instance, is a rough translation of one of Alexis Tolstoy's poems:

'Through the slush and the ruts of the road,
By the side of the dam of the stream;
Where the wet fishing nets are spread,
The carriage jogs on, and I muse.

I muse and I look at the road,
At the damp and the dull grey sky,
At the shelving bank of the lake,
And the far-off smoke of the villages.

By the dam, with a cheerless face,
Is walking a tattered old Jew.
From the lake, with a splashing of foam,
The waters rush through the weir.

A little boy plays on a pipe,
He has made it out of a reed.
The startled wild-ducks have flown,
And call as they sweep from the lake.

Near the old crumbling mill
Labourers sit on the grass.
An old worn horse in a cart,
Is lazily dragging some sacks.

And I know it all, oh! so well,
Although I have never been here;
The roof of that house over there,
And that boy, and the wood, and the weir,

And the mournful voice of the mill,
And the crumbling barn in the field—
I have been here and seen it before,
And forgotten it all long ago.

This very same horse plodded on,
It was dragging the very same sacks;
And under the mouldering mill
Labourers sat on the grass.

And the Jew, with his beard, walked by,
And the weir made just such a noise.
All this has happened before,
Only, I cannot tell when.'

I have said that Russian fairy tales and folk stories are full of the same spirit of matter-of-factness. And so essential do I consider this factor to be, so indispensable do I consider the comprehension of it by the would-be student of Russian literature, that I will quote a short folk story at length, which reveals this quality in its essence. The reader will only have to compare the following tale in his mind with a French, English, or German fairy tale to see what I mean.

THE FOOL

Once upon a time in a certain kingdom there lived an old man, and he had three sons. Two of them were clever, the third was a fool. The father died, and the sons drew lots for his property: the clever sons won every kind of useful thing; the fool only received an old ox, and that was a lean and bony one.

The time of the fair came, and the clever brothers made themselves ready to go and do a deal. The fool saw them doing this, and said:

'I also, brothers, shall take my ox to the market.'

And he led his ox by a rope tied to its horn, towards the town. On the way to the town he went through a wood, and in the wood there stood an old dried-up birch tree. The wind blew and the birch tree groaned.

'Why does the birch tree groan?' thought the fool. 'Does it perhaps wish to bargain for my ox? Now tell me, birch tree, if you wish to buy. If that is so, buy. The price of the ox is twenty roubles: I cannot take less. Show your money.'

But the birch tree answered nothing at all, and only groaned, and the fool was astonished that the birch tree wished to receive the ox on credit.

'If that is so, I will wait till tomorrow,' said the fool.

He tied the ox to the birch tree, said good-bye to it, and went home.

B

The clever brothers came to him and began to question him.

'Well, fool' they said, 'have you sold your ox?'

'I have sold it.'

'Did you sell it dear?'

'I sold it for twenty roubles.'

'And where is the money?'

'I have not yet got the money. I have been told I shall receive it tomorrow.'

'Oh, you simpleton!' said the clever brothers.

On the next day, early in the morning, the fool got up, made himself ready, and went to the birch tree for his money. He arrived at the wood; the birch tree was there, swaying in the wind, but the ox was not there any more—the wolves had eaten him in the night.

'Now, countryman,' said the fool to the birch tree, 'pay me the money. You promised you would pay it today.'

The wind blew, the birch tree groaned, and the fool said:

'Well, you are an untrustworthy fellow! Yesterday you said, "I will pay the money tomorrow," and today you are trying to get out of it. If this is so I will wait yet another day, but after that I shall wait no longer, for I shall need the money myself.'

The fool went home, and his clever brothers again asked him: 'Well, have you received your money?'

'No, brothers,' he answered, 'I shall have to wait still another little day.'

'Whom did you sell it to?'

'A dried old birch tree in the wood.'

'See what a fool!' said the brothers.

On the third day the fool took an axe and set out for the wood. He arrived and demanded the money.

The birch tree groaned and groaned.

'No, countryman,' said the fool, 'if you always put off everything till the morrow, I shall never get anything from you at all. I do not like joking, and I shall settle matters with you at once and for all.'

He took the axe and struck the tree, and the chips flew on all sides.

Now in the tree was a hollow, and in this hollow some

robbers had hidden a bag of gold. The tree was split into two parts, and the fool saw a heap of red gold; and he gathered the gold together in a heap and took some of it home and showed it to his brothers.

And his brothers said to him:

'Where did you get such a lot of money, fool?'

'A countryman of mine gave it to me for my ox,' he said, 'and there is still a great deal left. I could not bring half of it home. Let us go, brothers, and get the rest of it.'

They went into the wood and found the money, and brought it home.

'Now look you, fool,' said the clever brothers, 'do not tell anyone that we have so much money.'

'Of course not,' said the fool. 'I will not tell anyone, I promise you.'

But soon after this they met a deacon.

'What are you bringing from the wood, children?' said the deacon.

'Mushrooms,' said the clever brothers.

But the fool interrupted and said: 'They are not telling the truth—we are bringing gold. Look at it if you will.'

The deacon gasped with astonishment, fell upon the gold, and took as much as he could and stuffed his pockets full of it.

But the fool was annoyed at this, and struck him with an axe and beat him till he was dead.

'Oh fool, what have you done?' said his brothers. 'You will be ruined, and ruin us also. What shall we do now with this dead body?'

They thought and they thought, and then they took it to an empty cellar and threw it into the cellar.

Late in the evening the eldest brother said to the second: 'This is a bad business. As soon as they miss the deacon the fool is certain to tell them all about it. Let us kill a goat and hide it in the cellar and put the dead body in some other place.'

They waited until the night was dark; then they killed a goat, threw it into the cellar, and took the body of the deacon to another place and buried it in the earth.

A few days passed; people looked for the deacon every-where, and asked everybody they could about him. And the fool said to them:

'What do you want of him? I killed him with an axe, and my brothers threw the body into the cellar.'

They at once seized the fool and said to him:

'Take us and show us.'

The fool climbed into the cellar, took out the head of the goat, and said:

'Was your deacon black?'

'Yes,' they said.

'And had he got a beard?'

'Yes, he had a beard.'

'And had he got horns?'

'What sort of horns, you fool?'

'Well, look!' And he threw down the head.

The people looked and saw that it was a goat, and they spat at the fool and went home.

This story, more than pages of analysis and more than chap-ters of argument, illustrates what I mean: namely, that if the Russian poet and the Russian peasant, the one in his verse, the other in his folk tales and fairy stories, are matter-of-fact, alien to flights of exaggerated fancy, and above all things enamoured of the truth; if by their closeness to nature, their gift of seeing things as they are, and expressing these things in terms of the utmost simplicity, without fuss, without affectation and with-out artificiality—if, I say, all this entitles us to call them realists, then this realism is not and must never be thought of as being the fad of a special school, the theory of a limited clique, or the watchword of a literary camp, but it is rather the natural expression of the Russian temperament and the Russian character.

I will try throughout this book to attempt to illustrate this character and this temperament as best I can, but observing widely different manifestations of it; but all these manifesta-tions, however different they may be, contain one great quality in common: that is, the quality of reality of which I have been writing. And unless the student of Russian literature realizes this and appreciates what Russian realism consists of, and what it really means, he will be unable to understand either the men or the literature of Russia.

CHAPTER III

Gogol and the Cheerfulness of the Russian People

THE FIRST THING that strikes the English reader when he dips into translations of Russian literature, is the unrelieved gloom, the unmitigated pessimism of the characters and the circumstances described. Everything is grey, everybody is depressed; the atmosphere is one of hopeless melancholy. On the other hand, the first thing that strikes the English traveller when he arrives in Russia for the first time, is the cheerfulness of the Russian people. Nowhere have I seen this better described than in an article, written by Mr Charles Hands, which appeared in the summer of 1905 in the *Daily Mail*. Mr Hands summed up his idea of the Russian people, which he had gathered after living with them for two years, both in peace and in war, in a short article. His final impression was the same as that which he received on the day he arrived in Russia for the first time. That was in winter; it was snowing; the cold was intense. The streets of St Petersburg were full of people, and in spite of the driving snow, the bitter wind, and the cruel cold, everybody was smiling, everybody was making the best of it. Nowhere did you hear people grumbling, or come across a face stamped with a grievance.

I myself experienced an impression of the same kind, one evening in July 1906. I was strolling about the streets of St Petersburg. It was the Sunday of the dissolution of the Duma; the dissolution had been announced that very morning. The streets were crowded with people, mostly poor people. I was walking with an Englishman who had spent some years in Russia, and he said to me: 'It is all very well to talk of the calamities of this country. Have you ever in your life seen a more cheerful Sunday crowd?' I certainly had not.

The Russian character has an element of happy consent and submission to the inevitable; of adapting itself to any circumstance, however disagreeable, which I have never come across in any other country. The Russians have a faculty of making the best of things which I have never seen developed in so high a degree. I remember once in Manchuria during the war, some soldiers, who were under the command of a sergeant, preparing early one morning, just before the battle of Ta-Shi-Chiao, to make some tea. Suddenly a man in command said there would not be time to have tea. The men simply said, 'Today no tea will be drunk,' with a smile; it did not occur to any one to complain, and they put away the kettle, which was just on the boil, and drove away in a cart. I witnessed this kind of incident over and over again. I remember one night at a place called Lonely Tree Hill. I was with a battery. We had just arrived, and there were no quarters. We generally lived in Chinese houses, but on this occasion there were none to be found. We encamped on the side of a hill. There was no shelter, no food, and no fire, and presently it began to rain. The Cossacks, of whom the battery was composed, made a kind of shelter out of what straw and millet they could find, and settled themselves down as comfortably and as cheerfully as if they had been in barracks. They accomplished the difficult task of making themselves comfortable out of nothing, and of making me comfortable also.

Besides this power of making the best of things, the Russians have a keen sense of humour. The clowns in their circuses are inimitable. A type you frequently meet in Russia is the man who tells stories and anecdotes which are distinguished by simplicity and by a knack of just seizing on the ludicrous side of some trivial episode or conversation. Their humour is not unlike English humour in kind, and this explains the wide popularity of our humorous writers in Russia, beginning with Dickens, including such essentially English writers as W. W. Jacobs and the author of *The Diary of a Nobody*, and ending with Jerome K. Jerome, whose complete works can be obtained at any Russian railway station.'[1]

All these elements are fully represented in Russian literature; but the kind of Russian literature which is saturated with these qualities either does not reach us at all, or reaches us in scarce and inadequate translations.

The greatest humorist of Russian literature, the Russian Dickens, is Nikolai Vasilievitch Gogol. Translations of some of his stories and of his longest work, *Dead Souls*, were published in 1887 by Mr Vizetelly. These translations are now out of print, and the work of Gogol may be said to be totally unknown in England. In France some of his stories have been translated by no less a writer than Prosper Mérimée.

Gogol was a Little Russian, a Cossack by birth; he belonged to the Ukraine, that is to say, the frontier country, the district which lies between the north and the extreme south. It is a country of immense plains, rich harvests, and smiling farms; of vines, laughter, and song. He was born in 1809 near Poltava, in the heart of the Cossack country. He was brought up by his grandfather, who had been the regimental chronicler of the Zaporozhian Cossacks, who live in the region beyond the falls of the Dnieper. His childhood was nursed in the warlike traditions of that race, and fed with the tales of a heroic epoch, the wars against Poland and the deeds of the dwellers of the Steppes. Later he was sent to school, and in 1829, when he was twenty years old, he went to St Petersburg, where after many disillusions and difficulties he obtained a place in a Government office. The time that he spent in this office gave him the material for one of his best stories. He soon tired of office work, and tried to go on the stage, but no manager would engage him. He became a tutor, but was not a particularly successful one. At last some friends obtained for him the professorship of History at the University, but he failed in this profession also, and so he finally turned to literature. By the publication of his first efforts in the St Petersburg press, he made some friends, and through these he obtained an introduction to Pushkin, the

---

[1] I met a Russian doctor in Manchuria, who knew pages of a Russian translation of *Three Men in a Boat* by heart.

greatest of Russian poets, who was at that time in the fullness of his fame.

Pushkin was a character devoid of envy and jealousy, over-flowing with generosity, and prodigal of praise. Gogol subsequently became his favourite writer, and it was Pushkin who urged Gogol to write about Russian history and popular Russian scenes. Gogol followed his advice and wrote the *Evenings in a Farmhouse on the Dikanka*. These stories are supposed to be told by an old beekeeper; and in them Gogol puts all the memories of his childhood, the romantic traditions, the fairy tales, the legends, the charming scenery, and the cheerful life of the Little Russian country.

In these stories he revealed the twofold nature of his talent: a fantasy, a love of the supernatural, and a power of making us feel it, which reminds one of Edgar Allan Poe, of Hoffmann, and of Robert Louis Stevenson; and side by side with this fantastic element, the keenest power of observation, which is mixed with an infectious sense of humour and a rich and delightful drollery. Together with these gifts, Gogol possessed a third quality, which is a blend of his fantasy and his realism, namely, the power of depicting landscape and places, with their colour and their atmosphere, in warm and vivid language. It is this latter gift with which I shall deal first. Here, for instance, is a description of the river Dnieper:

'Wonderful is the Dnieper when in calm weather, smooth and wilful, it drives its full waters through the woods and the hills; it does not whisper, it does not boom. One gazes and gazes without being able to tell whether its majestic spaces are moving or not: one wonders whether the river is not a sheet of glass, when like a road of crystal azure, measureless in its breadth and unending in its length, it rushes and swirls across the green world. It is then that the sun loves to look down from the sky and to plunge his rays into the cool limpid waters; and the woods which grow on the banks are sharply reflected in the river.

'The green-tressed trees and the wild flowers crowd together at the water's edge; they bend down and gaze at themselves; they are never tired of their own bright image, but smile to it and greet it, as they incline their boughs. They dare not look into the midst of the Dnieper; no one save the sun and the blue sky looks into that. It is rare that a bird flies as far as the midmost waters. Glorious river, there is none other like it in the world!

'Wonderful is the Dnieper in the warm summer nights when all things are asleep: men and beasts and birds, and God alone in His majesty looks round on the heaven and the earth and royally spreads out His sacerdotal vestment and lets it tremble. And from this vestment the stars are scattered: the stars burn and shine over the world, and all are reflected in the Dnieper. The Dnieper receives them all into its dark bosom: not one escapes it. The dark wood with its sleeping ravens, and the old rugged mountains above them, try to hide the river with their long dark shadows, but it is in vain: there is nothing in all the world which could overshadow the Dnieper! Blue, infinitely blue, its smooth surface is always moving by night and by day, and is visible in the distance as far as mortal eye can see. It draws near and nestles in the banks in the cool of the night, and leaves behind it a silver trail, that gleams like the blade of a sword of Damascus. But the blue river is once more asleep. Wonderful is the Dnieper then, and there is nothing like it in the world!

'But when the dark clouds gather in the sky, and the black wood is shaken to its roots, the oak trees tremble, and the lightnings, bursting in the clouds, light up the whole world again, terrible then is the Dnieper. The crests of the waters thunder, dashing themselves against the hills; fiery with lightning, and loud with many a moan, they retreat and dissolve and overflow in tears in the distance. Just in such a way does the aged mother of the Cossack weep when she goes to say good-bye to her son, who is off to the wars. He rides off, wanton, debonair, and full of spirit; he rides on his black horse with his elbows well out at the side, and he waves his cap. And his mother sobs and runs after him; she clutches hold of his stirrup, seizes the snaffle, throws her arms round her son, and weeps bitterly.'

Another characteristic description of Gogol's is the picture he gives us of the Steppes:

'The farther they went, the more beautiful the Steppes became. At that time the whole of the country which is now Lower New Russia, reaching as far as the Black Sea, was a vast green wilderness. Never a plough had passed over its measureless waves of wild grass. Only the horses, which were hidden in it as though in a wood, trampled it down. Nothing in Nature could be more beautiful than this grass. The whole of the surface of the earth was like a gold and green sea, on which millions of flowers of different colours were sprinkled. Through the high and delicate stems of grass the cornflowers twinkled—light blue, dark blue, and lilac. The yellow broom pushed upward its pointed crests; the white milfoil, with its flowers like fairy umbrellas, dapples the surface of the grass; an ear of wheat, which had come Heaven knows whence, was ripening.

' At the roots of the flowers and the grass, partridges were running about everywhere, thrusting out their necks. The air was full of a thousand different bird-notes. Hawks hovered motionless in the sky, spreading out their wings, and fixing their eyes on the grass. The cry of a flock of wild geese was echoed in I know not what far-off lake. A gull rose from the grass in measured flight, and bathed wantonly in the blue air; now she has vanished in the distance, and only a black spot twinkles; and now she wheels in the air and glistens in the sun.'

Of course, descriptions such as these lose all their beauty in a translation, for Gogol's language is rich and native; full of diminutives and racial idiom, nervous and highly-coloured. To translate it into English is like translating Rabelais into English. I have given these two examples more to show the nature of the thing he describes than the manner in which he describes it.

Throughout this first collection of stories there is a blend of broad farce and poetical fancy; we are introduced to the

humours of the fair, the adventures of sacristans with the devil
and other apparitions; to the Russalka, a naiad, a kind of land-
mermaid, or Loreley, which haunts the woods and the lakes.
And every one of these stories smells of the South Russian
soil, and is overflowing with sunshine, good-humour, and a
mellow charm. This side of Russian life is not only wholly unknown in Europe, but it is not even suspected. The picture
most people have in their minds of Russia is a place of grey
skies and bleak monotonous landscape, weighed down by an
implacable climate. These things exist, but there is another side
as well, and it is this other side that Gogol tells of in his early
stories. We are told much about the Russian winter, but who
ever thinks of the Russian spring? And there is nothing more
beautiful in the world, even in the north and centre of Russia,
than the abrupt and sudden invasion of springtime which
comes shortly after the melting snows, when the woods are
carpeted with lilies-of-the-valley, and the green of the birch
trees almost hurts the eye with its brilliance.

Nor are we told much about the Russian summer, with its
wonderful warm nights, nor of the pageant of the plains when
they become a rippling sea of golden corn. If the spring and
the summer are striking in northern and central Russia, much
more is this so in the south, where the whole character of the
country is as cheerful and smiling as that of Devonshire or
Normandy. The farms are whitewashed and clean; sometimes
they are painted light blue or pink; vines grow on the walls;
there is an atmosphere of sunshine and laziness everywhere,
accompanied by much dancing and song.

Once when I was in St Petersburg I was talking to a peasant
member of the Duma who came from the south. After he had
declaimed for nearly twenty minutes of the terrible condition
of the peasants in the country, their needs, their wants, their
misery, their ignorance, he added thoughtfully: 'All the same
we have great fun in our village; you ought to come and stay
there. There is no such life in the world!' The sunshine and
laughter of the south of Russia rise before us from every page
of these stories of Gogol. Here, for instance, is a description of
a summer's day in Little Russia, the day of a fair:

'How intoxicating, how rich, is a summer's day in Little Russia! How overwhelmingly hot are those hours of noon-day silence and haze! Like a boundless azure sea, the dome of the sky, bending as though with passion over the world, seems to have fallen asleep, all drowned in softness, and clasps and caresses the beautiful earth with a celestial embrace. There is no cloud in the sky; and the stream is silent. Everything is as if it were dead; only aloft in the deeps of the sky a lark quivers, and its silvery song echoes down the vault of heaven, and reaches the love-sick earth. And from time to time the cry of the seagull or the clear call of the quail is heard in the plain.

'Lazily and thoughtlessly, as though they were idling vaguely, stand the shady oaks; and the blinding rays of the sun light up the picturesque masses of foliage, while the rest of the tree is in a shadow dark as night, and only when the wind rises, a flash of gold trembles across it.

'Like emeralds, topazes and amethysts, the diaphanous insects flutter in the many-coloured fruit gardens, which are shaded by stately sun-flowers. Grey haycocks and golden sheaves of corn stand in rows along the field like hillocks on the immense expanse. Broad boughs bend under their load of cherries, plums, apples, and pears. The sky is the transparent mirror of the day, and so is the river, with its high green frame of trees. . . . How luscious and how soft is the summer in Little Russia!

'It was just such a hot day in August 18—, when the road, ten versts from the little town of Sorochinetz, was seething with people hurrying from all the farms, far and near, to the fair. With the break of day an endless chain of waggons laboured along, carrying salt and fish. Mountains of pots wrapped in hay moved slowly on us if they were weary of being cut off from the sunshine. Only here and there some brightly-painted soup tureen or earthenware saucepan proudly emerged on the tilt of the high-heaped waggon, and attracted the eyes of lovers of finery; many passers-by looked with envy on the tall potter, the owner of all these treasures, who with slow steps walked beside his goods.'

Why are we never told of these azure Russian days, of these laden fruit-trees and jewelled insects?

In 1832, Gogol published a continuation of this series, entitled *Stories of Mirgorod*. This collection contains the masterpieces of the romantic, and the fantastic side of Gogol's genius. His highest effort in the romantic province is the historical history of *Taras Bulba*, which is a prose epic. It is the tale of an old Cossack chieftain whose two sons, Ostap and Andrii, are brought up in the Zaporozhian settlement of the Cossacks, and trained as warriors to fight the Poles. They lay siege to the Polish city of Dubno, and starve the city. Andrii, the younger son, discovers that a girl whom he had loved at Kiev, before his Cossack training, is shut up in the city. The girl's servant leads him into Dubno by an underground passage. Andrii meets his lady-love and abandons the Cossack cause, saying that his fatherland and his country is there where his heart is.

In the meantime the Polish troops arrive, reinforce the beleaguered garrison; Andrii is for ever lost to Cossack chivalry, and his country and his father's house shall know him no more. News then comes that in the absence of the Cossacks from their camp in the Ukraine, the Tartars have plundered it. So they send half their army to defend it, while half of it remains in front of the besieged city. The Poles attack the Cossacks who are left.

There is a terrific battle, in which Andrii fights against the Cossacks. He is taken prisoner by his own father, who bids him dismount. He dismounts obediently, and his father addresses him thus: 'I begot you, and now I shall kill you.'   And he shoots him dead.

Immediately after this incident Taras Bulba and his elder son, Ostap, are attacked by the enemy. Ostap, after inflicting deadly losses on the enemy, is separated from his father—who falls in a swoon, and owing to this escapes—and taken prisoner. Ostap is taken to the city and tortured to death. In the extremity of his torment, after having endured the long agonies without a groan, he cries out: 'Father, do you hear me?' And from the crowd a terrible voice is heard answering: 'I hear!' Later, Taras raises an army of Cossacks to avenge the death of his son, and lays waste the country; but at the end he is caught and put to death by the Poles.

This story is told with epic breadth and simplicity; the figure of the old warrior is Homeric, and Homeric, also is the character of the young traitor Andrii, who, although he betrays his own people, never loses sympathy, so strong is the impression you receive of his brilliance, his dash, and his courage.

In the domain of fantasy, Gogol's masterpiece is to be found in this same collection. It is called *Viy*. It is the story of a beautiful lady who is a witch. She casts her spell on a student in theology, and when she dies, her dying will is that he shall spend three nights in reading prayers over her body, in the church where her coffin lies. During his watch on the first night, the dead maiden rises from her coffin, and watches him with glassy, opaque eyes. He hears the flapping of the wings of innumerable birds, and in the morning is found half dead from terror. He attempts to avoid the ordeal on the second night, but the girl's father, an old Cossack, forces him to carry out his daughter's behest, and three nights are spent by the student in terrible conflict with the witch. On the third night he dies. The great quality of this story is the atmosphere of over-mastering terror that it creates.

With these two stories, *Taras Bulba* and *Viy*, Gogol took leave of Romanticism and Fantasy, and started on the path of Realism. In this province he was what the Germans call a *bahnbrecher*, and he discovered a new kingdom. It may be noticed that Gogol, roughly speaking, began where Dickens ended; that is to say, he wrote his *Tale of Two Cities* first, and his *Pickwick* last. But already in this collection of Mirgorod tales there are two stories in the humorous realistic vein, which Gogol never excelled; one is called *Old-fashioned Landowners*, and the other *How Ivan Ivanovitch quarrelled with Ivan Nikiforovitch*.

Old-fashioned Landowners is a simple story. It is about an old couple who lived in a low-roofed little house, with a veranda of blackened tree-trunks, in the midst of a garden of dwarfed fruit-trees covered with cherries and plums. The couple,

Athanasii Ivanovitch and his wife Pulcheria Ivanovna, are old.
He is sixty, she is fifty-five. It is the story of Philemon and
Baucis. Nothing happens in it, except that we are introduced to
these charming, kind, and hospitable people; that Pulcheria
dies, and that after her death everything in the house becomes
untidy and slovenly, because Athanasii cannot live without
her; and after five years he follows her to the grave, and is
buried beside her. There is nothing in the story, and there is
everything. It is amusing, charming, and infinitely pathetic.
Some of the touches of description remind one strongly of
Dickens. Here, for instance, is a description of the doors of the
house where the old couple lived:

'The most remarkable thing about the house was the
creaking of the doors. As soon as day broke, the singing of
these doors was heard throughout the whole house. I cannot
say why they made the noise: either it was the rusty hinges,
or else the workman who made them hid some secret in
them; but the remarkable thing was that each door had its
own special note. The door going into the bedroom sang in a
delicate treble; the door going into the dining-room had a
hoarse bass note; but that which led into the front hall made
a strange trembling, groaning noise, so that if you listened
to it intently you heard it distinctly saying, "Batiushka, I am
so cold!"'

The story of the two Ivans is irresistibly funny. The two
Ivans were neighbours; one of them was a widower and the
other a bachelor. They were the greatest friends. Never a
day passed without their seeing each other, and their greatest
pleasure was to entertain each other at big, Dickens-like meals.
But one day they quarrelled about a gun, and Ivan Nikiforovitch called Ivan Ivanovitch a goose. After this they would not
see each other, and their relations were broken off. Hitherto,
Ivan Nikiforovitch and Ivan Ivanovitch had sent every day to
inquire about each other's health, had conversed together
from their balconies, and had said charming things to each
other. On Sundays they had gone to church arm in arm, and

outdone each other in mutual civilities; but now they would not look at each other.

At length the quarrel went so far that Ivan Ivanovitch lodged a complaint against Ivan Nikiforovitch, saying that the latter had inflicted a deadly insult on his personal honour, firstly by calling him a goose, secondly by building a goose-shed opposite his porch, and thirdly by cherishing a design to burn his house down. Ivan Nikiforovitch lodged a similar petition against Ivan Ivanovitch. As bad luck would have it, Ivan Ivanovitch's brown sow ate Ivan Nikiforovitch's petition, and this, of course, made the quarrel worse.

At last a common friend of the pair attempts to bring about a reconciliation, and asks the two enemies to dinner. After much persuasion they consent to meet. They go to the dinner, where a large company is assembled; both Ivans eat their meal without glancing at each other, and as soon as the dinner is over they rise from their seats and make ready to go. At this moment they are surrounded on all sides, and are adjured by the company to forget their quarrel. Each says that he was innocent of any evil design, and the reconciliation is within an ace of being effected when, unfortunately, Ivan Nikiforovitch says to Ivan Ivanovitch: 'Permit me to observe, in a friendly manner, that you took offence because I called you a goose.' As soon as the fatal word 'goose' is uttered, all reconciliation is out of the question, and the quarrel continues to the end of their lives.

In 1835, Gogol retired definitely from the public service. At this point of his career he wrote a number of stories and comedies, of a varied nature, which he collected later in two volumes, *Arabesques*, 1834, and *Tales*, 1836. It was the dawn of his realistic phase, although he still indulged from time to time in the fantastic, as in the grotesque stories, *The Nose*—the tale of a nose which gets lost and wanders about—and *The Coach*. But the most remarkable of these stories is *The Overcoat*, which is the highest example of Gogol's pathos, and contains in embryo all the qualities of vivid realism which he was to develop later. It is the story of a clerk who has a passion for copying, and to whom caligraphy is a fine art. He is never warm enough; he is always shivering. The ambition, the dream of his life, is to have a warm overcoat. After years of privation he saves up the sum necessary to realize his dream and buy a new over-coat; but on the first day that he wears it, the coat is stolen from him.

The police, to whom he applies after the theft, laugh at him, and the clerk falls into a black melancholy. He dies unnoticed and his ghost haunts the squalid streets where he was wont to walk.

Nearly half of modern Russian literature descends directly from this story. The figure of this clerk and the way he is treated by the author is the first portrait of an endless gallery of the failures of this world, the flotsam and jetsam of a social system: grotesque figures, comic, pathetic, with a touch of tragedy in them, which, since they are handled by their creator with a kindly sympathy, and never with cruelty or disdain, win our sympathy and live in our hearts and our affections.

During this same period Gogol wrote several plays, among which the masterpiece is *The Inspector*. This play, which is still immensely popular in Russia, and draws crowded houses on Sundays and holidays, is a good-humoured, scathing satire on the Russian Bureaucracy. As a translation of this play is easily to be obtained, and as it has been performed in London by the Stage Society, I need not dwell on it here, except to mention for those who are unacquainted with it, that the subject of the play is a misunderstanding which arises from a traveller being mistaken for a government inspector who is expected to arrive incognito in a provincial town. A European critic in reading or seeing this play is sometimes surprised and unreasonably struck by the universal dishonesty of almost every single character in the play. For instance, one of the characters says to another: 'You are stealing above your rank.' One should re-member, however, that in a translation it is impossible not to lose something of the good-humour and the comic spirit of which the play is full. It has often been a matter of surprise that this play, at the time when Gogol wrote it, should have been passed by the censorship. The reason of this is that Gogol had for censor the Emperor of Russia himself, who read the play, was extremely amused by it, commanded its immediate performance, was present at the first night, and led the applause.

Hlestakov, the hero of *The Inspector*, is one of the most natural and magnificent liars in literature. Gogol himself, in his stage directions, describes him as a man 'without a Tsar in his head'—a man who speaks and acts without the slightest reflection, and who is not capable of consecutive thought, or of fixing his attention for more than a moment on any single idea.

In 1836, Gogol left Russia and settled in Rome. He had been working for some time at another book, which he intended should be his masterpiece, a book in which he intended to say *everything*, and express the whole of his message. Gogol was possessed by this idea. The book was to be divided into three parts. The first part appeared in 1842, the second part, which was never finished, Gogol threw in the fire in a fit of despair. It was, however, subsequently printed from an incomplete manuscript which had escaped his notice. The third part was never written. As it is, the first fragment of Gogol's great ambition remains his masterpiece, and the book by which he is best known. It is called *Dead Souls*. The hero of this book is a man called Chichikov. He has hit on an idea by which he can make money by dishonest means. Like all great ideas, it is simple. At the time at which the book was written the serfs in Russia had not yet been emancipated. They were called 'souls', and every landlord possessed so many 'souls'. A revision of the list of peasants took place every ten years, and the landlord had to pay a poll-tax for the souls that had died during that period, that is to say, for the men; women and children did not count. Between the periods of revision nobody looked at the lists. If there was any epidemic in the village the landlord lost heavily, as he had to continue paying a tax for the 'souls' who were dead.

Chichikov's idea was to take these 'dead souls' from the landlords, and pay the poll-tax, for them. The landlord would be only too pleased to get rid of a property which was fictitious, and a tax which was only too real. Chichikov could then register his purchases with all due formality, for it would never occur to a tribunal to think that he was asking them to legalize a sale of dead men; he could thus take the documents to a bank of St Petersburg or at Moscow, and mortgage the 'souls', which he presented as living in some desert place in the Crimea, at one hundred roubles apiece, and then be rich enough to buy living 'souls' of his own.

Chichikov travelled all over Russia in search of 'dead souls'. The book tells us the adventures he met with; and the scheme is particularly advantageous to the author, because it not only enables him to introduce us to a variety of types, but the transaction itself, the manner in which men behave when faced by the proposition, throws a searchlight on their characters. Chichikov starts from a large provincial town, which he makes his base, and thence explores the country; the success or failure of his transactions forms the substance of the book. Sometimes he is successful, sometimes the system breaks down because the people in the country want to know the market value of the 'dead souls' in the town.

The travels of Chichikov, like those of Mr Pickwick, form a kind of Odyssey. The types he introduces us to are extraordinarily comic; there are fools who give their 'souls' for nothing, and misers who demand an exorbitant price for them. But sometimes Chichikov meets with people who are as clever as himself, and who outwit him. One of the most amusing episodes is that where he comes across a suspicious old woman called Korobotchka. Chichikov, after arriving at her house late at night, and having spent the night there, begins his business transactions cautiously and tentatively. The old woman at first thinks he has come to sell her tea, or that he has come to buy honey. Then Chichikov comes to the point, and asks her if any peasants have died on her land. She says eighteen. He then asks her to sell them to him, saying that he will give her money for them. She asks if he wishes to dig them out of the ground. He explains that the transaction would only take place upon paper. She asks him why he wants to do this. That, he answers, is his own affair.

'But they are dead,' she says:

'Whoever said they were alive?' asked Chichikov. 'It is a loss to you that they are dead. You pay for them, and I will now save you the trouble and the expense, and not only save you this, but give you fifteen roubles into the bargain. Is it clear now?'

'I really can't say', the old woman replies. 'You see I never before sold *dead* "souls".' And she keeps on repeating: 'What bothers me is that they are *dead*.'

Chichikov again explains to her that she has to pay a tax on them just as though they were alive.

'Don't talk of it!' she says. 'Only a week ago I had to pay one hundred and fifty roubles.'

Chichikov again explains to her how advantageous it would be for her to get them off her hands, upon which she answers that she has never had occasion to sell dead souls; if they were alive, on the other hand, she would have been delighted to do it.

'But I don't want live ones! I want dead ones,' answers Chichikov.

'I am afraid,' she says, 'that I might lose over the bargain— that you may be deceiving me.'

Chichikov explains the whole thing over again, offering her fifteen roubles, and showing her the money; upon which she says she would like to wait a little, to find out what they are really worth.

'But who on earth will buy them from you?' asks Chichikov.

'They might be useful on the estate,' says the old woman.

'How can you use dead souls on the estate?' asks Chichikov.

Korobotchka suggests that she would rather sell him some hemp, and Chichikov loses his temper.

Equally amusing are Chichikov's adventures with the miser Plushkin, Nozderf, a swaggering drunkard, and Manilov, who is simply a fool. But when all is said and done, the most amusing person in the book is Chichikov himself.

At the end of the first volume, Gogol makes a defence of his hero. After having described the circumstances of his youth, his surroundings, and all the influences which made him what he was, the author asks: 'Who is he?' And the answer he gives himself is: 'Of course a rascal: but why a rascal?' He continues:

'Why should we be so severe on others? We have no rascals among us now, we have only well-thinking, pleasant people; we have, it is true, two or three men who have enjoyed the shame of being thrashed in public, and even these speak of virtue. It would be more just to call him a man who acquires; it is the passion for gain that is to blame for everything. This passion is the cause of deeds which the world characterizes as ugly. It is true that in such a character there is perhaps something repulsive. But the same reader who in real life will be friends with such a man, who will dine with him, and pass the time pleasantly with him, will look askance at the same character should he meet with him as the hero of a book or of a poem. That man is wise who is not offended by any character, but is able to look within it, and to trace the development of nature to its first causes. Everything in man changes rapidly. You have scarcely time to look round, before inside the man's heart a hateful worm has been born which absorbs the vital sap of his nature. And it often happens that not only a great passion, but some ridiculous whim for a trivial object, grows in a man who was destined to better deeds, and causes him to forget his high and sacred duty, and to mistake the most miserable trifle for what is most exalted and most holy. The passions of mankind are as countless as the sands of the sea, and each of them is different from the others; and all of them, mean or beautiful, start by being subject to man, and afterwards become his most inexorable master. Happy is the man who has chosen for himself a higher passion . . . but there are passions which are not chosen by man: they are with him from the moment of his birth, and strength is not given him to free himself from them. These passions are ordered according to a high plan, and there is something in them which eternally and incessantly summons him, and which lasts as long as life lasts. They have a great work to accomplish; whether they be sombre or whether they be bright, their purpose is to work for an ultimate good which is beyond the ken of man. And perhaps in this same Chichikov the ruling passion which governs him is not of his choosing, and in his cold existence there may be something which will one day cause us to humble ourselves on our knees and in the dust before the Divine wisdom.'

I quote this passage at length because it not only explains the point of view of Gogol towards his creation, but also that which nearly all Russian authors and novelists hold with regard to mankind in general. Gogol's *Dead Souls* is an extremely funny book; it is full of delightful situations, comic characters and situations. At the same time it has often struck people as being a sad book. When Gogol read out to Pushkin the first chapter, Pushkin, who at other times had always laughed when Gogol read his work to him, became sadder and sadder, and said when Gogol had reached the end: 'What a sad country Russia is!'

It is true, as Gogol himself says at the end of the first volume of *Dead Souls*, that there is probably not one of his readers who, after an honest self-examination, will not wonder whether he has not something of Chichikov in himself. And if at such a moment such a man should meet an acquaintance in the street, whose rank is neither too exalted for criticism nor too obscure for notice, he will nudge his companion, and say with a chuckle: 'There goes Chichikov!' Perhaps every Russian feels that there is something of Chichikov in him, and Chichikov is a rascal, and most of the other characters in *Dead Souls* are rascals also; people who try to cheat their neighbours, and feel no moral scruples or remorse after they have done so. But in spite of all this, the impression that remains with one after reading the book is not one of bitterness or of melancholy. For in all the characters there is a vast amount of good-nature and of humanity. Also, as Gogol has pointed out in the passage quoted above, the peculiar blend of faults and qualities on which moralists may be severe, may be a special part of the Divine scheme.

However this may be, what strikes the casual student most when he has read *Dead Souls*, is that Gogol is the only Russian author who has given us in literature the universal type of Russian; the Russian 'man in the street'. Tolstoy has depicted the upper classes. Dostoievsky has reached the innermost depths of the Russian soul in its extremest anguish and at its highest pitch. Tourgeniev has fixed on the canvas several striking portraits, which suffer from the defect either of being caricatures, or of being too deeply dyed in the writer's pessimism and self-consciousness. Gorky has painted in lurid colours one side of the common people. Andreev has given us the nightmares of the younger generation. Tchekov has depicted the pessimism and the ineffectiveness of the 'intelligentzia'.[1] But nobody except Gogol has given us the ordinary cheerful Russian man in the street, with his crying faults, his attractive good qualities, and his overflowing human nature. In fact, it is the work of Gogol that explains the attraction which the Russian character and the Russian country exercise over people who have come beneath their influence. At first sight the thing seems inexplicable. The country seems ugly, dreary and monotonous, without art, without beauty and without brilliance; the climate is either fiercely cold and damp, or excruciatingly dry and hot; the people are slow and heavy; there is a vast amount of dirt, dust, disorder, untidiness, slovenliness, squalor, and sordidness everywhere; and yet in spite of all this, even a foreigner who has lived in Russia (not to speak of the Russians themselves), and who has once come in contact with its people, can never be quite free from its over-mastering charm, and the secret fascination of the country.

In another passage towards the end of *Dead Souls*, Gogol writes about this very thing as follows:

'Russia' (he writes), 'I see you from the beautiful "far away" where I am. Everything in you is miserable, dis-

[1] The highly educated professional middle class.

ordered and inhospitable. There are no emphatic miracles of Nature to startle the eye, graced with equally startling miracles of art. There are no towns with high, many-windowed castles perched on the top of crags; there are no picturesque trees, no ivy-covered houses beside the ceaseless thunder and foam of waterfalls. One never strains one's neck back to look at the piled-up rocky crags soaring endlessly into the sky. There never shines, through dark and broken arches overgrown with grapes, ivy, and a million wild roses—there never shines, I say, from afar the eternal line of gleaming mountains standing out against transparent and silver skies. Everything in you is open and desert and level; like dots, your squatting towns lie almost unobserved in the midst of the plains. There is nothing to flatter or to charm the eye. What then is the secret and incomprehensible power which lies hidden in you? Why does your aching melancholy song, which wanders throughout the length and breadth of you, from sea to sea, sound and echo unceasingly in one's ears? What is there in this song? What is there that calls and sobs and captures the heart? What are the sounds which hurt as they kiss, pierce my very inmost soul and flood my heart? Russia, what do you want of me? What inexplicable bond is there between you and me?'

Gogol does not answer the question, and if he cannot put his finger on the secret it would be difficult for any one else to do so. But although he does not answer the question directly, he does so indirectly by his works. Any one who reads Gogol's early stories, even *Dead Souls*, will understand the inexplicable fascination hidden in a country which seems at first sight so devoid of outward and superficial attraction, and in a people whose defects are so obvious and unconcealed. The charm of Russian life lies in its essential goodness of heart, and in its absence of hypocrisy, and it is owing to this absence of hypocrisy that the faults of the Russian character are so easy to detect. It is for this reason that in Gogol's realistic and satirical work, as in *The Inspector* and *Dead Souls*, the characters startle the foreign observer by their frank and almost universal dishonesty. The truth is that they do not take the trouble to conceal their shortcomings; they are indulgent to the failings of others, and not only expect but know that they will find their own faults treated with similar indulgence. Faults, failings, and vices which in Western Europe would be regarded with uncompromising censure and merciless blame, meet in Russia either with pity or good-humoured indulgence.

This happy-go-lucky element, the good-natured indulgence and scepticism with which Russians regard many things which we consider of grave import, are, no doubt, to a great extent the cause of the evils which exist in the administrative system of the country—the cause of nearly all the evils of which Russian reformers so bitterly complain. On the other hand, it should not be forgotten that this same good-humour and this same indulgence, the results of which in public life are slackness, disorder, corruption, irresponsibility and arbitrariness, in private life produce results of a different nature, such as pity, charity, hospitality and unselfishness; for the good-humour and the good-nature of the Russian proceed directly from goodness, and from nothing else.

Gogol never finished *Dead Souls*. He went on working on the second and third parts of it until the end of his life, in 1852; and he twice threw the work, when it was completed, into the fire. All we possess is an incomplete copy of a manuscript of the second part, which escaped destruction. He had intended the second part to be more serious than the first; his ambition was to work out the moral regeneration of Chichikov, and in doing so to attain to a full and complete expression of his ideals and his outlook on life. The ambition pursued and persecuted him like a feverish dream, and not being able to realize it, he turned back upon himself and was driven inward. His nature was religious to the core, since it was based on a firm and unshaken belief in Providence; and there came a time when he began to experience that distaste of the world which ultimately leads to a man becoming an ascetic and a recluse.

He lived in Rome, isolated from the world; he became consumed with religious zeal; he preached to his friends and acquaintances the Christian virtues of humility, resignation and charity; he urged them not to resist authority, but to become contrite Christians. And in order that the world should hear him, in 1847 he published passages from a correspondence with friends. In these letters Gogol insisted on the paramount necessity of spiritual life; but instead of attacking the Church he defended it, and preached submission both to it and to the Government.

The book created a sensation, and raised a storm of abuse. Some of the prominent Liberals were displeased. It was, of course, easy for them to attack Gogol; for here, they said, was the man who had, more than any other, satirized and dis-credited the Russian Government and Russian administration, coming forward as an apostle of orthodoxy and officialdom. The intellectual world scorned him as a mystic, and considered the matter settled; but if the word 'mystic' had the signific-ance which these people seem to have attached to it, then Gogol was not a mystic. There was nothing extravagant or uncommon in his religion. He gave up writing, and devoted himself to religion and good works; but this does not constitute what the intellectuals seem to have meant by mysticism. Mysticism with them was equivalent to madness. If, on the other hand, we mean by mysticism the transcendent common sense which recognizes a Divine order of things, and the reality of an in-visible world, then Gogol was a mystic. Therefore, when Gogol ceased to write stories, he no more *became* a mystic than did Pascal when he ceased going into society, or than Racine did when he ceased to write plays. In the other sense of the word he was a mystic all his life; so was Racine.

At the age of thirty-three his creative faculties had dried up, and at the age of forty-three, in February 1852, he died of typhoid fever. The place of Gogol in Russian literature is a very high one. Prosper Mérimée places him among the best *English* humorists. Gogol's European reputation is less great than it should be, because his subject-matter is more remote. But of all the Russian prose writers of the last century, Gogol is perhaps the most national. His work smells of the soil of Russia; there is nothing imitative or foreign about it. When he published

The Inspector, the motto which he appended to it was: 'If your mouth is crooked, don't blame the looking-glass.' He was a great humorist. He was also a great satirist. He was a penetrating but not a pitiless observer; in his fun and his humour, there is often a note of sadness, an accent of pathos, and a tinge of wistful melancholy. His pathos and his laughter are closely allied one to another, but in his sadness there is neither bitterness nor gloom; there is no shadow of the powers of darkness, no breath of the icy terror which blows through the works of Tolstoy; there is no hint of the emptiness and the void, or of a fear of them. There is nothing akin to despair. For his whole outlook on life is based on faith in Providence, and the whole of his morality consists in Christian charity, and in submission to the Divine.

In one of his lectures, Gogol, speaking of Pushkin, singles out, as one of the qualities of Russian literature, the pity for all who are unfortunate. This, he says, is a truly Russian characteristic.

'Think,' he writes, 'of that touching spectacle which our people afford when they visit the exiles who are starting for Siberia, when every man brings something, either food or money, or a kind word. There is here no hatred of the criminal; no quixotic wish to make him a hero, or to ask for his autograph or his portrait, or to regard him as an object of morbid curiosity, as often happens in more civilized Europe. Here there is something more: it is not the desire to whitewash him, or to deliver him from the hands of the law, but to comfort his broken spirit, and to console him as a brother comforts a brother, or as Christ ordered us to console each other.'

This sense of pity is the greatest gift that the Russian nation possesses: it is likewise the cardinal factor of Russian literature, as well as its most precious asset; the inestimable legacy and contribution which Russian authors have made to the literature of the world. It is a thing which the Russians and no other people have given us. There is no better way of judging of this quality and of estimating its results, than to study the works of Russian's greatest humorist, satirist, and realist. For if realism can be so vivid without being cruel, if satire can be so cruel without being bitter, and a sense of the ridiculous so broad and so strong without being ill-natured, the soil of goodness out of which these things all grow must indeed be rich and deep, and the streams of pity with which it is watered must indeed be plentiful.

CHAPTER IV

Tolstoy and Tourgeniev

THE EIGHTIETH BIRTHDAY of Count Tolstoy, which was celebrated in Russia on August 28 (old style), 1908, was closely followed by the twenty-fifth anniversary of the death of Tourgeniev, who died on September 3, 1883, at the age of sixty-five. These two anniversaries followed close upon the publication of a translation into English of the complete works of Count Tolstoy by Professor Wiener; and it is not long ago that a new edition of the complete works of Tourgeniev, translated into English by Mrs Garnett, appeared. Both these translations have been made with great care, and are faithful and accurate. Thirty years go it is certain that European critics, and probable that Russian critics, would have observed, in commenting on the concurrence of these two events, that Tolstoy and Tourgeniev were the two giants of modern Russian literature. Is the case the same today? Is it still true that, in the opinion of Russia and of Europe, the names of Tolstoy and Tourgeniev stand pre-eminently above all their contemporaries?

With regard to Tolstoy the question can be answered without the slightest hesitation. Time, which has inflicted such mournful damage on so many great reputations in the last twenty-five years, has not only left the fame of Tolstoy's masterpieces unimpaired, but has increased our sense of their greatness. The question arises, whose work forms the complement to that of Tolstoy, and shares his undisputed dominion of modern Russian literature? Is it Tourgeniev? In Russia at the present day the answer would be 'No', it is not Tourgeniev. And in Europe, students of Russian literature who are acquainted with the Russian language—as we see in M. Emile Haumant's study of Tourgeniev's life and work, and in Professor Brückner's history of Russian literature—would also answer in the negative, although their denial would be less emphatic and not perhaps unqualified.

The other giant, the complement of Tolstoy, almost any Russian critic of the present day without hesitation would pronounce to be Dostoievsky; and the foreign critic who is thoroughly acquainted with Dostoievsky's work cannot but agree with him. I propose to go more fully into the question of the merits and demerits of Dostoievsky later on; but it is impossible not to mention him here, because the very existence of his work powerfully affects our judgment when we come to look at that of his contemporaries. We can no more ignore his presence and his influence than we could ignore the presence of a colossal fresco by Leonardo da Vinci in a room in which there were only two other religious pictures, one by Rembrandt and one by Vandyck. For anyone who is familiar with Dostoievsky, and has felt his tremendous influence, cannot look at the work of his contemporaries with the same eyes as before. To such a one, the rising of Dostoievsky's red and troubled planet, while causing the rays of Tourgeniev's serene star to pale, leaves the rays of Tolstoy's orb undiminished and undimmed. Tolstoy and Dostoievsky shine in the firmament of Russian literature like two planets, one of them as radiant as the planet Jupiter, the other as ominous as the planet Mars. Beside either of these the light of Tourgeniev twinkles, pure indeed, and full of pearly lustre, like the moon faintly seen in the east at the end of an autumnal day.

It is rash to make broad generalizations. They bring with them a certain element of exaggeration which must be discounted. Nevertheless I believe that I am stating a fundamental truth in saying that the Russian character can, roughly speaking, be divided into two types, and these two types dominate the whole of Russian literature. The first is that which I shall call, for want of a better name, Lucifer, the fallen angel. The second type is that of the hero of all Russian folk-tales, Ivan Durak, Ivan the Fool, or the Little Fool. There are innumerable folk-tales in Russian which tell the adventures of Ivan the

Fool, who, by his very simplicity and foolishness, outwits the wisdom of the world. This type is characteristic of one Russian ideal. The simple fool is venerated in Russia as something holy. It is acknowledged that his childish innocence is more precious than the wisdom of the wise. Ivan Durak may be said to be the hero of all Dostoievsky's novels. He is the aim and ideal of Dostoievsky's life, an aim and ideal which he fully achieves. He is also the aim and ideal of Tolstoy's teaching, but an aim and ideal which Tolstoy recommends to others and only partly achieves himself.

The first type I have called, for want of a better name, since I can find no concrete symbol of it in Russian folk-lore, Lucifer, the fallen angel. This type is the embodiment of stubborn and obdurate pride, the spirit which cannot bend; such is Milton's Satan, with his

> '*Courage never to submit or yield,*
> *And what is else not to be overcome.*'

This type is also widely prevalent in Russia, although it cannot be said to be a popular type, embodied, like Ivan the Fool, in a national symbol. One of the most striking instances of this, the Lucifer type, which I have come across, was a peasant called Nazarenko, who was a member of the first Duma. He was a tall, powerfully built, rugged-looking man, spare and rather thin, with clear-cut prominent features, black penetrating eyes, and thick black tangled hair. He looked as if he had stepped out of a sacred picture by Velasquez. This man had the pride of Lucifer. There was at that time, in July 1905, an Inter-parliamentary Congress sitting in London. Five delegates of the Russian Duma were chosen to represent Russia. It was proposed that Nazarenko should represent the peasants. I asked him once if he were going. He answered:

'I shan't go unless I am unanimously chosen by the others. I have written down my name and asked, but I shall not ask twice. I never ask twice for anything. When I say my prayers, I only ask God once for a thing, and if it is not granted, I never ask again. So it is not likely I would ask my fellow-men twice for anything. I am like that. I leave out that passage in the prayers about being a miserable slave. I am not a miserable slave, either of man or of Heaven.'

Such a man recognizes no authority, human or divine. Indeed he not only refuses to acknowledge authority, but it will be difficult for him to admire or bow down to any of those men or ideas which the majority have agreed to believe worthy of admiration, praise, or reverence.

Now, while Dostoievsky is the incarnation of the first type, of Ivan the Fool, Tolstoy is the incarnation of the second. It is true that, at a certain stage of his career, Tolstoy announced to the world that the ideal of Ivan Durak was the only ideal worth following. He perceives this aim with clearness, and, in preaching it, he has made a multitude of disciples; the only thing he has never been able to do is to make the supreme submission, the final surrender, and to become the type himself.

We know everything about Tolstoy, not only from the biographical writings of Fet and Behrs, but from his own autobiography, his novels, and his *Confession*. He gives us a panorama of events down to the smallest detail of his long career, as well as of every phase of feeling, and every shade and mood of his spiritual existence. The English reader who wishes to be acquainted with all the important facts of Tolstoy's material and spiritual life cannot do better than read Mr Aylmer Maude's *Life of Tolstoy*, which compresses into one well-planned and admirably executed volume all that is of interest during the first fifty years of Tolstoy's career. In reading this book a phrase of Tourgeniev's occurs to one. 'Man is the same, from the cradle to the grave.' Tolstoy had been called inconsistent; but the student of his life and work, far from finding inconsistency, will rather be struck by the unvarying and obstinate consistency of his ideas. Here, for instance, is an event recorded in Tolstoy's *Confession* (p. 1):

'I remember how, when I was about eleven, a boy, Vladimir Miliutin, long since dead, visited us one Sunday, and announced as the latest novelty a discovery made at his

c

school. The discovery was that there is no God at all, and all we are taught about Him is a mere invention. I remember how interested my elder brothers were in this news. They called me to their council, and we all, I remember, became animated, and accepted the news as something very interesting and fully possible.'

There is already the germ of the man who was afterwards to look with such independent eyes on the accepted beliefs and ideas of mankind, to play havoc with preconceived opinions, and to establish to his own satisfaction whether what was true for others was true for himself or not. Later he says:

'I was baptized and brought up in the Orthodox Christian faith. I was taught it in childhood and all through my boyhood and youth. Before I left the university, in my second year, at the age of eighteen, I no longer believed anything I had been taught.'[1]

A Russian writer, M. Kurbski, describes how, when he first met Tolstoy, he was overwhelmed by the look in Tolstoy's eyes. They were more than eyes, he said; they were like electric searchlights, which penetrated into the depths of your mind, and, like a photographic lens, seized and retained for ever a positive picture. In his *Childhood and Youth*, Tolstoy gives us the most vivid, the most natural, the most sensitive picture of childhood and youth that has ever been penned by the hand of man. And yet, after reading it, one is left half-unconsciously with the impression that the author feels there is something wrong, something unsatisfactory behind it all.

Tolstoy then passes on to describe the life of a grown-up man, in *The Morning of a Landowner*, in which he tells how he tried to work in his own home, on his property, and to teach the peasants, and how nothing came of his experiments. And again we have the feeling of something unsatisfactory, and something wanting, something towards which the man is straining, and which escapes him.

A little later, Tolstoy goes to the Caucasus, to the war,

[1] *Life of Tolstoy*, p. 38.

where life is primitive and simple, where he is nearer to nature, and where man himself is more natural. And then we have *The Cossacks*, in which Tolstoy's searchlights are thrown upon the primitive life of the old huntsman, the Cossack, Yeroshka, who lives as the grass lives, without care, without grief, and without reflection. Once more we feel that the soul of the writer is dissatisfied, still searching for something he has not found.

In 1854, Tolstoy took part in the Crimean War, which supplied him with the stuff for what are perhaps the most truthful pictures of war that have ever been written. But even here, we feel he has not yet found his heart's desire. Something is wrong. He was recommended for the St George's Cross, but owing to his being without some necessary official document at the time of his recommendation, he failed to receive it. This incident is a symbol of the greater failure, the failure to achieve the inward happiness that he is seeking—a solid ground to tread on, a bridge to the infinite, a final place of peace. In his private diary there is an entry made at the commencement of the war, while he was at Silistria, which runs as follows:

'I have no modesty; that is my great defect. . . . I am ugly, awkward, uncleanly, and lack society education. I am irritable, a bore to others, not modest; intolerant, and as shamefaced as a child. . . . I am almost an ignoramus. What I do know I have learnt anyhow, by myself, in snatches, without sequence, without a plan, and it amounts to very little. I am incontinent, undecided, inconstant, and stupidly vain and vehement, like all characterless people. I am not brave. . . . I am clever, but my cleverness has as yet not been thoroughly tested on anything. . . . I am honest; that is to say, I love goodness. . . . There is a thing I love more than goodness, and that is fame. I am so ambitious, and so little has this feeling been gratified, that, should I have to choose between fame and goodness, I fear I may often choose the former. Yes, I am not modest, and therefore I am proud at heart, shamefaced, and shy in society.'

At the time that Tolstoy wrote this he was a master, as Mr Aylmer Maude points out, of the French and German languages besides having some knowledge of English, Latin, Arabic, and Turco-Tartar. He had published stories which had caused the editors of the best Russian magazines to offer him the rate of pay accorded to the best-known writers. Therefore his discontent with his position, both intellectual and social, was in reality quite unfounded.

After the Crimean War, Tolstoy went abroad. He found nothing in Western Europe to satisfy him. On his return he settled down at Yasnaya Polyana, and married; and the great patriarchal phase of his life began, during which every gift and every happiness that man can be blessed with seemed to have fallen to his lot. It was then that he wrote *War and Peace*, in which he describes the conflict between one half of Europe and the other. He takes one of the largest canvases ever attacked by man; and he writes a prose epic on a period full of tremendous events. His piercing glance sees through all the fictions of national prejudice and patriotic bias; and he gives us what we feel to be the facts as they were, the very truth. No detail is too small for him, no catastrophe too great. He traces the growth of the spreading tree to its minute seed, the course of the great river to its tiny source. He makes a whole vanished generation of public and private men live before our eyes in such a way that it is difficult to believe that these people are not a part of our actual experience; and that his creations are not men and women we have seen with our own eyes, and whose voices we have heard with our own ears.

But when we put down this wonderful book, unequalled as a prose epic, as a panorama of a period and a gallery of a thousand finished portraits, we are still left with the impression that the author has not yet found what he is seeking. He is still asking why? and wherefore? What does it all mean? why all these horrors, why these sacrifices? Why all this conflict and suffering of nations? What do these high deeds, this heroism, mean? What is the significance of these State problems, and the patriotic self-sacrifice of nations? We are aware that the soul of Tolstoy is alone in an awful solitude, and that it is shivering on the heights, conscious that all round it is emptiness, darkness and despair.

Again, in *War and Peace* we are conscious that Tolstoy's proud nature, the 'Lucifer' type in him, is searching for another ideal; and that in the character of Pierre Bezuhov he is already setting up before us the ideal of Ivan Durak as the model which we should seek to imitate. And in Pierre Bezuhov we feel that there is something of Tolstoy himself. Manners change but man, faced by the problem of life, is the same throughout all ages; and, whether consciously or unconsciously, Tolstoy proves this in writing *Anna Karenina*. Here again, on a large canvas, we see unrolled before us the contemporary life of the upper classes in Russia, in St Petersburg, and in the country, with the same sharpness of vision, which seizes every outward detail, and reveals every recess of the heart and mind. Nearly all characters in all fiction seem bookish beside those of Tolstoy. His men and women are so real and so true that, even if his psychological analysis of them may sometimes err and go wrong from its oversubtlety and its desire to explain too much, the characters themselves seem to correct this automatically, as though they were independent of their creator. He creates a character and gives it life. He may theorize on a character, just as he might theorize on a person in real life; and he may theorize wrong, simply because sometimes no theorizing is necessary, and the very fact of a theory being set down in words may give a false impression; but, as soon as the character speaks and acts, it speaks and acts in the manner which is true to itself, and corrects the false impression of the theory, just as though it were an independent person over whom the author had no control.

Nearly every critic, at least nearly every English critic,[1] in dealing with *Anna Karenina*, has found fault with the author for the character of Vronsky. Anna Karenina, they say, could never have fallen in love with such an ordinary commonplace man. Vronsky, one critic has said (in a brilliant article), is only a glorified 'Steerforth'. The answer to this is that if you go to St Petersburg or to London, or to any other town you like to mention, you will find that the men with whom the Anna Kareninas of this world fall in love are precisely the Vronskys,

[1] Matthew Arnold is a notable exception.

and no one else, for the simple reason that Vronsky is a man. He is not a hero, and he is not a villain; he is not what people call 'interesting', but a man, as masculine as Anna is feminine, with many good qualities and many limitations, but above all things alive. Nearly every novelist, with the exception of Fielding, ends, in spite of himself, by placing his hero either above or beneath the standard of real life. There are many Vronskys today in St Petersburg, and for the matter of that, *mutatis mutandis*, in London. But no novelist except Tolstoy has ever had the power to put this simple thing, an ordinary man, into a book. Put one of Meredith's heroes next to Vronsky, and Meredith's hero will appear like a figure dressed up for a fancy-dress ball. Put one of Bourget's heroes next to him, with all his psychological documents attached to him, and, in spite of all the analysis in the world, side by side with Tolstoy's human being he will seem but a plaster-cast. Yet, all the time, in *Anna Karenina* we feel, as in *War and Peace*, that the author is still unsatisfied and hungry, searching for something he has not yet found; and once again, this time in still sharper outline and more living colours, he paints an ideal of simplicity which is taking us towards Ivan Durak in the character of Levin. Into this character, too, we feel that Tolstoy has put a great deal of himself; and that Levin, if he is not Tolstoy himself, is what Tolstoy would like to be. But the loneliness and the void that are round Tolstoy's mind are not yet filled; and in that loneliness and in that void we are sharply conscious of the brooding presence of despair, and the power of darkness.

We feel that Tolstoy is afraid of the dark; that to him there is something wrong in the whole of human life, a radical mistake. He is conscious that, with all his genius, he has only been able to record the fact that all that he has found in life is not what he is looking for, but something irrelevant and unessential; and, at the same time, that he has not been able to determine the thing in life which is not a mistake, nor where the true aim, the essential thing, is to be found, nor in what it consists. It is at this moment that the crisis occurred in Tolstoy's life which divides it outwardly into two sections, although it constitutes no break in his inward evolution. The fear of the dark, of the abyss yawning in front of him, was so strong that he felt he must rid himself of it at all costs.

'I felt terror' (he writes) 'of what was awaiting me, though I knew that this terror was more terrible than my position itself; I could not wait patiently for the end; my horror of the darkness was too great, and I felt I must rid myself of it as soon as possible by noose or bullet.'

This terror was not a physical fear of death, but an abstract fear, arising from the consciousness that the cold mists of decay were rising round him. By the realization of the nothingness of everything, of what Leopardi calls 'l'infinita vanità del tutto', he was brought to the verge of suicide. And then came the change which he describes thus in his *Confession*: 'I grew to hate myself; and now all has become clear to me.' This was the preliminary step of the development which led him to believe that he had at last found the final and everlasting truth. 'A man has only got not to desire lands or money, in order to enter into the kingdom of God.' Property, he came to believe, was the source of all evil. 'It is not a law of nature, the will of God, or a historical necessity; rather a superstition, neither strong nor terrible, but weak and contemptible.' To free oneself from this superstition he thought was as easy as to stamp on a spider. He desired literally to carry out the teaching of the Gospels, to give up all he had and to become a beggar.

This ideal he was not able to carry out in practice. His family, his wife, opposed him: and he was not strong enough to face the uncompromising and terrible sayings which speak of a man's foes being those of his own household, of father being divided against son, and household against household, of the dead being left to bury their dead. He put before him the ideal of the Christian saints, and of the early Russian martyrs who literally acted upon the saying of Christ; 'Whoso leaveth not house and lands and children for My sake, is not worthy of Me.' Tolstoy, instead of crushing the spider of property, shut his eyes to it. He refused to handle money, or to have anything to do with it; but this does not alter the fact that it was handled for him, so that he retained its advantages, and this without any

of the harassment which arises from the handling of property.
His affairs were, at all times, managed for him; and he continued to live as he had done before. No sane person would
think of blaming Tolstoy for this. He was not by nature a St
Francis; he was not by nature a Russian martyr, but the reverse.
What one does resent is not that his practice is inconsistent with
his teaching, but that his teaching is inconsistent with the ideal
which it professes to embody. He takes the Christian teaching,
and tells the world that it is the only hope of salvation, the only
key to the riddle of life. At the same time he neglects the first
truth on which that teaching is based, namely, that man must be
born again; he must humble himself and become as a little child.
It is just this final and absolute surrender that Tolstoy has been
unable to make. Instead of loving God through himself, and
loving himself for the God in him, he hates himself, and refuses
to recognize the gifts that God has given him. It is for this
reason that he talks of all his great work, with the exception of
a few stories written for children, as being worthless. It is for
this reason that he ceased writing novels, and attempted to
plough the fields. And the cause of all this is simply spiritual
pride, because he was unwilling 'to do his duty in that state of
life to which it had pleased God to call him'. Providence had
made him a novelist and a writer, and not a tiller of the fields.
Providence had made him not only a novelist, but perhaps the
greatest novelist that has ever lived; yet he deliberately turns
upon this gift, and spurns it, and spits upon it, and says that it
is worth nothing.

The question is, has a human being the right to do this,
especially if, for any reasons whatever, he is not able to make
the full and complete renunciation, and to cut himself off from
the world altogether? The answer is that if this be the foundation of Tolstoy's teaching, people have a right to complain of
there being something wrong in it. If he had left the world and
become a pilgrim, like one of the early Russian saints, not a
word could have been said; or if he had remained in the world,
preaching the ideals of Christianity and carrying them out as
far as he could, not a word could have been said. But, while he
has not followed the first course, he has preached that the second

course is wrong. He has striven after the ideal of Ivan Durak, but has been unable to find it, simply because he has been unable to humble himself; he has re-written the Gospels to suit his own temperament. The cry of his youth, 'I have no modesty,' remains true of him after his conversion. It is rather that he has no humility; and, instead of acknowledging that every man is appointed to a definite task, and that there is no such thing as a superfluous man or a superfluous task, he has preached that all tasks are superfluous except what he himself considers to be necessary; instead of preaching the love of the divine 'image of the King', with which man is stamped like a coin, he has told us to love the maker of the coin by hatred of His handiwork, quite regardless of the image with which it is stamped.

This all arises from the dual personality in the man, the conflict between the titanic 'Lucifer' and the other element in him, for ever searching for the ideal of Ivan Durak. The Titan is consumed with desire to become Ivan Durak; he preaches to the whole world that they should do so, but he cannot do it himself. Other proud and titanic natures have done it; but Tolstoy cannot do what Dante did. Dante was proud and a Titan, but Dante divested himself of his pride, and seeing the truth, said: 'In la sua volontade è nostra pace.' Nor can Tolstoy attain to Goethe's great cry of recognition of the 'himmlische Mächte', 'Wer nie sein Brod mit Thränen ass'. He remains isolated in his high and terrible solitude:

'*In the cold starlight where thou canst not climb.*'

Tourgeniev said of Tolstoy, 'He never loved any one but himself.' Merejkowski, in his *Tolstoy as Man and Artist,* a creative work of criticism, is nearer the truth when he says, 'He has never loved any man, *not even himself*!' But Merejkowski considers that the full circle of Tolstoy's spiritual life is not closed. He does not believe he has found the truth which he has sought for all his life, nor that he is, as yet, at rest.

'I cannot refuse to believe him' (he writes) 'when he speaks of himself as a pitiable fledgling fallen from the nest.

Yes, however terrible, it is true. This Titan, with all his vigour, is lying on his back and wailing in the high grass, as you and I and all the rest of us. No, he has found nothing; no faith, no God. And his whole justification is solely in his hopeless prayer, this piercing and plaintive cry of boundless solitude and dread. . . . Will he at last understand that there is no higher or lower in the matter; that the two seemingly contradictory and equally true paths, leading to one and the same goal, are not two paths, but one path which merely seems to be two; and that it is not by going against what is earthly or fleeing from it, but only through what is earthly, that we can reach the Divine; that it is not by divesting ourselves of the flesh, but through the flesh, that we can reach that which is beyond the flesh? Shall we fear the flesh? we, the children of Him who said, "My blood is drink indeed, and My flesh is meat indeed"; we, whose God is that God whose Word was made flesh?'[1]

Yet, whatever the mistakes of Tolstoy's teaching may be, they do not detract from the moral authority of the man. All his life he has searched for the truth, and all his life he has said exactly what he thought; and though he has fearlessly attacked all constituted authorities, nobody has dared to touch him. He is too great. This is the first time independent thought has prevailed in Russia; and this victory is the greatest service he has rendered to Russia *as a man*.

Neither Tolstoy nor Dostoievsky could endure Tourgeniev; their dislike of him is interesting, and helps us to understand the nature of their work and of their artistic ideals, and the nature of the distance that separates the work of Tourgeniev from that of Tolstoy. 'I despise the man,' Tolstoy wrote of Tourgeniev to Fet. Dostoievsky, in his novel *The Possessed*,[2] draws a scathing portrait of Tourgeniev, in which every defect of the man is noted but grossly exaggerated. This portrait is not uninstructive.

[1] *Tolstoy as Man and Artist*, pp. 93, 95. This passage is translated from the Russian edition.

[2] It should be said that this portrait is so unfair, and yet contains elements of truth so acutely observed, that for some people it spoils the whole book.

'I read his works in my childhood,' Dostoievsky writes, 'I even revelled in them. They were the delight of my boyhood and my youth. Then I gradually grew to feel colder towards his writing.' He goes on to say that Tourgeniev is one of those authors who powerfully affect one generation, and are then put on the shelf, like the scene of a theatre. The reason of this dislike, of the inability to admire Tourgeniev's work, which was shared by Tolstoy and Dostoievsky, is perhaps that both these men, each in his own way, reached the absolute truth of the life which was round them. Tolstoy painted the outer and the inner life of those with whom he came in contact, in a manner such as has never been seen before or since; and Dostoievsky painted the inner life (however fantastic he made the outer machinery of his work) with an insight that has never been attained before or since. Now Tourgeniev painted people of the same epoch, the same generation; he dealt with the same material; he dealt with it as an artist and as a poet, as a great artist, and as a great poet. But his vision was weak and narrow compared with that of Tolstoy, and his understanding was cold and shallow compared with that of Dostoievsky. His characters, beside those of Tolstoy, seem caricatures, and beside those of Dostoievsky they are conventional.

In Europe no foreign writer has ever received more abundant praise from the most eclectic judges than has Tourgeniev. Flaubert said of him: 'Quel gigantesque bonhomme que ce Scythe!' George Sand said, 'Maître, il nous faut tous aller à votre école.' Taine speaks of Tourgeniev's work as being the finest artistic production since Sophocles. Twenty-five years have now passed since Tourgeniev's death; and, as M. Haumant points out in his book, the period of reaction and of doubt, with regard to his work, has now set in even in Europe. People are beginning to ask themselves whether Tourgeniev's pictures are true, whether the Russians that he describes ever existed, and whether the praise which was bestowed upon him by his astonished contemporaries all over Europe was not a gross exaggeration.

One reason of the abundant and perhaps excessive praise which was showered on Tourgeniev by European critics is that

it was chiefly through Tourgeniev's work that Europe discovered Russian literature, and became aware that novels were
being written in which dramatic issues, as poignant and terrible
as those of Greek tragedy, arose simply out of the clash of certain characters in everyday life. The simplicity of Russian
literature, the naturalness of the characters in Russian fiction,
came like a revelation to Europe; and, as this revelation came
about partly through the work of Tourgeniev, it is not difficult
to understand that he received the praise not only due to him
as an artist, but the praise for all the qualities which are inseparable from the work of any Russian.

Heine says somewhere that the man who first came to Germany was astonished at the abundance of ideas there. 'This
man,' he says, 'was like the traveller who found a nugget of
gold directly he arrived in El Dorado; but his enthusiasm died
down when he discovered that in El Dorado there was nothing
but nuggets of gold.' As it was with ideas in Germany, according to Heine, so was it with the naturalness of Tourgeniev.
Compared with the work of Tolstoy and that of all other
Russian writers, Tourgeniev's naturalness is less astonishing,
because he possesses the same qualities that they possess, only
in a less degree.

When all is said, Tourgeniev was a great poet. What time
has not taken away from him, and what time can never take
away, is the beauty of his language and the poetry in his work.
Every Russian schoolboy has read the works of Tourgeniev
before he has left school; and every Russian schoolboy will
probably continue to do so, because Tourgeniev's prose remains a classic model of simple, beautiful, and harmonious
language, and as such it can hardly be excelled. Tourgeniev
never wrote anything better than the book which brought him
fame, the *Sportsman's Sketches*. In this book nearly the whole of
his talent finds expression. One does not know which to admire more—the delicacy of the art in choosing and recording
his impressions, or the limpid and musical utterance with which
they are recorded. To the reader who only knows his work
through a translation, three-quarters of the beauty are lost;
yet so great is the truth, and so moving is the poetry of these

sketches, that even in translation they will strike a reader as unrivalled.

There is, perhaps, nothing so difficult in the world to translate as stories dealing with Russian peasants. The simplicity and directness of their speech are the despair of the translator; and to translate them properly would require literary talent at once as great and as delicate as the author's. Mrs Garnett's version of Tourgeniev's work is admirable; yet in reading the translation of the *Sportsman's Sketches*, and comparing it with the original, one feels that the task is an almost impossible one. Some writers, Rudyard Kipling for instance, succeed in conveying to us the impression which is made by the conversation of men in exotic countries. When Rudyard Kipling gives us the speech of an Indian, he translates it into simple and biblical English. There is no doubt this is the right way to deal with the matter; it is the method which was adopted with perfect success by the great writers of the eighteenth century, the method of Fielding and Smollett in dealing with the conversation of simple men. One cannot help thinking that it is a mistake, in translating the speech of people like Russian peasants, or Indians, or Greeks, however familiar the speech may be, to try to render it by the equivalent colloquial or slang English. For instance, Mrs Garnett, in translating one of Tourgeniev's masterpieces, *The Singers*, turns the Russian words 'nie vryosh' (Art thou not lying?) by 'Isn't it your humbug?' In the same story she translates the Russian word 'molchat' by the slang expression 'shut up'. Now 'shut up' might, in certain circumstances, be the colloquial equivalent of 'molchat'; but the expression conveyed is utterly false, and it would be better to translate it simply 'be silent'; because to translate the talk of the Russian peasant into English colloquialisms conveys precisely the same impression, to any one familiar with the original, which he would receive were he to come across the talk of a Scotch gillie translated into English cockney slang.

This may seem a small point, but in reality it is the chief problem of all translation, and especially of that translation which deals with the talk and the ways of simple men. It is therefore of cardinal importance, when the material in question happens to be the talk of Russian peasants; and I have seen no translation in which this mistake is not made. How great the beauty of the original must be is proved by the fact that even in a translation of this kind one can still discern it, and that one receives at least a shadow of the impression which the author intended to convey. If the *Sportsman's Sketches* be the masterpiece of Tourgeniev, he rose to the same heights once more at the close of his career, when he wrote the incomparable *Poems in Prose*. Here once more he touched the particular vibrating string which was his special secret, and which thrills and echoes in the heart with so lingering a sweetness.

So much for Tourgeniev as a poet. But Tourgeniev was a novelist, he was famous as a novelist, and must be considered as such. His three principal novels. *A House of Gentlefolk, Fathers and Sons,* and *Virgin Soil,* laid the foundation of his European fame. Their merits consist in the ideal character of the women described, the absence of tricks of mechanism and melodrama, the naturalness of the sequence of the events, the harmony and proportion of the whole, and the vividness of the characters. No one can deny that the characters of Tourgeniev live; they are intensely vivid. Whether they are true to life is another question. The difference between the work of Tolstoy and Tourgeniev is this: that Tourgeniev's characters are as living as any characters ever are in books, but they belong, comparatively speaking, to bookland, and are thus conventional; whereas Tolstoy's characters belong to life. The fault which Russian critics find with Tourgeniev's characters is that they are exaggerated, that there is an element of caricature in them; and that they are permeated by the faults of the author's own character, namely, his weakness, and, above all, his self-consciousness. M. Haumant points out that the want of backbone in all Tourgeniev's characters does not prove that types of this kind must necessarily be untrue or misleading pictures of the Russian character, since Tourgeniev was not only a Russian, but an exceptionally gifted and remarkable Russian. Tourgeniev himself divides all humanity into two types, the Don Quixotes and the Hamlets. With but one notable exception, he almost exclusively portrayed the Hamlets. Feeble, nerveless people, full of ideas, enthusiastic in speech, capable by their words of exciting enthusiasm and even of creating belief in themselves, but incapable of action and devoid of will; they lack both the sublime simplicity and the weakness of Ivan Durak, which is not weakness but strength, because it proceeds from a profound goodness.

To this there is one exception. In *Fathers and Sons*, Tourgeniev drew a portrait of the 'Lucifer' type, of an unbending and inflexible will, namely, Bazarov. There is no character in the whole of his work which is more alive; and nothing that he wrote ever aroused so much controversy and censure as this figure. Tourgeniev invented the type of the intellectual Nihilist in fiction. If he was not the first to invent the word, he was the first to apply it and to give it currency. The type remains, and will remain, of the man who believes in nothing, bows to nothing, bends to nothing, and who retains his invincible pride until death strikes him down. Here again, compared with the Nihilists whom Dostoievsky has drawn in his *Possessed*, we feel that, so far as the inner truth of this type is concerned, Tourgeniev's Bazarov is a book-character, extraordinarily vivid and living though he be; and that Dostoievsky's Nihilists, however outwardly fantastic they may seem, are inwardly not only truer, but the very quintessence of truth. Tourgeniev never actually saw the real thing as Tolstoy might have seen it and described it; nor could he divine by intuition the real thing as Dostoievsky divined it, whether he saw it or not. But Tourgeniev evolved a type out of his artistic imagination, and made a living figure which, to us at any rate, is extraordinarily striking. This character has proved, however, highly irritating to those who knew the prototype from which it was admittedly drawn, and considered him not only a far more interesting character than Tourgeniev's conception, but quite different from it. But whatever fault may be found with Bazarov, none can be found with the description of his death. Here Tourgeniev reaches his highwater mark as a novelist, and strikes a note of manly pathos which, by its reserve, suggests an infinity of things all the more striking for being left unsaid. The death of Bazarov is one of the great pages of the world's fiction.

In *Virgin Soil*, Tourgeniev attempts to give a sketch of underground life in Russia—the revolutionary movement, helpless in face of the ignorance of the masses and the unpreparedness of the nation at large for any such movement. Here, in the opinion of all Russian judges, and of most latter-day critics who have knowledge of the subject, he failed. In describing the official class, although he does this with great skill and cleverness, he makes a gallery of caricatures; and the revolutionaries whom he sets before us as types, however good they may be as fiction, are not the real thing.[1] Nevertheless, in spite of Tourgeniev's limitations, these three books, *A House of Gentlefolk, Fathers and Sons,* and *Virgin Soil*, must always have a permanent value as reflecting the atmosphere of the generation which he paints, even though his pictures be marred by caricatures, and feeble when compared with those of his rivals.

Of his other novels, the most important are *On the Eve, Smoke, Spring Waters,* and *Rudin* (the most striking portrait in his gallery of Hamlets). In *Spring Waters*, Tourgeniev's poetry is allowed free play; the result is therefore an entrancing masterpiece. With regard to *On the Eve*, Tolstoy writes thus:[2]

'These are excellent negative characters, the artist and the father. The rest are not types; even their conception, their position, is not typical, or they are quite insignificant. That, however, is always Tourgeniev's mistake. The girl is hopelessly bad. 'Ah, how I love thee! . . . Her eyelashes were long.' In general it always surprises me that Tourgeniev, with his mental powers and poetic sensibility, should, even in his methods, not be able to refrain from banality. There is no humanity or sympathy for the characters, but the author exhibits monsters whom he scolds and does not pity.'

Again, in writing of *Smoke*, Tolstoy says:[3]

[1] With the exception of Marianna, one of his most beautiful and noble characters.
[2] *Life*, p. 189.
[3] *Life*, p. 312.

'About *Smoke*, I think that the strength of poetry lies in love; and the direction of that strength depends on character. Without strength of love there is no poetry; but strength falsely directed—the result of the poet's having an unpleasant weak character—creates dislike. In *Smoke* there is hardly any love of anything, and very little pity; there is only love of light and playful adultery; and therefore the poetry of that novel is repulsive.'

These criticisms, especially the latter, may be said to sum up the case of the 'Advocatus Diaboli' with regard to Tourgeniev. I have quoted them because they represent what many educated Russians feel at the present day about a great part of Tourgeniev's work, however keenly they appreciate his poetical sensibility and his gift of style. The view deserves to be pointed out, because all that can be said in praise of Tourgeniev has not only been expressed with admirable nicety and discrimination by widely different critics of various nationalities, but their praise is constantly being quoted; whereas the other side of the question is seldom mentioned. Yet in the case of *On the Eve*, Tolstoy's criticism is manifestly unfair. Tolstoy was unable by his nature to do full justice to Tourgeniev. Perhaps the most impartial and acute criticism of Tourgeniev's work that exists is to be found in M. de Vogüé's *Roman Russe*. M. de Vogüé is not indeed blind to Tourgeniev's defects; he recognizes the superiority both of Tolstoy and Dostoievsky, but he nevertheless gives Tourgeniev his full meed of appreciation.

The lapse of years has only emphasized the elements of banality and conventionality which are to be found in Tourgeniev's work. He is a masterly landscape painter; but even here he is not without convention. His landscapes are always orthodox Russian landscapes, and are seldom varied. He seems never to get face to face with nature, after the manner of Wordsworth; he never gives us any elemental pictures of nature, such as Gorky succeeds in doing in a phrase; but he rings the changes on delicate arrangements of wood, cloud, mist and water, vague backgrounds and diaphanous figures, after the manner of Corot. This does not detract from the beauty of his pictures, and our admiration for them is not lessened; but all temptation to exaggerate its merits vanishes when we turn from his work to that of stronger masters.

To sum up, it may be said that the picture of Russia obtained from the whole of Tourgeniev's work has been incomplete, but it is not inaccurate; and such as it is, with all its faults, it is invaluable. In 1847, Bielinski, in writing to Tourgeniev, said: 'It seems to me that you have little or no creative genius. Your vocation is to depict reality.' This criticism remained true to the end of Tourgeniev's career, but it omits his greatest gift, his poetry, the magical echoes, the 'unheard melodies', which he sets vibrating in our hearts by the music of his utterance. The last of Tourgeniev's poems in prose is called 'The Russian Language.' It runs as follows:

'In days of doubt, in the days of burdensome musing over the fate of my country, thou alone art my support and my mainstay, oh great, mighty, truthful, and unfettered Russian language! Were it not for thee, how should I not fall into despair at the sight of all that is being done at home? But how can I believe that such a tongue was given to any but a great people?'

No greater praise can be given to Tourgeniev than to say that he was worthy of his medium, and that no Russian prose writer ever handled the great instrument of his inheritance with a more delicate touch or a surer execution.

When Tourgeniev was dying, he wrote to Tolstoy and implored him to return to literature. 'That gift,' he wrote, 'came whence all comes to us. Return to your literary work, great writer of our Russian land!'

All through Tourgeniev's life, in spite of his frequent quarrels with Tolstoy, he never ceased to admire the works of his rival. Tourgeniev had the gift of admiration. Tolstoy is absolutely devoid of it. The 'Lucifer' spirit in him refuses to bow down before Shakespeare or Beethoven, simply because it is incapable of bending at all. To justify this want, this incapacity to admire the great masterpieces of the world, Tolstoy wrote a book called *What is Art*, in which he condemned theories he had himself enunciated years before. In this, and in a book on Shakespeare, he treats all art, the very greatest, as if it were in the same category with that of æsthetes who confine themselves to prattling of 'Art for Art's sake'. Beethoven he brushes aside because, he says, such music can only appeal to specialists. 'What proportion of the world's population,' he asks, 'have ever heard the Ninth Symphony or seen *King Lear*? And how many of them enjoyed the one or the other?' If these things be the highest art, and yet the bulk of men live without them, and do not need them, then the highest art lacks all claim to such respect as Tolstoy is ready to accord to art. In commenting on this, Mr Aylmer Maude writes: 'The case of the specialists, when Tolstoy calls in question the merits of *King Lear* or of the Ninth Symphony, is an easy one.'

But the fallacy does not lie here. The fallacy lies in thinking the matter is a case for specialists at all. It is not a case for specialists. Beethoven's later quartets may be a case for the specialist, just as the obscurer passages in Shakespeare may be a case for the specialist. This does not alter the fact that the whole of the German nation, and multitudes of people outside Germany, meet together to hear Beethoven's symphonies played, and enjoy them. It does not alter the fact that Shakespeare's plays are translated into every language and enjoyed, and, when they are performed, are enjoyed by the simplest and the most uneducated people. The highest receipts are obtained at the Théâtre Français on holidays and feast days, when the plays of Molière are given. Tolstoy leaves out the fact that very great art, such as that of Homer, Shakespeare, Dante, Milton, Beethoven, Mozart, appeals at the same time, and possibly for different reasons, to the highly trained specialist and to the most uncultivated ignoramus. This, Dr Johnson points out, is the great merit of Bunyan's *Pilgrim's Progress*: the most cultivated man cannot find anything to praise more highly, and a child knows nothing more amusing. This is also true of *Paradise Lost*, an appreciation of which is held in England to be the highest criterion of scholarship. And *Paradise Lost*, translated into simple prose, is sold in cheap editions, with

coloured pictures, all over Russia,[1] and greedily read by the
peasants, who have no idea that it is a poem, but enjoy it as a
tale of fantastic adventure and miraculous events. It appeals at
the same time to their religious feeling and to their love of fairy
tales, and impresses them by a certain elevation in the language (just as the chants in church impress them) which they
unconsciously feel does them good.

It is this inability to admire which is the whole defect of
Tolstoy, and it arises from his indomitable pride, which is the
strength of his character, and causes him to tower like a giant
over all his contemporaries. Therefore, in reviewing his whole
work and his whole life, and in reviewing it in connection with
that of his contemporaries, one comes to this conclusion. If
Tolstoy, being as great as he is, has this great limitation, we can
only repeat the platitude that no genius, however great, is
without limitations; no ruby without a flaw. Were it otherwise—had there been combined with Tolstoy's power and
directness of vision and creative genius, the large love and the
childlike simplicity of Dostoievsky—we should have had,
united in one man, the complete expression of the Russian race;
that is to say, we should have had a complete man—which is
impossible.

Tourgeniev, on the other hand, is full to the brim of the
power of admiration and appreciation which Tolstoy lacks;
but then he also lacks Tolstoy's strength and power. Dostoievsky has a power different from Tolstoy's, but equal in scale,
and titanic. He has a power of admiration, an appreciation
wider and deeper than Tourgeniev's, and the humility of a man
who has descended into hell, who has been face to face with the
sufferings and the agonies of humanity and the vilest aspects of
human nature; who, far from losing his faith in the divine, has
detected it in every human being, however vile, and in every
circumstance, however hideous; and who in dust and ashes has
felt himself face to face with God. Yet, in spite of all this,
Dostoievsky is far from being the complete expression of the
Russian genius, or a complete man. His limitations are as great
as Tolstoy's; and no one was ever more conscious of them than

[1] Written in 1910.

himself. They do not concern us here. What does concern us is that in modern Russian literature, in the literature of this century, leaving the poets out of the question, the two great figures, the two great columns which support the temple of Russian literature, are Tolstoy and Dostoievsky. Tourgeniev's place is inside that temple; there he has a shrine and an altar which are his own, which no one can dispute with him, and which are bathed in serene radiance and visited by shy visions and voices of haunting loveliness. But neither as a writer nor as a man can he be called the great representative of even half the Russian genius; for he complements the genius of neither Tolstoy nor Dostoievsky. He possesses in a minor degree qualities which they both possessed; and the qualities which are his and his only, exquisite as they are, are not of the kind which belong to the greatest representatives of a nation or of a race.

CHAPTER V

The Place of Tourgeniev

IN THE PRECEDING I have tried very briefly to point out the state of the barometer of public opinion (the barometer of the average educated man and not of any exclusive clique) with regard to Tourgeniev's reputation in Russia at the present day.

That and no more. I have not devoted a special chapter in this book to Tourgeniev for the reasons I have already stated: namely, that his work is better known in England than most other Russian classics, and that admirable appreciations of his work exist already, written by famous critics, such as Mr Henry James and M. Melchior de Vogüé. There is in England, among people who care for literature and who study the literature of Europe, a perfectly definite estimate of Tourgeniev. It is for this reason that I confined myself to trying to elucidate what the average Russian thinks today about Tourgeniev compared with other Russian writers, and to noticing any changes which have come about with regard to the estimate of his work in Russia and in Europe during the last twenty years. I thought this was sufficient.

But I now realize from several able criticisms on my study of Tolstoy and Tourgeniev when it appeared in the *Quarterly Review,* that I had laid myself open to be misunderstood. It was taken for granted in several quarters not only that I underrated Tourgeniev as a writer, but that I wished to convey the impression that his reputation was a bubble that had burst. Nothing was farther from my intention than this. And here lies the great danger of trying to talk of any foreign writer from the point of view of that writer's country and not from that of your own country. You are instantly misunderstood. For instance, if you say Alfred de Musset is not so much admired now in France as he used to be in the sixties, the English reader, who may only recently have discovered Alfred de Musset, and, indeed, may be approaching French poetry as a whole for the first time, at once retorts: 'There is a man who is depreciating one of France's greatest writers!'

Now what I wish to convey with regard to Tourgeniev is simply this:

Firstly, that although he is and always will remain a Russian classic, he is not, rightly or wrongly, so enthusiastically admired as he used to be: new writers have risen since his time (not necessarily better ones, but men who have opened windows on undreamed-of-vistas); and not only this, but one of his own contemporaries, Dostoievsky, has been brought into a larger and clearer light of fame than he enjoyed in his lifetime, owing to the dissipation of the mists of political prejudices and temporary and local polemics, differences, quarrels and controversies.

But the English reader has, as a general rule, never got farther than Tourgeniev. He is generally quite unacquainted with the other Russian classics; and so when it is said that there are others greater than he—Dostoievsky and Gogol, for instance—the English reader thinks an attempt is being made to break a cherished and holy image. And if he admires Tourgeniev—which, if he likes Russian literature at all he is almost sure to do—it makes him angry.

Secondly, I wish to say that owing to the generally prevailing limited view of the educated intellectual Englishman as to the field of Russian literature as a whole, I do think he is inclined to overrate the genius and position of Tourgeniev in Russian literature, great as they are. There is, I think, an exaggerated cult for Tourgeniev among intellectual Englishmen.[1] The case of Tennyson seems to me to afford a very close parallel to that of Tourgeniev.

Mr Gosse pointed out not long ago in a subtle and masterly article that Tennyson, although we were now celebrating his centenary, had not reached that moment when a poet is rapturously rediscovered by a far younger generation than his

[1] See, for instance, Mr Frank Harris in his *Shakespeare the Man: His Tragedy.* See footnote, p. 124.

own, but that he had reached that point when the present generation felt no particular excitement about his work. This seems to me the exact truth about Tourgeniev's reputation in Russia at the present day. Everybody has read him, and everybody will always read him because he is a classic and because he has written immortal things, but now, in the year 1909, there is no particular excitement about *Fathers and Sons* in Russia: just as now there is no particular excitement about the 'Idylls of the King' or 'In Memoriam' in England today. Tourgeniev has not yet been rediscovered.

Of course, there are some critics who in 'the fearless old fashion' say boldly that Tennyson's reputation is dead; that he exists no longer, and that we need not trouble to mention him. I read some such sweeping pronouncement not long ago by an able journalist. There are doubtless Russian critics who say the same about Tourgeniev. As to whether they are right or wrong, I will not bother myself or my readers, but I do wish to make it as clear as daylight that I myself hold no such opinion either with regard to Tourgeniev or to Tennyson.

I believe Tennyson to have written a great quantity of immortal and magnificently beautiful verse. I believe that Tennyson possesses an enduring throne in the Temple of English poets. I believe Tourgeniev to have written a great quantity of immortal and inexpressibly beautiful prose, and I believe that he will hold an enduring seat in the Temple of Russian literature. I think this is clear. But supposing a Russian critic were to write on the English literature and the English taste of the present day, and supposing he were to say, 'Of course, as we Russians all feel, there is only one English poet in the English literature of the last hundred years, and that is Tennyson. Tennyson is the great and only representative of English art; the only writer who has expressed the English soul.' We should then suspect he had never studied the world of Wordsworth, Shelley, Byron, Keats, Coleridge, Browning and Swinburne. Well, this, it seems to me, is exactly how Tourgeniev is treated in England. All I wished to point out was that the point of view of a Russian was necessarily different, owing to his larger field of vision and to the greater extent and depth of his knowledge, and to his closer communion with the work of his national authors.

But, as I have said, it was taken for granted by some people that I wished to show that Tourgeniev was not a classic. I will therefore, at the risk of wearying my readers, repeat—with as much variation as I can muster—what I consider to be some of Tourgeniev's special claims to enduring fame.

I have said he was a great poet; but the words seem bare and dead when one considers the peculiar nature of the shy and entrancing poetry that is in Tourgeniev's work. He has the magic that water gives to the reflected images of trees, hills and woods; he touches the ugly facts of life, softens and transfigures them so that they lose none of their reality, but gain a majesty and a mystery that comes from beyond the world, just as the moonlight softens and transfigures the wrinkled palaces and decaying porticoes of Venice, hiding what is sordid, heightening the beauty of line, and giving a quality of magic to every stately building, to each delicate pillar and chiselled arch.

Then there is in his work a note of wistful tenderness that steals into the heart and fills it with an incommunicable pleasureable sadness, as do the songs you hear in Russia on dark summer nights in the villages, or, better still, on the broad waters of some huge silent river—songs aching with an ecstasy of homesickness, songs which are something half-way between the whining sadness of Oriental music and the rippling plaintiveness of Irish and Scotch folk-song; songs that are imperatively melodious, but strange to us in their rhythm, constantly changing yet subordinated to definite law, varying indeed with an invariable law; songs whose notes, without being definitely sharp or flat, seem a little bit higher, or a shade lower than you expect, and in which certain notes come over and over again with an insistent appeal, a heartbreaking iteration, and an almost intolerable pathos; songs which end abruptly and suddenly, so that you feel that they are meant to begin again at once and to go on for ever.

This is how Tourgeniev's poetical quality—as manifested in his *Sportsman's Sketches*, his *Poems in Prose*, and in many other of his works—strikes me. But I doubt if any one unacquainted with the Russian language would derive such impressions, for it is above all things Tourgeniev's language—the words he uses and the way in which he uses them—that is magical. Every sentence is a phrase of perfect melody; limpid, simple and sensuous. And all this must necessarily half disappear in a translation, however good.

But then Tourgeniev is not only a poet. He is a great novelist and something more than a great novelist. He has recorded for all time the atmosphere of a certain epoch. He has done for Russia what Trollope did for England: he has exactly conveyed the atmosphere and the tone of the fifties. The characters of Trollope and Tourgeniev are excelled by those of other writers—and I do not mean to put Tourgeniev on the level of Trollope, because Tourgeniev is an infinitely greater writer and an artist of an altogether higher order—; but for giving the general picture and atmosphere of England during the fifties, I do not believe any one has excelled Trollope; and for giving the general atmosphere of the fifties in Russia, of a certain class, I do not believe anyone—with the possible exception of Aksakov, the Russian Trollope—has excelled what Tourgeniev did in his best known books, *Fathers and Sons, Virgin Soil,* and *A House of Gentlefolk.*

Then, of course, Tourgeniev has gifts of shrewd characterization, the power of creating delightful women, gifts of pathos and psychology, and artistic gifts of observation and selection, the whole being always illumined and refined by the essential poetry of his temperament, and the magical manner in which, like an inspired conductor leading an orchestra of delicate wood and wind instruments, he handles the Russian language. But when it comes to judging who has interpreted more truly Russian life as a whole, and who has gazed deepest into the Russian soul and expressed most truly and fully what is there, then I can but repeat that I think he falls far short of Tolstoy, in the one case, and of Dostoievsky, in the other. Judged as a whole, I think he is far excelled, for different reasons, by Tolstoy, Dostoievsky, and by Gogol, who surpasses him immeasurably alike in imagination, humour and truth. I have endeavoured to explain why in various portions of this book. I will not add anything further here, and I only hope that I have made it sufficiently clear that although I admire other Russian writers more than Tourgeniev, I am no image-breaker; and that although I worship more fervently at other altars, I never for a moment intended either to deny or to depreciate the authentic ray of divine light that burns in Tourgeniev's work.[1]

[1] The most striking instance I have come across lately of the cult for Tourgeniev in England is in Mr Frank Harris's remarkable book on Shakespeare. He illustrates his thesis that Shakespeare could not create a manly character, by saying that Shakespeare could not have drawn a *Bazarov* or a *Marianna*. Leaving the thesis out of the discussion, it is to me almost incredible that any one could think Tourgeniev's characters manly, compared with those of Shakespeare. Tourgeniev played a hundred variations on the theme of the minor Hamlet. He painted a whole gallery of little Hamlets. *Bazarov* attains his strength at the expense of intellectual nihilism, but he is a neuropath compared with Mercutio. And *Bazarov* is the only one of Tourgeniev's characters (and Tourgeniev's acutest critics agree with this—see Brückner and Vogüé) that has strength. Tourgeniev could no more have created a Falstaff than he could have flown. Where are these manly characters of Tourgeniev? Who are they? Indeed a Russian critic lately pointed out, *à propos* of Tchekov, that the whole of Russian politics, literature, and art, during the latter half of the nineteenth century, suffered from the misfortune of there being so many such Hamlets and so few Fortinbrases. I am convinced that had Mr Harris been a Russian, or had Tourgeniev been an Englishman, Mr Harris would not have held these views. (*Written in 1910.*)

CHAPTER VI

Dostoievsky

'In nobler books we are moved with something like the emotions of
life; and this emotion is very variously provoked. We are moved when
Levine labours in the field, when André sinks beyond emotion, when
Richard Feverel and Lucy Desborough meet beside the river, when
Antony, not cowardly, puts off his helmet, when Kent has infinite pity on
the dying Lear, when in Dostoievsky's *Despised and Rejected*, the uncom-
plaining hero drains his cup of suffering and virtue. These are notes
which please the great heart of man.'

R. L. STEVENSON, *Across the Plains*

'Raskolnikoff (*Crime and Punishment*) is easily the greatest book I have
read in ten years. . . . I divined . . . the existence of a certain impotence in
many minds of today which prevents them from living in a book or a
character and keeps them afar off, spectators of a puppet show. To such I
suppose the book may seem empty in the centre; to the others it is a room,
a house of life, into which they themselves enter, and are tortured and
purified. . . .

'Another has been translated—*Humiliés et offensés*. It is even more in-
coherent than *Le Crime et le Châtiment*, but breathes much of *the same
lovely goodness*.'[1]

R. L. STEVENSON, *Letters*

I

INTRODUCTORY

IN THE AUTUMN of 1897 I was staying in the South of Russia
at the house of a gentleman who has played no unimportant
part in Russian politics. We were sitting one evening at tea, a
party of nearly thirty people round the table, consisting of
country gentlemen, neighbours and friends. The village doctor
was present: he was an ardent Tolstoyist, and not only an admirer of Tolstoy's genius, but a disciple, and a believer in his

---

[1] These italics are mine.

religious teaching. He had been talking on this subject for some time, and expressing his hero-worship in emphatic terms, when the son of my host, a boy at school, only seventeen years of age, yet familiar with the literature of seven languages, a writer, moreover, of both English and Russian verse, fired up and said:

'In fifty years' time we Russians shall blush with shame to think that we gave Tolstoy such fulsome admiration, when we had at the same time a genius like Dostoievsky, the latchet of whose shoes Tolstoy is not worthy to unloose.'

A few months after this I read an article on Dostoievsky in one of the literary weeklies in England, in which the writer stated that Dostoievsky was a mere *feuilletonist*, a concocter of melodrama, to be ranked with Eugene Sue and Xavier de Montépin. I was struck at the time by the divergence between English and Russian views on this subject. I was amazed by the view of the English critic in itself; but the reason that such a view could be expressed at all is not far to seek, since there is at this moment no complete translation of Dostoievsky's works in England, and no literary translation of the same. Only one of his books, *Crime and Punishment*, is known at all, and the rest of them are difficult even to obtain in the English language.

However this may be, at the present time Dostoievsky's fame in Russia is every day becoming more universally and more emphatically recognized. The present generation are inclined to consider him the greatest of all their novelists; and although they as a rule, with the critic Merejkowski, put him equal with Tolstoy as one of the two great pillars which uphold the Temple of Russian literature, they are for the most part agreed in thinking that he was a unique product, a more startling revelation and embodiment of genius, a greater elemental force, than Tolstoy or any other Russian writer of fiction. In fact, they hold the same view about him that we do with regard to Shelley in our poetical literature. We may not think that Shelley is a greater poet than Keats, Wordsworth, Coleridge or Byron, but he certainly is a more exceptional incarnation of poetical genius. We can imagine poets like Keats arising again—one nearly akin to him and almost equally exquisite did appear in the shape of Tennyson. We can imagine there being other writers who would attain to Wordsworth's simplicity and communion with nature, but Shelley has as yet been without kith or kindred, without mate or equal, in the whole range of the world's literary history. He does not appear to us like a plant that grows among others, differing from them only in being more beautiful and striking, which is true even of poets like Shakespeare, Dante and Goethe, who reveal in the highest degree qualities which other poets possess in a lesser degree, and complete and fulfil what the others aim at and only partially achieve; but Shelley is altogether different in kind: he aims at and achieves something which is beyond the range and beyond the ken of other poets. It is as though he were not a man at all, but an embodiment of certain elemental forces.

So it is with Dostoievsky. And for this reason those who admire him do so passionately and extravagantly. It must not be thought that they do not discern his faults, his incompleteness, and his limitations, but the positive qualities that he possesses seem to them matchless, and so precious, so rare, so tremendous, that they annihilate all petty criticism. The example of Shelley may again serve us here. Only a pedant, in the face of such flights of genius as 'The Cloud', the 'Ode to the West Wind', 'The Sensitive Plant', or that high pageant of grief, fantasy, or 'thoughts that breathe and words that burn,'—'Adonais'—would apply a magnifying glass to such poems and complain of the occasional lapses of style or of the mistakes in grammar which may be found in them. These poems may be full of trivial lapses of this kind, but such matters are of small account when a poet has evoked for us a vision of what dwells beyond the veil of the senses, and struck chords of a music which has the power and the wonder of a miracle.

With Dostoievsky the case is somewhat but not in all respects similar. He possesses a certain quality which is different in kind from those of any other writer, a power of seeming to get nearer to the unknown, to what lies beyond the flesh, which is perhaps the secret of his amazing strength; and, besides this, he has certain great qualities which other writers, and notably other Russian writers, possess also; but he has them in so far higher a degree that when seen with other writers he annihilates them. The combination of this difference in kind and this difference in degree makes something so strong and so tremendous, that it is not to be wondered at when we find many critics saying that Dostoievsky is not only the greatest of all Russian writers, but one of the greatest writers that the world has ever seen. I am not exaggerating when I say that such views are held; for instance, Professor Brückner, a most level-headed critic, in his learned and exhaustive survey of Russian literature, says that it is not in *Faust*, but rather in *Crime and Punishment*, that the whole grief of mankind takes hold of us.

Even making allowance for the enthusiasm of his admirers, it is true to say that almost any Russian judge of literature at the present day would place Dostoievsky as being equal to Tolstoy and immeasurably above Tourgeniev; in fact, the ordinary Russian critic at the present day no more dreams of comparing Tourgeniev with Dostoievsky, than it would occur to an Englishman to compare Charlotte Yonge with Charlotte Brontë.

Dostoievsky's fame came late, although his first book, *Poor Folk*, made a considerable stir, and the publication of his *Crime and Punishment* ensured his popularity. But when I say 'fame', I mean the universal recognition of him by the best and most competent judges. This recognition is now an accomplished fact in Russia and also in Germany. The same cannot be said positively of France, although his books are for the most part well translated into French, and have received the warmest and the most acute appreciation at the hands of a French critic, namely, M. de Vogüé in *Le Roman Russe*.[1] In England, Dostoievsky cannot be said to be known at all, since the translations of his works are not only inadequate, but scarce and difficult to obtain, and it is possible to come across the most amazing judgments pronounced on them by critics whose judgment on other subjects is excellent.[2] The reason of this tardy recognition of Dostoievsky in his own country is that he

[1] The reader should remember that Maurice Baring wrote this paragraph in 1910.

[2] This is, of course, not universal. See Mr Gosse's *Questions at Issue*.

was one of those men whose innate sense of fairness and hatred
of cant prevent them from whole-heartedly joining a political
party and swallowing its tenets indiscriminately, even when
some of these tenets are nonsensical and iniquitous. He was one
of those men who put truth and love higher than any political
cause, and can fight for such a cause only when the leaders of it,
in practice as well as in theory, never deviate from the one or
the other. He was between two fires: the Government considered him a revolutionary, and the revolutionaries thought
him a retrograde; because he refused to be blind to the merits
of the Government, such as they were, and equally refused to be
blind to the defects of the enemies of the Government. He
therefore attacked not only the Government, but the Government's enemies; and when he attacked, it was with thunder-
bolts. The Liberals never forgave him this. Dostoievsky was un-
justly condemned to spend four years in penal servitude for a
political crime; for having taken part in a revolutionary propaganda. He returned from Siberia a Slavophil, and, I will not
say a Conservative, as the word is misleading; but a man convinced not only of the futility of revolution, but also of the
worthlessness of a great part of the revolutionaries. Nor did the
Liberals ever forgive him this. They are only just beginning to
do so now. Moreover, in one of his most powerful books, *The
Possessed*, he draws a scathing picture of all the flotsam and
jetsam of revolution, and not only of the worthless hangers-
on who are the parasites of any such movement, but he reveals
the decadence and worthlessness of some of the men, who by
their dominating character played leading parts and were popular heroes. Still less did the Liberals forgive him this book; and
even now, few Liberal writers are fair towards it. Again,
Dostoievsky was, as I shall show later, by nature an antagonist
of Socialism and a hater of materialism; and since all the leading men among the Liberals of his time were either one or the
other, if not both, Dostoievsky aroused the enmity of the whole
Liberal camp, by attacking not only its parasites but its leaders,
men of high principle such as Bielinsky, who were obviously
sincere and deserving of the highest consideration and respect.
One can imagine a similar situation in England if at the present

time there were an autocratic government, a backward and ignorant peasantry, and a small and Liberal movement carried on by a minority of extremely intellectual men, headed, let us say, by Mr Bernard Shaw, Lord Morley, Professor Raleigh, and Sir J. J. Thomson. I purposely take men of widely different opinions, because in a country where there is a fight going on for a definite thing, such as a Constitution, there is a moment when men, who under another régime would be split up into Liberals and Conservatives, are necessarily grouped together in one big Liberal camp. Now, let us suppose that the men who were carrying on this propaganda for reform were undergoing great sacrifices; let us likewise suppose them to be Socialists and materialists to the core. Then suppose there should appear a novelist of conspicuous power, such as George Meredith or Mr Thomas Hardy or Mr H. G. Wells, who by some error was sent to Botany Bay for having been supposed to be mixed up with a revolutionary propaganda, and on his return announced that he was an Anti-Revolutionary, violently attacked Mr Shaw, wrote a book in which he caricatured him, and drew a scathing portrait of all his disciples—especially of the less intelligent among them. One can imagine how unpopular such an author would be in Liberal circles. This was the case of Dostoievsky in Russia. It is only fair to add that his genius has now obtained full recognition, even at the hands of Liberals, though they still may not be able to tolerate his book, *The Possessed*. But considering the magnitude of his genius, this recognition has been, on the whole, a tardy one. For instance, even in so valuable a book as Prince Kropotkin's *Ideals and Realities in Russian Literature*, Dostoievsky receives inadequate treatment and scanty appreciation. On the other hand, in Merejkowsky's *Tolstoy and Dostoievsky*, Merejkowsky, who is also a Liberal, praises Dostoievsky with complete comprehension and with brilliance of thought and expression.

DOSTOIEVSKY'S LIFE

Dostoievsky was the son of a staff-surgeon and a trades-man's daughter. He was born in a charity hospital, the 'Maison de Dieu,' at Moscow, in 1821. He was, as he said, a member of a stray family. His father and five children lived in a flat consisting of two rooms and a kitchen. The nursery of the two boys, Michael and Fedor, consisted of a small part of the entrance hall, which was partitioned off. His family belonged to the lowest ranks of the nobility, to that stratum of society which supplied the bureaucracy with its minor public servants. The poverty surrounding his earliest years was to last until the day of his death.

Some people are, as far as money is concerned, like a negative pole—money seems to fly away from them, or rather, when it comes to them, to be unable to find any substance it can cleave to. Dostoievsky was one of these people; he never knew how much money he had, and when he had any, however little, he gave it away. He was what the French call a *panier percé*: money went through him as through a sieve. And however much money he had, it was never he but his friends who benefited by it.

He received his earliest education at a small school in Moscow, where a schoolmaster who taught Russian inspired him and his brother with a love of literature, of Pushkin's poetry and other writers, introduced him also to the works of Walter Scott, and took him to see a performance of Schiller's *Robbers*. When his preliminary studies were ended, he was sent with his brother to a school of military engineers at St Petersburg. Here his interest in literature, which had been first aroused by coming into contact with Walter Scott's works, was further developed by his discovery of Balzac, George Sand, and Homer. Dostoievsky developed a passionate love of literature and poetry. His favourite author was Gogol. He left this school in 1843 at the age of twenty-three, with the rank of sub-lieutenant.

His first success in literature was his novel, *Poor Folk* (published in 1846), which he possibly began to write while he was still at school. He sent this work to a review and awaited the result, utterly hopeless of its being accepted. One day, at four o'clock in the morning, just when Dostoievsky was despairing of success and thinking of suicide, Nekrasov the poet, and Grigorovitch the critic, came to him and said: 'Do you understand yourself what you have written? To have written such a book you must have possessed the direct inspiration of an artist.'

This, said Dostoievsky, was the happiest moment of his life. The book was published in Nekrasov's newspaper, and was highly praised on all sides. He thus at once made a name in literature. But as though Fate wished to lose no time in proving to him that his life would be a series of unending struggles, his second story, *The Double*, was a failure, and his friends turned from him, feeling that they had made a mistake. From that time onward, his literary career was a desperate battle, not only with poverty but also with public opinion, and with political as well as with literary critics.

Dostoievsky suffered all his life from epilepsy. It has been said that this disease was brought on by his imprisonment. This is not true: the complaint began in his childhood, and one of his biographers gives a hint of its origin: 'It dates back,' he writes, 'to his earliest youth, and is connected with a *tragic event* in their family life.' This sentence affords us an ominous glimpse into the early years of Dostoievsky, for it must indeed have been a tragic event which caused him to suffer from epileptic fits throughout his life.

In 1849 came the most important event in Dostoievsky's life. From 1840 to 1847 there was in St Petersburg a group of young men who met together to read and discuss the Liberal writers such as Fourier, Louis Blanc and Prudhon. Towards 1847 these circles widened, and included officers and journalists: they formed a club under the leadership of Petrachevsky, a former student, the author of a Dictionary of Foreign Terms.

The club consisted, on the one hand, of certain men, followers of the Decembrists of 1825, who aimed at the emancipation of the serfs and the establishment of a Liberal Constitution; and, on the other hand, of men who were predecessors of the Nihilists, and who looked forward to a social revolution. The special function of Dostoievsky in this club was to preach the Slavophil doctrine, according to which Russia, sociologically speaking, needed no Western models, because in her work-men's guilds and her system of mutual reciprocity for the pay-ment of taxes, she already possessed the means of realizing a superior form of social organization.

The meetings of this club took place shortly after the revolutionary movement which convulsed Western Europe in 1848. The Emperor Nicholas, who was a strong-minded and just man, imbued with a religious conviction that he was appointed by God to save the crumbling world, was dreaming of the emancipation of the serfs, and by a fatal misunderstand-ing was led to strike at men whose only crime was that they shared his own aims and ideals. One evening at a meeting of this club, Dostoievsky had declaimed Pushkin's Ode on the Abolition of Serfdom, when someone present expressed a doubt of the possibility of obtaining this reform except by in-surrectionary means. Dostoievsky is said to have replied: 'Then insurrection let it be!' On the 23rd of April 1849, at five o'clock in the morning, thirty-four suspected men were arrested. The two brothers Dostoievsky were among them. They were imprisoned in a citadel, where they remained for eight months. On the 22nd of December, Dostoievsky was conducted, with twenty-one others, to the public square, where a scaffold had been erected. The other prisoners had been released. While they were taking their places on the scaffold, Dostoievsky communicated the idea of a book which he wished to write to Prince Monbelli, one of his fellow-prisoners, who related the incident later. There were, that day, 21 degrees of frost (Réaumur); the prisoners were stripped to their shirts, and had to listen to their sentence; the reading lasted over twenty minutes: the sentence was that they were to be shot. Dostoi-evsky could not believe in the reality of the event. He said to one of his comrades: 'Is it possible that we are going to be executed?' The friend of whom he asked the question pointed to a car laden with objects which, under the tarpaulin that covered them looked like coffins. The Registrar walked down from the scaffold; the Priest mounted it, taking the cross with him, and bade the condemned men make their last confession. Only one man, of the shopkeeper class, did so: the others contented themselves with kissing the cross. Dostoievsky thus relates the close of the scene in a letter to his brother:

'They snapped swords above our heads, they made us put on the long white shirts worn by persons condemned to death. We were bound in parties of three to stakes to suffer execution. Being third in the row, I concluded that I had only a few minutes to live. I thought of you and your dear ones, and I managed to kiss Pleshtcheev and Dourov, who were next to me, and to bid them farewell.'

The officer in charge had already commanded his firing party to load; the soldiers were already preparing to take aim, when a white handkerchief was waved in front of them. They lowered their guns, and Dostoievsky and the other twenty-one learned that the Emperor had cancelled the sentence of the military tribunal, and commuted the sentence of death to one of hard labour for four years. The carts really contained convict uniforms, which the prisoners had to put on at once, and they started then and there for Siberia. When the prisoners were unbound, one of them, Grigoriev, had lost his reason. Dostoievsky, on the other hand, afterwards affirmed that this episode was his salvation; and never, either on account of this or of his subsequent imprisonment, did he ever feel or express anything save gratitude. 'If this catastrophe had not occurred,' said Dostoievsky, alluding to his sentence, his reprieve and his subsequent imprisonment, 'I should have gone mad.' The moments passed by him in the expectation of immediate death had an ineffaceable effect upon his entire after-life. They shifted his angle of vision with regard to the whole world. He knew something that no man could know who had not been through such moments. He constantly alludes to the episode in his novels, and in *The Idiot* he describes it thus, through the mouth of the principal character:

'I will tell you of my meeting last year with a certain man; this man was connected with a strange circumstance, strange because it is a very unusual one. He was once led, together with others, on to the scaffold, and a sentence was read out which told him that he was to be shot for a political crime. He spent the interval between the sentence and the reprieve, which lasted twenty minutes, or at least á quarter of an hour, with the certain conviction that in a few minutes he should die. I was very anxious to hear how he would recall his impressions. He remembered everything with extraordinary clearness, and said that he would never forget a single one of those minutes. Twenty paces from the scaffold round which the crowd and the soldiers stood, three stakes were driven into the ground, there being several prisoners. The first three were led to the stakes and bound, and the white dress of the condemned was put on them. This consisted of a long white shirt, and over their eyes white bandages were bound so that they should not see the guns. Then in front of each stake a firing party was drawn up. My friend was No. 8, so he went to the stake in the third batch. A priest carried the cross to each of them. My friend calculated that he had five minutes more to live, not more. He said that these five minutes seemed to him an endless period, infinitely precious. In these five minutes it seemed to him that he would have so many lives to live that he need not yet begin to think about his last moment, and in his mind he made certain arrangements. He calculated the time it would take him to say good-bye to his comrades; for this he allotted two minutes. He assigned two more minutes to think one last time of himself, and to look round for the last time. He remembered distinctly that he made these three plans, and that he divided his time in this way. He was to die, aged twenty-seven, healthy and strong, after having said good-bye to his companions. He remembered that he asked one of them a somewhat irrelevant question, and was much interested in the answer. Then, after he had said good-bye to his comrades, came the two minutes which he had set aside for thinking of himself. He knew beforehand of what he would think: he wished to represent to himself as quickly and as clearly as possible how this could be: that now he was breathing and living, and that in three minutes he would already be something else, someone or something, but what? and where? All this he felt he could decide in those two minutes. Not far away was the church, and the cathedral with its gilded dome was glittering in the sunshine. He remembered that he looked at the dome with terrible persistence, and on its glittering rays. He could not tear his gaze away from the rays. It seemed to him somehow that these rays were his new nature, and that in three minutes he would be made one with them. The uncertainty and the horror of the unknown, which was so near, were terrible. But he said that during this time there was nothing worse than the unceasing thought: "What if I do not die? What if life were restored to me now? What an eternity! And all this would be mine. I would in that case make every minute into a century, lose nothing, calculate every moment, and not spend any atom of the time fruitlessly." He said that this thought at last made him so angry that he wished that they would shoot him at once.'

Dostoievsky's sentence consisted of four years' hard labour in the convict settlement in Siberia, and this ordeal was doubtless the most precious boon which Providence could have bestowed on him. When he started for prison he said to A. Milioukov, as he wished him good-bye: 'The convicts are not wild beasts, but men probably better, and perhaps much worthier, than myself. During these last months (the months of his confinement in prison) I have gone through a great deal, but I shall be able to write about what I shall see and experience in the future.' It was during the time he spent in prison that Dostoievsky really found himself. To share the hard labour of the prisoners, to break up old ships, to carry loads of bricks, to sweep up heaps of snow, strengthened him in body and calmed his nerves, while the contact with murderers and criminals and prisoners of all kinds, whose inmost nature he was able to reach gave him a priceless opportunity of developing the qualities which were especially his own both as a writer and as a man.

With the criminals he was not in the position of a teacher,

but of a disciple; he learnt from them, and in his life with them he grew physically stronger, and found faith, certitude and peace.

At the end of the four years (in 1853) he was set free and returned to ordinary life, strengthened in body and better balanced in mind. He had still three years to serve in a regiment as a private soldier, and after this period of service three years more to spend in Siberia. In 1859 he crossed the frontier and came back to Russia, and was allowed to live first at Tver and then at St Petersburg. He brought a wife with him, the widow of one of his former colleagues in the Petrachevsky conspiracy, whom he had loved and married in Siberia. Until 1865 he worked at journalism.

Dostoievsky's nature was alien to Socialism, and he loathed the moral materialism of his Socialistic contemporaries. Petrachevsky repelled him because he was an atheist and laughed at all belief; and the attitude of Bielinsky towards religion, which was one of flippant contempt, awoke in Dostoievsky a passion of hatred which blazed up whenever he thought of the man. Dostoievsky thus became a martyr, and was within an ace of losing his life for the revolutionary cause; a movement in which he had never taken part, and in which he disbelieved all his life.

Dostoievsky returned from prison just at the time of the emancipation of the serfs, and the trials which awaited him on his release were severer than those which he endured during his captivity. In January 1861 he started a newspaper called the *Vremya*. The venture was a success. But just as he thought that Fortune was smiling upon him, and that freedom from want was drawing near, the newspaper, by an extraordinary misunderstanding, was prohibited by the censorship for an article on Polish affairs. This blow, like his condemnation to death, was due to a casual blunder in the official machinery. After considerable efforts, in 1864 he started another newspaper called the *Epocha*. This newspaper incurred the wrath, not of the Government censorship, but of the Liberals; and it was now that his peculiar situation, namely, that of a man between two fires, became evident. The Liberals abused him in every kind of manner, went so far as to hint that the *Epocha* and its staff were Government spies, and declared that Dostoievsky was a scribbler with whom the police should deal. At this same time his brother Michael, his best friend Grigoriev, who was on the staff of his newspaper, and his first wife, Marie, died one after another. Dostoievsky was now left all alone; he felt that his whole life was broken, and that he had nothing to live for. His brother's family was left without resources of any kind. He tried to support them by carrying on the publication of the *Epocha*, and worked day and night at this, being the sole editor, reading all the proofs, dealing with the authors and the censorship, revising articles, procuring money, sitting up till six in the morning, and sleeping only five out of the twenty-four hours. But this second paper came to grief in 1865, and Dostoievsky was forced to own himself temporarily insolvent. He had incurred heavy liabilities, not only to the subscribers of the newspaper, but in addition a sum of £1400 in bills and £700 in debts of honour. He writes to a friend at this period: 'I would gladly go back to prison if only to pay off my debts and to feel myself free once more.'

A publishing bookseller, Stellovsky, a notorious rascal, threatened to have him taken up for debt. He had to choose between the debtors' prison and flight: he choose the latter, and escaped abroad, where he spent four years of inexpressible misery, in the last extremity of want.

His *Crime and Punishment* was published in 1866, and this book brought him fame and popularity; yet in spite of this, on an occasion in 1869, he was obliged to pawn his overcoat and his last shirt in order with difficulty to obtain two thalers.

During all this time his attacks of epilepsy continued. He was constantly in trouble with his publishers, and bound and hampered by all sorts of contracts. He writes at this epoch: 'In spite of all this I feel as if I were only just beginning to live. It is curious, isn't it? I have the vitality of a cat.' And on another occasion he talks of his stubborn and inexhaustible vitality. He also says through the mouth of one of his characters, Dimitri Karamazov, 'I can bear anything, any suffering, if I can only keep on saying to myself: "I live; I am in a thousand torments, but I live! I am on the pillory, but I exist! I see the sun, or I do not see the sun, but I know that it is there. And to know that there *is* a sun is enough.'"

It was during these four years, overwhelmed by domestic calamity, perpetually harassed by creditors, attacked by the authorities on the one hand and the Liberals on the other, misunderstood by his readers, poor, almost starving, and never well, that he composed his three great masterpieces: *Crime and Punishment* in 1866, *The Idiot* in 1868, and *The Possessed* in 1871–2; besides planning *The Brothers Karamazov.* He had married a second time, in 1867. He returned to Russia in July 1871: his second exile was over. His popularity had increased, and the success of his books enabled him to free himself from debt. He became a journalist once more, and in 1873 edited Prince Meschtcherki's newspaper, *The Grazjdanin.* In 1876 he started a monthly review called *The Diary of a Writer,* which sometimes appeared once a month and sometimes less often. The appearance of the last number coincided with his death. This review was a kind of encyclopaedia, in which Dostoievsky wrote all his social, literary and political ideas, related any stray anecdotes, recollections and experiences which occurred to him, and commented on the political and literary topics of the day. He never ceased fighting his adversaries in this review; and during this time he began his last book, *The Brothers Karamazov,* which was never finished. In all his articles he preached his Slavophil creed, and on one occasion he made the whole of Russia listen to him and applaud him as one man. This was on June 8, 1880, when he made a speech at Moscow in memory of Pushkin, and aroused to frenzy the enthusiasm even of those men whose political ideals were the exact opposite of his own. He made people forget they were 'Slavophils' or 'Westernizers,' and remember only one thing—that they were Russians.

In the latter half of 1880, when he was working on *The Brothers Karamazov,* Strakhov records: 'He was unusually thin and exhausted; his body had become so frail that the first slight blow might destroy it. His mental activity was untiring, although work had grown very difficult for him. In the beginning of 1881 he fell ill with a severe attack of emphysema, the result of catarrh in the lung. On January 28 he had haemorrhage from the throat. Feeling the approach of death, he wished to confess and to receive the Blessed Sacrament. He gave the New Testament used by him in prison to his wife to read aloud. The first passage chanced to be Matthew iii, 14: 'But John held Him back and said, "It is I that should be baptized by Thee and dost Thou come to me?" And Jesus answered and said unto him, "Detain Me not; for thus it behoves us to fulfil a great truth."'

When his wife had read this, Dostoievsky said: 'You hear: Do not detain me. That means that I am to die.' And he closed the book. A few hours later he did actually die, instantaneously, from the rupture of an artery in the lungs.

This was on the 28th of January 1881; on the 30th he was buried in St Petersburg. His death and his funeral had about them an almost mythical greatness, and his funeral is the most striking comment on the nature of the feeling which the Russian public had for him both as a writer and as a man. On the day after his death, St Petersburg witnessed a most extraordinary sight: the little house in which he had lived suddenly became for the moment the moral centre of Russia. Russia understood that with the death of this struggling and disease-stricken novelist, she had lost something inestimably precious, rare and irreplaceable. Spontaneously, and without any organized preparation, the most imposing and triumphant funeral ceremony was given to Dostoievsky's remains; and this funeral was not only the greatest and most inspiring which had ever taken place in Russia, but as far as its inward significance was concerned there can hardly ever have been a greater one in the world. Other great writers and other great men have been buried with more gorgeous pomp and with a braver show of outward display, but never, when such a man has been followed to the grave by a mourning multitude, have the trophies and tributes of grief been so real; for striking as they were by their quantity and their nature, they seemed but a feeble and slender evidence of the sorrow and the love to which they bore witness. There were deputations bearing countless wreaths, there were numerous choirs singing religious chants, there were thousands of people following in a slow stream along the streets of St Petersburg, there were men and women of every class, but mostly poor people, shabbily dressed, of the lower middle or the lower classes. The dream of Dostoievsky, that the whole of Russia should be united by a bond of fraternity and brotherly love, seemed to be realized when this crowd of men, composed of such various and widely differing elements, met together in common grief by his grave. Dostoievsky had lived the life of a pauper, and of a man who had to fight with all his strength in order to win his daily bread. He had been assailed by disease and hunted by misfortune; his whole life seemed to have rushed by before he had had time to sit down quietly and write the great ideas which were seething in his mind. Everything he had written seemed to have been written by chance, haphazardly, to have been jotted down against time, between wind and water. But in spite of this, in his work, however incomplete, however fragmentary and full of faults it may have been, there was a voice speaking, a particular message being delivered, which was different from that of other writers, and at times more precious. While it was there, the public took it for granted, like the sun; and it was only when Dostoievsky died that the hugeness of the gap made by his death, caused them to feel how great was the place he had occupied both in their hearts and in their minds. It was only when he died that they recognized how great a man he was, and how warmly they admired and loved him. Everybody felt this from the highest to the lowest. Tolstoy, in writing of Dostoievsky's death, says: 'I never saw the man, and never had any direct relations with him, yet suddenly when he died I understood that he was the nearest and dearest and most necessary of men to me. Everything that he did was of the kind that the more he did of it the better I felt it was for men. And all at once I read that he is dead, and a prop has fallen from me.' This is what the whole of Russia felt, that a support had fallen from them; and this is what they expressed when they gave to Dostoievsky a funeral such as no king nor Captain has ever had, a funeral whose very shabbiness was greater than any splen-

dour, and whose trophies and emblems were the grief of a
nation and the tears of thousands of hearts united together in
the admiration and love of a man whom each one of them regarded as his brother.

• III

DOSTOIEVSKY'S CHARACTER

Such, briefly, are the main facts of Dostoievsky's crowded life.
Unlike Tolstoy, who has himself told us in every conceivable
way everything down to the most intimate detail which is to be
known about himself, Dostoievsky told us little of himself,
and all that we know about him is gathered from other people
or from his letters; and even now we know comparatively little
about his life. He disliked talking about himself; he could not
bear to be pitied. He was modest, and shielded his feelings with
a lofty shame. Strakhov writes about him thus:

'In Dostoievsky you could never detect the slightest bitterness or hardness resulting from the sufferings he had under-
gone, and there was never in him a hint of posing as a martyr.
He behaved as if there had been nothing extraordinary in his
past. He never represented himself as disillusioned, or as not
having an equable mind; but, on the contrary, he appeared
cheerful and alert, when his health allowed him to do so. I
remember that a lady coming for the first time to Michael
Dostoievsky's (his brother's) evenings at the newspaper office,
looked long at Dostoievsky, and finally said: "As I look at you
it seems to me that I see in your face the sufferings which you
have endured." These words visibly annoyed Dostoievsky.
"What sufferings?" he said, and began to joke on indifferent
matters.'

Long after his imprisonment and exile, when some friends
of his tried to prove to him that his exile had been a brutal act of
injustice, he said: 'The Socialists are the result of the followers
of Petrachevsky. Petrachevsky's disciples sowed many seeds.'
And when he was asked whether such men deserved to be

exiled, he answered: 'Our exile was just; the *people* would have condemned us.'

The main characteristics of his nature were generosity, catholicity, vehement passion, and a 'sweet reasonableness'. Once when he was living with Riesenkampf, a German doctor, he was found living on bread and milk; and even for that he was in debt at a little milk shop. This same doctor says that Dostoievsky was 'one of those men to live with whom is good for every one, but who are themselves in perpetual want.' He was mercilessly robbed, but he would never blame any one who took advantage of his kindness and his trustfulness. One of his biographers tells us that his life with Riesenkampf proved expensive to him, because no poor man who came to see the doctor went away without having received something from Dostoievsky. One cannot read a page of his books without being aware of the 'sweet reasonableness' of his nature. This pervaded his writings with fragrance like some precious balm, and is made manifest to us in the touching simplicity of some of his characters, such as the Idiot and Alexis Karamazov, to read of whom is like being with some warm and comforting influence, something sweet and sensible and infinitely human. His catholicity consists in an almost boundless power of appreciation, an appreciation of things, persons and books widely removed from himself by accidents of time, space, class, nationality and character. Dostoievsky is equally able to appreciate the very essence of a performance got up by convicts in his prison, and the innermost beauty of the plays of Racine. This last point is singular and remarkable. He was universal and cosmopolitan in his admiration of the literature of foreign countries; and he was cosmopolitan, not because he wished to cut himself away from Russian traditions and to become European and Westernized, but because he was profoundly Russian, and had the peculiarly Russian plastic and receptive power of understanding and assimilating things widely different from himself.

When he was a young man, Shakespeare and Schiller were well known, and it was the fashion to admire them. It was equally the fashion to despise the French writers of the seventeenth century. But Dostoievsky was just as enthusiastic in his admiration of Racine and Corneille and all the great classics of the seventeenth century. Thus he writes: 'But Phédre, brother! You will be the Lord knows what if you say this is not the highest and purest nature and poetry; the outline of it is Shakespearian, but the statue is in plaster, not in marble.' And again of Corneille: 'Have you read *The Cid*? Read it, you wretch, read it, and go down in the dust before Corneille!'

Dostoievsky was constantly 'going down in the dust' before the great masterpieces, not only of his own, but of other countries, which bears out the saying that 'La valeur morale de l'homme est en proportion de sa faculté d'admirer'.

Dostoievsky never theorized as to how alms should be given, or as to how charity should be organized. He gave what he had, simply and naturally, to those who he saw had need of it; and he had a right to this knowledge, for he himself had received alms in prison. Neither did he ever theorize as to whether a man should leave the work which he was fitted by Providence to do (such as writing books), in order to plough fields and to cut down trees. He had practised hard labour, not as a theoretic amateur, but as a constrained professional. He had carried heavy loads of bricks and broken up ships and swept up heaps of snow, not out of philosophy or theory, but because he had been obliged to do so; because if he had not done so he would have been severely punished. All that Tolstoy dreamed of and aimed at, which was serious in theory but not serious in practice, that is to say, giving up his property, becoming one with the people, ploughing the fields, was a reality to Dostoievsky when he was in prison. He knew that hard labour is only real when it is a necessity, when you cannot leave off doing it when you want to; he had experienced this kind of hard labour for four years, and during his whole life he had to work for his daily bread. The result of this is that he made no theories about what work a man *should* do, but simply did as well as he could the work he *had* to do. In the words of a ballade written by Mr Chesterton, he might have said:

' We eat the cheese—you scraped about the rind,
You lopped the tree—we eat the fruit instead.
You were benevolent, but we were kind,
You know the laws of food, but we were fed.'

And this is the great difference between Dostoievsky and Tolstoy. Tolstoy was benevolent, but Dostoievsky was kind. Tolstoy theorized on the distribution of food, but Dostoievsky was fed and received alms like a beggar. Dostoievsky, so far from despising the calling of an author, or thinking that it was an occupation 'thin sown with aught of profit or delight' for the human race, loved literature passionately. He was proud of his profession: he was a great man of letters as well as a great author. 'I have never sold,' he wrote, 'one of my books without getting the price down beforehand. I am a literary proletarian. If anybody wants my work he must ensure me by prepayment.'

There is something which resembles Dr Johnson in the way he talks of his profession and his attitude towards it. But there is, nevertheless, in the phrase just quoted, something bitterly ironical when one reflects that he was a poor man all his life and incessantly harassed by creditors, and that he derived almost nothing from the great popularity and sale of his books.

'Dostoievsky,' writes Strakov, 'loved literature; he took her as she was, with all her conditions; he never stood apart from literature, and he never looked down upon her. This absence of the least hint of literary snobbishness is in him a beautiful and touching characteristic. Russian literature was the one lodestar of Dostoievsky's life, and he cherished for it a passionate love and devotion. He knew very well that when he entered the lists he would have to go into the public market-place, and he was never ashamed of his trade nor of his fellow-workers. On the contrary, he was proud of his profession, and considered it a great and sacred one.'

He speaks of himself as a literary hack: he writes at so much a line, three and a half printed pages of a newspaper in two days and two nights. 'Often,' he says, 'it happened in my literary career that the beginning of the chapter of a

novel or story was already set up, and the end was still in my
mind and had to be written by the next day.' Again: 'Work
from want and for money has crushed and devoured me. Will
my poverty ever cease? Ah, if I had money, then I should be
free!'

I have said that one of the main elements of Dostoievsky's
character was vehement passion. There was more than a
vehement element of passion in Dostoievsky; he was not only
passionate in his loves and passionate in his hates, but his passion was unbridled. In this he resembles the people of the
Renaissance. There were perilous depths in his personality;
black pools of passion; a seething whirlpool that sent up every
now and then great eddies of boiling surge; yet this passion
has nothing about it which is undefinably evil; it never smells
of the pit. The reason of this is that although Dostoievsky's
soul descended into hell, it was purged by the flames, and no
poisonous fumes ever came from it. There was something of
St Francis in him, and something of Velasquez. Dostoievsky
was a violent hater. I have already told how he hated Bielinsky,
the Socialists and the materialists whom he attacked all his life,
but against Tourgeniev he nourished a blind and causeless
hatred. This manifests itself as soon as he leaves prison, in
the following outburst: 'I know very well,' he writes, 'that I
write worse than Tourgeniev, but not so very much worse,
and after all I hope one day to write quite as well as he does.
Why, with my crying wants, do I receive only 100 roubles a
sheet, and Tourgeniev, who possesses two thousand serfs,
receives 400 roubles? Owing to my poverty I am *obliged* to
hurry, to write for money, and consequently to spoil my work.'
In a postscript he says that he sends Katkov, the great Moscow
editor, fifteen sheets at 100 roubles a sheet, that is, 1500 roubles
in all. 'I have had 500 roubles from him, and besides, when I
had sent three-quarters of the novel, I asked him for 200 to help
me along, or 700 altogether. I shall reach Tver without a
farthing. But, on the other hand, I shall shortly receive from
Katkov seven or eight hundred roubles.'

It must not be forgotten that the whole nature of Dostoievsky, both as man and artist, was profoundly modified by the

disease from which he suffered all his life, his epilepsy. He had therefore two handicaps against him; disease and poverty. But it is his epilepsy which was probably the cause of his dislikes, his hatreds and his outbreaks of violent passion. The attacks of epilepsy came upon him about once a month, and sometimes, though not often, they were more frequent. He once had two in a week. His friend Strakov describes one of them thus: 'I once saw one of his ordinary attacks: it was, I fancy, in 1863, just before Easter. Late in the evening, about eleven o'clock, he came to see me, and we had a very animated conversation. I cannot remember the subject, but I know that it was important and abstruse. He became excited, and walked about the room while I sat at the table. He said something fine and jubilant. I confirmed his opinion by some remark, and he turned to me a face which positively glowed with the most transcendent inspiration. He paused for a moment, as if searching for words, and had already opened his lips to speak. I looked at him all expectant for fresh revelation. Suddenly from his open mouth issued a strange, prolonged and inarticulate moan. He sank senseless on the floor in the middle of the room.'

The ancients called this 'the sacred sickness'. Just before the attacks, Dostoievsky felt a kind of rapture, something like what people say they feel when they hear very great music, a perfect harmony between himself and the world, a sensation as if he had reached the edge of a planet, and were falling off it into infinite space. And this feeling was such that for some seconds of the rapture, he said, you might give ten years of your life, or even the whole of it. But after the attack his condition was dreadful, and he could hardly sustain the state of low-spirited dreariness and sensitiveness into which he was plunged. He felt like a criminal, and fancied there hung over him an invisible guilt, a great transgression. He compares both sensations, suddenly combined and blended in a flash, to the famous falling pitcher of Mahomet, which had not time to empty itself while the Prophet on Allah's steed was girdling heaven and hell. It is no doubt the presence of this disease and the frequency of the attacks, which were responsible for the want of balance in his nature and in his artistic conceptions, just as his grinding poverty and the merciless conditions of his existence are responsible for the want of finish in his style. But Dostoievsky had the qualities of his defects, and it is perhaps owing to his very illness, and to its extraordinary nature, that he was able so deeply to penetrate into the human soul. It is as if the veil of flesh and blood dividing the soul from that which is behind all things, was finer and more transparent in Dostoievsky than in other men: by his very illness he may have been able to discern what is invisible to others. It is certainly owing to the combined poverty and disease which made up his life, that he had such an unexampled insight into the lives and hearts of the humble, the rejected, the despised, the afflicted, and the oppressed. He sounded the utmost depths of human misery, he lived face to face with the lowest representatives of human misfortune and disgrace, and he was neither dispirited nor dismayed. He came to the conclusion that it was all for the best, and like Job in dust and ashes consented to the eternal scheme. And though all his life he was one of the conquered, he never ceased fighting, and never for one moment believed that life was not worth living. On the contrary, he blessed life and made others bless it.

His life was 'a long disease', rendered harder to bear and more difficult by exceptionally cruel circumstances. In spite of this, Dostoievsky was a happy man: he was happy and he was cheerful; and he was happy not because he was a saint, but because, in spite of all his faults, he radiated goodness; because his immense heart overflowed in kindness, and having suffered much himself, he understood the sufferings of others; thus although his books are terrible, and deal with the darkest clouds which can overshadow the human spirit, the descent into hell of the human soul, yet the main impression left by them is not one of gloom but one of comfort. Dostoievsky is, above all things, a healer and a comforter, and this is because the whole of his teaching, his morality, his art, his character, are based on the simple foundation of what the Russians call 'dolgoterpjenie', that is, forbearance, and 'smirenie', that is to say, resignation. In the whole history of the world's literature there is no literary man's life which was so arduous and so hard; but Dostoiesvsky never complained, nor, we can be sure, would he have wished his life to have been otherwise. His life was a martyrdom, but he enjoyed it. Although no one more nearly than he bears witness to Heine's saying that 'where a great spirit is, there is Golgotha', yet we can say without hesitation that Dostoievsky was a happy man, and he was happy because he never thought about himself, and because, consciously or unconsciously, he relieved and comforted the sufferings of others. And his books continued to do so long after he ceased to live.

All this can be summed up in one word: the value of Dostoievsky's life. And the whole reason that his books, although they deal with the tragedies of mankind, bring comfort to the reader instead of gloom, hope instead of despair, is, firstly, that Dostoievsky was an altruist, and that he fulfilled the most difficult precept of Christianity—to love others better than oneself; and, secondly, that in leading us down in the lowest depths of tragedy, he shows us that where man ends, God takes up the tale.

IV

POOR FOLK AND THE LETTERS FROM A DEAD HOUSE

In his first book, *Poor Folk*, which was published in 1846, we have the germ of all Dostoievsky's talent and genius. It is true that he accomplished far greater things, but never anything more characteristic. It is the story of a poor official, a minor clerk in a Government office, already aged and worn with cares, who battles against material want. In his sombre and monotonous life there is a ray of light: in another house as poor and as squalid as his own, there lives a girl, a distant relation of his, who is also in hard and humble circumstances, and who has nothing in the world save the affection and friendship of this poor clerk. They write to each other daily. In the man's

letters a discreet unselfishness is revealed, a rare delicacy of
feeling, which is in sharp contrast to the awkwardness of his
everyday actions and ideas, which verge on the grotesque. At
the office, he has to cringe and sacrifice his honour in order not
to forfeit the favour of his superiors. He stints himself, and
makes every kind of small sacrifice, in order that this woman
may be relieved of her privations. He writes to her like a father
or brother; but it is easy for us to see in his simple phrases that
he is in love with her, although she does not realize it. The
character of the woman is equally clear to us: she is superior to
him in education and mind, and she is less resigned to her fate
than he is. In the course of their correspondence we learn all
that is to be known about their past, their melancholy history
and the small incidents of their everyday life, the struggle that
is continually working in the mind of the clerk between his
material want and his desire not to lose his personal honour.
This correspondence continues day by day until the crisis
comes, and the clerk loses the one joy of his life, and learns that
his friend is engaged to be married. But she has not been
caught up or carried off in a brilliant adventure: she married a
middle-aged man, very rich and slightly discredited, and all her
last letters are full of commissions which she trusts to her
devoted old friend to accomplish. He is sent to the dress-
makers about her gowns, and to the jeweller about her rings;
and all this he accepts and does with perfect self-sacrifice; and
his sacrifice seems quite accidental, a matter of course: there is
not the slightest pose in it, nor any fuss, and only at the end, in
his very last letter, and even then only in a veiled and discreet
immense sorrow which the blow is bringing to him.

The woman's character is as subtly drawn as the man's; she
is more independent than he, and less resigned; she is kind and
good, and it is from no selfish motives that she grasps at the im-
provement in her fortunes. But she is still young, and her
youth rises within her and imperatively claims its natural
desires. She is convinced that by accepting the proposal which
is made to her she will alleviate her friend's position as much as
her own; moreover, she regards him as a faithful friend, and
nothing more. But we, the outsiders who read his letters, see

clearly that what he feels for her is more than friendship: it is simply love and nothing else.

The second important book which Dostoievsky wrote (for the stories he published immediately after *Poor Folk* were not up to his mark) was the *Letters from a Dead House*, which was published on his return to Russia in 1861. This book may not be his finest artistic achievement, but it is certainly the most humanly interesting book which he ever wrote, and one of the most interesting books which exist in the whole of the world's literature. In this book he told his prison experiences: they were put forward in the shape of the posthumous records of a nobleman who had committed murder out of jealousy, and was condemned to spend some years in the convict prison. The book is supposed to be the papers which this nobleman left behind him. They cover a period of four years, which was the term of Dostoievsky's sentence. The most remarkable characteristic of the book is the entire absence of egotism in the author. Many authors in similar circumstances would have written volumes of self-analysis, and filled pages with their lamentations and in diagnosing their sensations. Very few men in such a situation could have avoided a slight pose of martyrdom. In Dostoievsky there is nothing of this. He faces the horror of the situation, but he has no grievance; and the book is all about other people and as little as possible about himself. And herein lies its priceless value, for there is no other book either of fiction or travel which throws such a searching light on the character of the Russian people, and especially on that of the Russian peasants. Dostoievsky got nearer to the Russian peasant than any one has ever done, and necessarily so, because he lived with them on equal terms as a convict. But this alone would not suffice to produce so valuable a book; something else was necessary, and the second indispensable factor was supplied by Dostoievsky's peculiar nature, his simplicity of mind, his kindness of heart, his sympathy and understanding. In the very first pages of this book we are led into the heart of a convict's life: the *milieu* rises before us in startling vividness. The first thing which we are made aware of is that this prison life has a peculiar character of its own. The strange family or colony which was gathered together in this Siberian prison consisted of criminals of every grade and description, and in which not only every class of Russian society, but every shade and variety of the Russian people was represented; that is to say, there were here assassins by profession, and men who had become assassins by chance, robbers, brigands, tramps, pick-pockets, smugglers, peasants, Armenians, Jews, Poles, Mussulmans, soldiers who were there for insubordination and even for murder; officers, gentlemen, and political prisoners, and men who were there no one knew why.

Now Dostoievsky points out that at a first glance you could detect one common characteristic in this strange family. Even the most sharply defined, the most eccentric and original personalities, who stood out and towered above their comrades, even these did their best to adopt the manners and customs, the unwritten code, the etiquette of the prison. In general, he continues, these people with a very few exceptions (innately cheerful people who met with universal contempt) were surly, envious, extraordinarily vain, boastful, touchy, and in the highest degree punctilious and conventional. To be astonished at nothing was considered the highest quality; and in all of them the one aim and obsession was outward demeanour and the wish to keep up appearances. There were men who pretended to have either great moral or great physical strength and boasted of it, who were in reality cowards at heart, and whose cowardice was revealed in a flash. There were also men who possessed really strong characters; but the curious thing was, Dostoievsky tells us, that these really strong characters were abnormally vain. The main and universal characteristic of the criminal was his vanity, his desire, as the Italians say, to *fare figura* at all costs. I have been told that this is true of English prisons, where prisoners will exercise the most extraordinary ingenuity in order to shave. The greater part of these people were radically vicious, and frightfully quarrelsome. The gossip, the backbiting, the tale-bearing, and the repeating of small calumnies were incessant; yet in spite of this not one man dared to stand up against the public opinion of the prison, according to whose etiquette and unwritten law a particular kind of demeanour was observed. In other words, these prisoners were exactly like private schoolboys or public schoolboys. At a public school, boys will create a certain etiquette, which has its unwritten law; for instance, let us take Eton. At Eton you may walk on one side of the street but not on the other, unless you are a person of sufficient importance. When you wear a greatcoat, you must always turn the collar up, unless you are a person of a particular importance. You must likewise never go about with an umbrella unrolled; and, far more important than all these questions, there arrives a psychological moment in the career of an Eton boy when, of his own accord, he wears a stick-up collar instead of a turned-down collar, by which act he proclaims to the world that he is a person of considerable importance. These rules are unwritten and undefined. Nobody tells another boy not to walk on the wrong side of the road; no boy will ever dream of turning down his collar, if he is not important enough; and in the third and more special case, the boy who suddenly puts on a stick-up collar must feel himself by instinct when that psychological moment has arrived. It is not done for any definite reason, it is merely the expression of a kind of atmosphere. He knows at a given moment that he can or cannot go into stick-ups. Some boys can go into stick-ups for almost nothing, if they have in their personality the necessary amount of imponderable prestige; others, though the possessors of many trophies and colours, can only do so at the last possible minute. But all must have some definite reason for going into stick-ups: no boy can go into stick-ups merely because he is clever and thinks a lot of himself—that would not only be impossible, but unthinkable.

Dostoievsky's account of the convicts reminds me so strongly of the conduct of private and public schoolboys in England, that, with a few slight changes, his *Letters from a Dead House* might be about an English school, as far as the mere etiquette of the convicts is concerned. Here, for instance, is a case in point: Dostoievsky says that there lived in this prison men of dynamic personalities, who feared neither God nor man, and had never obeyed any one in their lives; and yet they at once fell in with the standard of behaviour expected of them.

There came to the prison men who had been the terror of their village and their neighbourhood. Such a 'new boy' looked round, and at once understood that he had arrived at a place where he could astonish no one, and that the only thing to do was to be quiet and fall in with the manners of the place, and into what Dostoievsky calls the universal etiquette, which he defines as follows: 'This etiquette,' he says, 'consisted outwardly of a kind of peculiar dignity with which every inhabitant of the prison was impregnated, as if the fact of being a convict was, *ipso facto*, a kind of rank, and a respectable rank.' This is exactly the point of view of a schoolboy at a private school. A schoolboy prefers to be at home rather than at school. He knows that he is obliged to be at school, he is obliged to work against his will, and to do things which are often disagreeable to him; at the same time his entire efforts are strained to one object, towards preserving the dignity of his status. That was the great ambition of the convicts, to preserve the dignity of the status of a convict. Throughout this book one receives the impression that the convicts behaved in many ways like schoolboys; in fact, in one place Dostoievsky says that in many respects they were exactly like children. He quotes, for instance, their delight in spending the little money they could get hold of on a smart linen shirt and a belt, and walking round the whole prison to show it off. They did not keep such finery long, and nearly always ended by selling it for almost nothing; but their delight while they possessed it was intense. There was, however, one curious item in their code of morals, which is singularly unlike that of schoolboys in England, in Russia, or in any other country: they had no horror of a man who told tales to the authorities, who, in schoolboy language, was a sneak. 'The Sneak' did not expose himself to the very smallest loss of caste. Indignation against him was an unthinkable thing: nobody shunned him, people were friends with him; and if you had explained in the prison the whole odiousness of his behaviour, they would not have understood you at all.

'There was one of the gentlemen prisoners, a vicious and mean fellow, with whom from the first moment I would have nothing to do. He made friends with the major's orderly, and became his spy; and this man told everything he heard about the prisoners to the major. We all knew this, and nobody ever once thought of punishing or even of blaming the scoundrel.'

This is the more remarkable from the fact that in Russian schools, and especially in those schools where military discipline prevails, sneaking is the greatest possible crime. In speaking of another man who constantly reported everything to the authorities, Dostoievsky says that the other convicts despised him, not because he sneaked, but because he did not know how to behave himself properly.

The convicts, although they never showed the slightest signs of remorse or regret for anything they had done in the past, were allowed by their etiquette to express, as it were officially, a kind of outward resignation, a peaceful logic, such as, 'We are a fallen people. We could not live in freedom, and now we must break stones. . . . We could not obey father and mother, and now we must obey the beating of the drum.' The criminals abused each other mercilessly; they were adepts in the art, more than adepts, artists. Abuse in their hands became a science and a fine art; their object was to find not so much the word that would give pain, as the offensive thought, the spirit, the idea, as to who should be most venomous, the most razor-like in his abuse.

Another striking characteristic which also reminds one of schoolboys, was that the convict would be, as a rule, obedient and submissive in the extreme. But there were certain limits beyond which his patience was exhausted, and when once this limit was overstepped by his warders or the officer in charge, he was ready to do anything, even to commit murder, and feared no punishment.

Dostoievsky tells us that during all the time he was in prison he never noticed among the convicts the slightest sign of remorse, the slightest burden of spirit with regard to the crimes they had committed; and the majority of them in their hearts considered themselves perfectly justified. But the one thing they could not bear, not because it roused feelings of emotion in them, but because it was against the etiquette of the place, was that people should dwell upon their past crimes. He quotes

one instance of a man who was drunk—the convicts could get
wine—beginning to relate how he had killed a child of five
years old. The whole prison, which up till then had been
laughing at his jokes, cried out like a man, and the assassin was
obliged to be silent. They did not cry out from indignation,
but because it was not *the thing* to speak of *that*, because to speak
of *that* was considered to be violating the unwritten code of the
prison. The two things which Dostoievsky found to be the
hardest trials during his life as a convict were, first, the absolute absence of privacy, since during the whole four years he
was in prison he was never for one minute either by day or night
alone; and, secondly, the bar which existed between him and
the majority of the convicts, owing to the fact that he was a
gentleman. The convicts hated people of the upper class; although such men were on a footing of social equality with
them, the convicts never recognized them as comrades. Quite
unconsciously, even sincerely, they regarded them as gentlemen, although they liked teasing them about their change of
circumstance. They despised them because they did not know
how to work properly, and Dostoievsky says that he was two
years in prison before he won over some of the convicts,
though one can see from his accounts of what they said to
him, how much they must have liked him, and he admits that
the majority of them recognized, after a time, that he was a
good fellow. He points out how much harder such a sentence
was on one of his own class than on a peasant. The peasant
arrives from all ends of Russia, no matter where it be, and
finds in prison the *milieu* he is accustomed to, and into which he
falls at once without difficulty. He is treated as a brother and an
equal by the people who are there. With a gentleman it is
different, and especially, Dostoievsky tells us, with a political
offender, whom the majority of the convicts hate. He never becomes an equal; they may like him, as they obviously did in
Dostoievsky's case, but they never regard him as being on a
footing of equality with themselves. They preferred even
foreigners, Germans for instance, to the Russian gentlemen;
and the people they disliked most of all were the gentlemen
Poles, because they were almost exaggeratedly polite towards

the convicts, and at the same time could not conceal their innate hatred of them. With regard to the effect of this difference of class, Dostoievsky, in the course of the book, tells a striking story. Every now and then, when the convicts had a grievance about their food or their treatment, they would go on strike, and assemble in the prison yard. Dostoievsky relates that one day there was a strike about the food. As all the convicts were gathered together in the yard, he joined them, whereupon he was immediately told that that was not his place, that he had better go to the kitchen, where the Poles and the other gentlemen were. He was told this kindly by his friends, and men who were less friendly to him made it plain by shouting out sarcastic remarks to him. Although he wished to stay, he was told that he must go. Afterwards the strike was dispersed and the strikers punished, and Dostoievsky asked a friend of his, one of the convicts, whether they were not angry with the gentlemen convicts.

'Why?' asked this man.

'Why, because we did not join in the strike.'

'Why should you have joined in the strike?' asked the convict, trying to understand, 'You buy your own food.'

'Many of us eat the ordinary food,' answered Dostoievsky, 'but I should have thought that apart from this we ought to have joined, out of fellowship, out of comradeship.'

'But you are not our comrade,' said the other man quite simply; and Dostoievsky saw that the man did not even understand what he meant. Dostoeivsky realized that he could never be a real comrade of these men; he might be a convict for a century, he might be the most experienced of criminals, the most accomplished of assassins, the barrier existing between the classes would never disappear: to them he would always be a gentleman, it would always be a case of 'You go your way, we go ours'. And this, he said, was the saddest thing he experienced during the whole of his prison life.

The thing which perhaps caused him the most pleasure was the insight he gained into the kindness shown to convicts by outsiders. Alluding to the doctors in the prison hospital, he says: 'It is well known to prisoners all over Russia that the men who sympathize with them the most are the doctors: they never make the slightest difference in their treatment of prisoners, as nearly all outsiders do, except perhaps the Russian poor. The Russian poor man never blames the prisoner for his crime, however terrible it may be; he forgives him everything for the punishment that he is enduring, and for his misfortune in general. It is not in vain that the whole of the Russian people call crime a misfortune and criminals "unfortunates". This definition has a deep meaning; it is all the more valuable in that it is made unconsciously and instinctively.'

It is an incident revealing this pity for the unfortunate which gave Dostoievsky more pleasure than anything during his stay in prison. It was the first occasion on which he directly received alms. He relates it thus:

'It was soon after my arrival in the prison: I was coming back from my morning's work, accompanied only by the guard. There met me a mother and her daughter. The little girl was ten years old, as pretty as a cherub; I had already seen them once; the mother was the wife of a soldier, a widow; her husband, a young soldier, had been under arrest, and had died in the hospital in the same ward in which I had lain ill. The wife and the daughter had come to say good-bye to him, and both had cried bitterly. Seeing me, the little girl blushed, whispered something to her mother, and she immediately stopped and took out of her bundle a quarter of a kopeck and gave it to the little girl. The child ran after me and called out, "Unfortunate! For the sake of Christ, take this copper." I took the piece of money, and the little girl ran back to her mother quite contented. I kept that little piece of money for a very long time.'

What is most remarkable about the book, are the many and various discoveries which Dostoievsky made with regard to human nature: his power of getting behind the gloomy mask of the criminal to the real man underneath, his success in detecting the 'soul of goodness' in the criminals. Every single one of the characters he describes stands out in startling relief; and if one began to quote these one would never end. Nevertheless I will quote a few instances.

There is Akim Akimitch, an officer who had earned his sentence thus: He had served in the Caucasus, and been made governor of some small fortress. One night a neighbouring Caucasian prince attacked his fortress and burnt it down, but was defeated and driven back. Akim Akimitch pretended not to know who the culprit was. A month elapsed, and Akim Akimitch asked the prince to come and pay him a visit. He came without suspecting any evil. Akim Akimitch marched out his troops, and in their presence told him it was exceedingly wrong to burn down fortresses; and after giving him minute directions as to what the behaviour of a peaceful prince should be, shot him dead on the spot, and reported the case to his superiors. He was tried and condemned to death, but his sentence was commuted to twelve years' hard labour. Akim Akimitch had thus once in his life acted according to his own judgment, and the result had been penal servitude. He had not common sense enough to see where he had been guilty, but he came to the conclusion that he never under any circumstances ought to judge for himself. He thenceforth renounced all initiative of any kind or sort, and made himself into a machine. He was uneducated, extremely accurate, and the soul of honesty; very clever with his fingers, he was by turn carpenter, bootmaker, shoemaker, gilder, and there was no trade which he could not learn. Akim Akimitch arranged his life in so methodical a manner in every detail, with such pedantic accuracy, that at first he almost drove Dostoievsky mad, although Akim Akimitch was kindness itself to him, and helped him in every possible way during the first days of his imprisonment. Akim Akimitch appeared to be absolutely indifferent as to whether he was in prison or not. He arranged everything as though he were to stay there for the rest of his life; everything, from his pillow upwards, was arranged, as though no change could possibly occur to him. At first Dostoievsky found the ways of this automaton a severe trial, but he afterwards became entirely reconciled to him.

Then there was Orlov, one of the more desperate criminals. He was a soldier who had deserted. He was of small stature and slight build, but he was absolutely devoid of any sort of fear.

Dostoievsky says that never in his life had he met with such a strong, such an iron character as this man had. There was, in this man, a complete triumph of the spirit over the flesh. He could bear any amount of physical punishment with supreme indifference. He was consumed with boundless energy, a thirst for action, for revenge, and for the accomplishment of the aim which he set before him. He looked down on everybody in prison. Dostoievsky says he doubts whether there was any one in the world who could have influenced this man by his authority. He had a calm outlook on the world, as though there existed nothing that could astonish him; and although he knew that the other convicts looked up to him with respect, there was no trace of swagger about him: he was not at all stupid, and terribly frank, although not talkative. Dostoievsky would ask him about his adventures. He did not much like talking about them, but he always answered frankly. When once he understood, however, that Dostoievsky was trying to find out whether he felt any pangs of conscience or remorse for what he had done, he looked at him with a lofty and utter contempt, as though he suddenly had to deal with some stupid little boy who could not reason like grown-up people. There was even an expression of pity in his face, and after a minute or two he burst out in the simplest and heartiest laugh, without a trace of irony, and Dostoievsky was convinced that when left to himself he must have laughed again time after time, so comic did the thought appear to him.

One of the most sympathetic characters Dostoievsky describes is a young Tartar called Alei, who was not more than twenty-two years old. He had an open, clever, and even beautiful face, and a good-natured and naïve expression which won your heart at once. His smile was so confiding, so childlike and simple, his big black eyes so soft and kind, that it was a consolation merely to look at him. He was in prison for having taken part in an expedition made by his brothers against a rich Armenian merchant whom they had robbed. He retained his softness of heart and simplicity and his strict honesty all the time he was in prison; he never quarrelled, although he knew quite well how to stand up for himself, and everybody liked

him. 'I consider Alei,' writes Dostoievsky, 'as being far from
an ordinary personality, and I count my acquaintance with
him as one of the most valuable events of my life. There are
characters so beautiful by nature, so near to God, that even the
very thought that they may some day change for the worse
seems impossible. As far as they are concerned you feel absolutely secure, and I now feel secure for Alei. Where is he
now?'

I cannot help quoting two incidents in Dostoievsky's prison
life which seem to me to throw light on the characteristics of
the people with whom he mixed, and their manner of behaviour; the first is a story of how a young soldier called
Sirotkin came to be a convict. Here is the story which Dostoievsky gives us in the man's own words:

'My mother loved me very much. When I became a recruit,
I have since heard, she lay down on her bed and never rose
again. As a recruit I found life bitter. The colonel did not like
me, and punished me for everything. And what for? I was
obedient, orderly, I never drank wine, I never borrowed, and
that, Alexander Petrovitch, is a bad business, when a man
borrows. All round me were such hard hearts, there was no
place where one could have a good cry. Sometimes I would
creep into a corner and cry a little there. Once I was standing on
guard as a sentry; it was night. The wind was blowing, it was
autumn, and so dark you could see nothing. And I was so
miserable, so miserable! I took my gun, unscrewed the bayonet,
and laid it on the ground; then I pulled off my right boot, put
the muzzle of the barrel to my heart, leaned heavily on it and
pulled the trigger with my big toe. It was a miss-fire. I exam-
ined the gun, cleaned the barrel, put in another cartridge
and again pressed it to my breast. Again a miss-fire. I put on
my boot again, fixed the bayonet, shouldered my gun, and
walked up and down in silence; and I settled that whatever
might happen I would get out of being a recruit. Half an
hour later the colonel rode by, at the head of the patrol, right
past me.

'Is that the way to stand on guard?' he said.

'I took the gun in my hand and speared him with the bayonet

right up to the muzzle of the gun. I was severely flogged, and was sent here for life.'

The second story is about a man who 'exchanged' his sentence. It happened thus: A party of exiles were going to Siberia. Some were going to prison, some were merely exiled; some were going to work in factories, but all were going together. They stopped somewhere on the way in the Government of Perm. Among these exiles there was a man called Mikhailov, who was condemned to a life sentence for murder. He was a cunning fellow, and made up his mind to exchange his sentence. He comes across a simple fellow called Shushilov, who was merely condemned to a few years' transportation, that is to say, he had to live in Siberia and not in European Russia for a few years. This latter man was naïve, ignorant, and, moreover, had no money of his own, Mikhailov made friends with him and finally made him drunk, and then proposed to him an exchange of sentences. Mikhailov said: 'It is true that I am going to prison, but I am going to some *special department*,' which he explained was a particular favour, as it was a kind of first class. Shushilov, under the influence of drink, and being simple-minded, was full of gratitude for the offer, and Mikhailov taking advantage of his simplicity bought his name from him for a red shirt and a silver rouble, which he gave him on the spot, before witnesses. On the following day Shushilov spent the silver rouble and sold the red shirt for drink also, but as soon as he became sober again he regretted the bargain. Then Mikhailov said to him: 'If you regret the bargain give me back my money.' This he could not do; it was impossible for him to raise a rouble. At the next *étape* at which they stopped, when their names were called and the officer called out Mikhailov, Shushilov answered and Mikhailov answered to Shushilov's name, and the result was that when they left Tobolsk, Mikhailov was sent somewhere to spend a few years in exile, and Shushilov became a 'lifer'; and the special department which the other man talked of as a kind of superior class, turned out to be the department reserved for the most desperate criminals of all, those who had no chance of ever leaving prison, and who were most strictly watched and guarded. It was no good

E

complaining; there was no means of rectifying the mistake. There were no witnesses. Had there been witnesses they would have perjured themselves. And so Shushilov, who had done nothing at all, received the severest sentence the Russian Government had power to inflict, whereas the other man, a desperate criminal, merely enjoyed a few years' change of air in the country. The most remarkable thing about this story is this: Dostoievsky tells us that the convicts despised Shushilov, not because he had exchanged his sentence, but because he had made so bad a bargain, and had only got a red shirt and a silver rouble. Had he exchanged it for two or three shirts and two or three roubles, they would have thought it quite natural.

The whole book is crammed with such stories, each one of which throws a flood of light on the character of the Russian people.

These *Letters from a Dead House* are translated into French, and a good English translation of them by Marie von Thilo was published by Messrs. Longmans in 1881. But it is now, I believe, out of print. Yet if there is one foreign book in the whole world which deserves to be well known, it is this one. Not only because it throws more light on the Russian people than any other book which has ever been written, but also because it tells in the simplest possible way illuminating things about prisoners and prison life. It is a book which should be read by all legislators; it is true that the prison life it describes is now obsolete. It deals with convict life in the fifties, when everything was far more antiquated, brutal and severe than it is now. Yet although prisoners had to run the gauntlet between a regiment of soldiers, and were sometimes beaten nearly to death, in spite of the squalor of the prison and in spite of the dreariness and anguish inseparable from their lives, the life of the prisoners stands out in a positively favourable contrast to that which is led by our convicts in what Mr Chesterton calls our 'clean and cruel prisons', where our prisoners pick oakum today in solitary confinement. The proof of this is that Dostoievsky was able to write one of the most beautiful studies of human nature that have ever been written out of his prison experiences. In the

¹ *Publishers Note :* A translation is now published by Oxford University Press.

first place, the prisoners enjoyed human fellowship. They all had tobacco; they played cards; they could receive alms, and, though this was more difficult, they could get wine. There were no rules forbidding them to speak. Each prisoner had an occupation of his own, a hobby, a trade, in which he occupied all his leisure time. Had it not been for this, Dostoievsky says, the prisoners would have gone mad. One wonders what they would think of an English prison, where the prisoners are not even allowed to speak to each other. Such a régime was and is and probably always will be perfectly unthinkable to a Russian mind. Indeed this point reminds me of a startling phrase of a Russian revolutionary, who had experiences of Russian prisons. He was a member of the second Russian Duma; he had spent many years in prison in Russia. In the winter of 1906 there was a socialistic conference in London which he attended. When he returned to Russia he was asked by his fellow-politicians to lecture on the liberty of English institutions. He refused to do so. 'A Russian,' he said, 'is freer in prison than an Englishman is at large.'

The secret of the merit of this extraordinary book is also the secret of the unique quality which we find in all Dostoievsky's fiction. It is this: Dostoievsky faces the truth; he faces what is bad, what is worst, what is most revolting in human nature; he does not put on blinkers and deny the existence of evil, like many English writers, and he does not, like Zola, indulge in filthy analysis and erect out of his beastly investigations a pseudo-scientific theory based on the belief that all human nature is wholly bad. Dostoievsky analyses, not in order to experiment on the patient and to satisfy his own curiosity, but in order to cure and to comfort him. And having faced the evil and recognized it, he proceeds to unearth the good from underneath it; and he accepts the whole because of the good, and gives thanks for it. He finds God's image in the worst of the criminals, and shows it to us, and for that reason this book is one of the most important books ever written. Terrible as it is, and sad as it is, no one can read it without feeling better and stronger and more hopeful. For Dostoievsky proves to us—so far from complaining of his lot—that life in the Dead House is not only worth living, but full of unsuspected and unexplored riches, rare pearls of goodness, shining gems of kindness, and secret springs of pity. He leaves prison with something like regret, and he regards his four years' experience there as a special boon of Providence, the captain jewel of his life. He goes out saved for ever from despair, and full of that wisdom more precious than rubies which is to be found in the hearts of children.

V

CRIME AND PUNISHMENT

Crime and Punishment was published in 1866. It is a book which brought Dostoievsky fame and popularity, and by which, in Europe at any rate, he is still best known. It is the greatest tragedy about a murderer that has been written since *Macbeth*.

In the chapter on Tolstoy and Tourgeniev, I pointed out that the Russian character could roughly be divided into two types, which dominate the whole of Russian fiction, the two types being Lucifer, the embodiment of invincible pride, and Ivan Durak, the wise fool. This is especially true with regard to Dostoievsky's novels. Nearly all the most important characters in his books represent one or other of these two types. Raskolnikov, the hero of *Crime and Punishment*, is the embodiment of the Lucifer type, and the whole motive and mainspring of his character is pride.

Raskolnikov is a Nihilist in the true sense of the word, not a political Nihilist nor an intellectual Nihilist like Tourgeniev's Bazarov, but a moral Nihilist; that is to say, a man who strives to act without principle and to be unscrupulous, who desires to put himself beyond and above human moral conventions. His idea is that if he can trample on human conventions, he will be a sort of Napoleon. He goes to pawn a jewel at an old woman pawnbroker's, and the idea which is to affect his whole future vaguely takes root in his mind, namely, that an intelligent man, possessed of the fortune of this pawnbroker, could do anything, and that the only necessary step is to suppress this useless and positively harmful old woman. He thus expresses the idea later:

'I used to put myself this question: If Napoleon had found himself in my position and had not wherewith to begin his career, and there was neither Toulon, nor Egypt, nor the passage of the Alps, and if there were, instead of these splendid and monumental episodes, simply some ridiculous old woman, a usurer whom he would have to kill in order to get her money, would he shrink from doing this if there were no other alternative, merely because it would not be a fine deed and because it would be sinful? Now I tell you that I was possessed by this problem for a long time, and that I felt deeply ashamed when I at last guessed, suddenly as it were, that not only would he not be frightened at the idea, but that the thought that the thing was not important and grandiose enough would not even enter into his head: he would not even understand where the need for hesitation lay; and if there were no other way open to him, he would kill the woman without further reflection. Well, I ceased reflecting, and I killed her, following the example of my authority.'

Raskolnikov is obsessed by the idea, just as Macbeth is obsessed by the prophecy of the three witches, and circumstances seem to play the part of Fate in a Greek tragedy, and to lead him against his will to commit a horrible crime. 'He is mechanically forced,' says Professor Brückner in his *History of Russian Literature*, 'into performing the act, as if he had gone too near machinery in motion, had been caught by a bit of his clothing, and cut to pieces.' As soon as he has killed the old woman, he is fatally led into committing another crime immediately after the first crime is committed. He thinks that by committing this crime he will have trampled on human conventions, that he will be above and beyond morality, a Napoleon, a Superman. The tragedy of the book consists in his failure, and in his realizing that he has failed. Instead of becoming stronger than mankind, he becomes weaker than mankind; instead of having conquered convention and morality, he is himself vanquished by them. He finds that as soon as the

crime is committed the whole of his relation towards the world
is changed, and his life becomes a long struggle with himself,
a revolt against the moral consequences of his act. His instinct
of self-preservation is in conflict with the horror of what he has
done and the need for confession. Raskolnikov, as I have said,
is the embodiment of pride; pride is the mainspring of his
character. He is proud enough to build gigantic conceptions, to
foster the ambition of placing himself above and beyond
humanity, but his character is not strong enough to bear the
load of his ideas. He thinks he has the makings of a great man
in him, and in order to prove this to himself he commits a
crime that would put an ordinary man beyond the pale of
humanity, because he thinks that being an extraordinary man
he will remain within the pale of humanity and not suffer.
His pride suffers a mortal blow when he finds that he is weak,
and that the moral consequences of his act face him at every
turn. He fights against this, he strives not to recognize it; he
deliberately seeks the company of detectives; he discusses
murder and murderers with them minutely, and with a reck-
lessness which leads him to the very brink of the precipice,
when it would need but a word more for him to betray himself.

The examining magistrate, indeed, guesses that he has committed the crime, and plays with him as a cat plays with a
mouse, being perfectly certain that in the long-run he will confess of his own accord. The chapters which consist of the
duel between these two men are the most poignant in anguish
which I have ever read. I have seen two of these scenes acted on
the stage, and several people in the audience had hysterics
before they were over. At last the moment of expiation comes,
though that of regeneration is still far distant. Raskolnikov
loves a poor prostitute named Sonia. His act, his murder, has
affected his love for Sonia, as it has affected the rest of his life,
and has charged it with a sullen despair. Sonia, who loves him
as the only man who has never treated her with contempt, sees
that he has some great load on his mind, that he is tortured by
some hidden secret. She tries in vain to get him to tell her what
it is, but at last he comes to her with the intention of telling her,
and she reads the speaking secret in his eyes. As soon as she

knows, she tells him that he must kiss the earth which he has
stained, and confess to the whole world that he has committed
murder. Then, she says, God will send him a new life. At first
he refuses: he says that society is worse than he, that greater
crimes than his are committed every day; that those who commit them are highly honoured. Sonia speaks of his suffering,
and of the torture he will undergo by keeping his dread secret,
but he will not yet give in, nor admit that he is not a strong
man, that he is really a *louse* – which is the name he gives to all
human beings who are not 'Supermen'. Sonia says that they
must go to exile together, and that by suffering *together* they
will expiate his deed. This is one of Dostoievsky's principal
ideas, or rather it is the interpretation and conception of
Christianity which you will most frequently meet with among
the Russian people—that suffering is good in itself, and
especially suffering in common with someone else.

After Raskolnikov has confessed his crime to Sonia, he
still hovers round and round the police, like a moth fatally
attracted by a candle, and at last he makes open confession, and
is condemned to seven years' penal servitude. But although he
has been defeated in the battle with his idea, although he has
not only failed, but failed miserably, even after he has confessed
his crime and is paying the penalty for it in prison, his pride still
survives. When he arrives in prison, it is not the hardships of
prison life, it is not the hard labour, the coarse food, the
shaven head, the convict's dress, that weigh on his spirit; nor
does he feel remorse for his crime. But here once more in
prison he begins to criticize and reflect on his former actions,
and finds them neither foolish nor horrible as he did before. 'In
what,' he thinks, 'was my conception stupider than many conceptions and theories which are current in the world? One need
only look at the matter from an independent standpoint, and
with a point-of-view unbiased by conventional ideas, and the
idea will not seem so strange. And why does my deed,' he
thought to himself, 'appear so ugly? In what way was it an evil
deed? My conscience is at rest. Naturally I committed a criminal offence, I broke the letter of the law and I shed blood.
Well, take my head in return for the letter of the law and make

an end of it! Of course, even many of those men who have benefited mankind and who were never satiated with power, after they had seized it for themselves, ought to have been executed as soon as they had taken their first step, but these people succeeded in taking further steps, and therefore they are justified: I did not succeed, and therefore perhaps I had not the right to take the first step.'

Raskolnikov accordingly considered that his crime consisted solely in this, that he was not strong enough to carry it through to the end, and not strong enough to confess it. He also tortured himself with another thought: why did he not kill himself as soon as he recognized the truth? Why did he prefer the weakness of confession?

The other convicts in the prison disliked him, distrusted him, and ended by hating him. Dostoievsky's own experience of convict life enables him in a short space to give us a striking picture of Raskolnikov's relations with the other convicts. He gradually becomes aware of the vast gulf which there is between him and the others. The class barrier which rises between him and them, is more difficult to break down than that caused by a difference in nationality. At the same time, he noticed that in the prison there were political prisoners, Poles, for instance, and officers, who looked down on the other convicts as though they were insects, ciphers of ignorance, and despised them accordingly. But he is unable to do this, he cannot help seeing that these 'ciphers' are far cleverer in many cases than the men who look down on them. On the other hand, he is astonished that they all love Sonia, who has followed him to the penal settlement where his prison is, and lives in the town. The convicts rarely see her, meeting her only from time to time at their work; and yet they adore her, because she has followed Raskolnikov. The hatred of the other convicts against him grows so strong that one day at Easter, when he goes to church with them, they turn on him and say: 'You have no right to go to church: you do not believe in God, you are an atheist, you ought to be killed.' He had never spoken with them of God or of religion, and yet they wished to kill him as an atheist. He only narrowly escaped being killed by the timely interference of a sentry. To the truth of this incident I can testify by personal experience, as I have heard Russian peasants and soldiers say that such and such a man was religious and that such and such a man was 'godless', although these men had never mentioned religion to them; and they were always right.

Then Raskolnikov fell ill and lay for some time in delirium in the hospital. After his recovery he learns that Sonia has fallen ill herself, and has not been near the prison, and a great sadness comes over him. At last she recovers, and he meets her one day at his work. Something melts in his heart, he knows not how or why; he falls at her feet and cries; and from that moment a new life begins for him. His despair has rolled away like a cloud: his heart has risen as though from the dead.

Crime and Punishment, the best known of all Dostoievsky's works, is certainly the most powerful. The anguish of mind which Raskolnikov goes through tortures the reader. Dostoievsky seems to have touched the extreme limit of suffering which the human soul can experience when it descends into hell. At the same time, he never seems to be gloating over the suffering, but, on the contrary, to be revealing the agonies of the human spirit in order to pour balm upon them. There is an episode earlier in the story, when Raskolnikov kneels down before Sonia, and speaks words which might be taken as the motto of this book, and indeed of nearly all of Dostoievsky's books: 'It is not before you that I am kneeling, but before all the suffering of mankind.'

It is in this book more than in any of his other books that one has the feeling that Dostoievsky is kneeling down before the great agonies that the human soul can endure: and in doing this, he teaches us how to endure and how to hope. Apart from the astounding analysis to be found in the book, and the terrible network of details of which the conflict between Raskolnikov and his obsession consists: apart from the duel of tongues between the examining magistrate, who is determined that the criminal shall be condemned, not on account of any circumstantial evidence, but by his own confession, and who drives the criminal to confession by playing upon his obsession: apart from all this main action, there is a wealth of minor characters, episodes and scenes, all of which are indispensable to the main thread of tragedy which runs through the whole. The book, as has been pointed out, did not receive anything like its full recognition in 1866 when it appeared, and now, in 1909, it stands higher in the estimation of all those who are qualified to judge it than it did then. This can be said of very few books published in Europe in the sixties. For all the so-called psychological and analytical novels which have been published since 1866 in France and in England not only seem pale and lifeless compared with Dostoievsky's fierce revelations, but not one of them has a drop of his large humanity, or a breath of his fragrant goodness.

VI

THE IDIOT

Although *Crime and Punishment* is the most powerful, and probably the most popular of Dostoievsky's books, I do not think it is the most characteristic; that is to say, I do not think it possesses in so high a degree those qualities which are peculiar to his genius. More characteristic still is *The Idiot*, in the main character of which the very soul and spirit of Dostoievsky breathe and live. The hero of *The Idiot*, Prince Mwishkin, is the type of Ivan Durak, the simple fool who by his simplicity outwits the wisdom of the wise.

We make his acquaintance in a third-class railway carriage of the train which is arriving at St Petersburg from Warsaw. He is a young man about twenty-six years old, with thick fair hair, sloping shoulders, and a very slight fair beard; his eyes are large, light-blue, and penetrating; in his expression there is something tranquil but burdensome, something of that strange look which enables physicians to recognize at a first glance a victim of the falling sickness. In his hand he is carrying a bundle made of old *foulard*, which is his whole luggage. A fellow-traveller enters into conversation with him. He answers with unusual alacrity. Being asked whether he has been absent long, he says that it is over four years since he was in Russia, that he was sent abroad on account of his health—on account of some strange nervous illness like St Vitus' dance. As he listens, his fellow-traveller laughs several times, and especially when to the question, 'Did they cure you?' the fair-haired man answers, 'No, they did not cure me.' The dark-haired man is Rogozhin, a merchant. These two characters are the two figures round which the drama of the book centres and is played.

The purpose of Prince Mwishkin in coming to St Petersburg is to find a distant relation of his, the wife of a General Epanchin. He has already written to her from Switzerland, but has received no answer. He presents himself at the general's house with his bundle. A man in livery opens the door and regards him with suspicion. At last, after he has explained clearly and at some length that he is Prince Mwishkin, and that it is necessary for him to see the general on important business, the servant leads him into a small front-hall into which the anteroom (where guests are received) of the general's study opens. He delivers him into the hands of another servant who is dressed in black. This man tells the prince to wait in the anteroom and to leave his bundle in the front hall. He sits down in his armchair and looks with severe astonishment at the prince, who, instead of taking the suggestion, sits down beside him on a chair, with his bundle in his hands.

'If you will allow me,' said the prince, 'I would rather wait here with you. What should I do there alone?'

'The hall,' answered the servant, 'is not the place for you, because you are a visitor, or in other words, a guest. You wish to see the general himself?' The servant obviously could not reconcile himself with the idea of showing in such a visitor, and decided to question him further.

'Yes, I have come on business,' began the prince.

'I do not ask you what is your business. My business is simply to announce you. But without asking the secretary I said I would not announce you.' The suspicions of the servant continually seemed to increase. The prince was so unlike the ordinary run of everyday visitors. '. . . You are, so to speak, from abroad?' asked the servant at last, and hesitated as if he wished to say, 'You are really Prince Mwishkin?'

'Yes, I have this moment come from the train. I think that you wished to ask me whether I am really Prince Mwishkin, and that you did not ask me out of politeness.'

'H'm!' murmured the astonished servant.

'I assure you that I was not telling lies, and that you will not get into trouble on account of me. That I am dressed as I am and carrying a bundle like this is not astonishing, for at the present moment my circumstances are not flourishing.'

'H'm! I am not afraid of that. You see I am obliged to announce you, and the secretary will come to see you unless . . . the matter is like this: You have not come to beg from the general, may I be so bold as to ask?'

'Oh no, you may rest assured of that. I have come on other business.'

'Pardon me. Please wait for the secretary; he is busy . . .'

'Very well. If I shall have to wait long I should like to ask you whether I might smoke. I have a pipe and some tobacco.'

'Smoke!' The servant looked at him with contempt, as if he could not believe his ears. 'Smoke? No, you cannot smoke here. And what is more, you should be ashamed of thinking of such a thing. Well, this is queer!'

'I did not mean in this room, but I would go somewhere if you would show me, because I am accustomed to it, and I have not smoked now for three hours. But as you like.'

'Now, how shall I announce you?' murmured the servant as though almost unwillingly to himself. 'In the first place you ought not to be here, but in the ante-room, because you are a visitor, that is to say, a guest, and I am responsible. Have you come to live here?' he asked, looking again at the prince's bundle, which evidently disturbed him.

'No, I don't think so; even if they invited me, I should not stay. I have simply come to make acquaintance, nothing more.'

'How do you mean, to make acquaintance?' the servant asked, with trebled suspicion and astonishment. 'You said at first that you had come on business.'

'Well, it's not exactly business; that is to say, if you like, it *is* business—it is only to ask advice. But the chief thing is that I have come to introduce myself, because I and the general's wife are both descendants from the Mwishkins, and besides, myself there are no Mwishkins left.'

'So, what's more you are a relation!' said the frightened servant.

'No, not exactly a relation—that is to say, if you go back far enough, we are, of course, relations; but so far back that it doesn't count! I wrote to the general's wife a letter from abroad, but she did not answer me. All the same, I considered it necessary to make her acquaintance as soon as I arrived. I am explaining all this to you so that you should not have any doubts, because I see that you are disquieted. Announce that it is Prince Mwishkin, and that will be enough to explain the object of my visit. If they will see me, all will be well. If they do not, very likely all will be well too. But I don't think they can help receiving me, because the general's wife will naturally wish to see the oldest, indeed the only representative of her family; and she is most particular about keeping up relations with her family, as I have heard.'

'The conversation of the prince seemed as simple as possible, but the simpler it was, the more absurd it became under the circumstances; and the experienced footman could not help feeling something which was perfectly right between man and man, and utterly wrong between man and servant. Servants are generally far cleverer than their masters think, and this one thought that two things might be possible; either the prince had come to ask for money, or that he was simply a fool without ambition—because an ambitious prince would not remain in the front hall talking of his affairs with a footman, and would he not probably be responsible and to blame in either the one case or the other?'

I have quoted this episode, which occurs in the second chapter of the book, in full, because in it the whole character of the prince is revealed. He is the wise fool. He suffers from epilepsy, and this 'sacred' illness which has fallen on him has destroyed all those parts of the intellect out of which our faults grow, such as irony, arrogance and egoism. He is absolutely simple. He has the brains of a man, the tenderness of a woman and the heart of a child. He knows nothing of any barriers, either of class or character. He is the same and absolutely himself with every one he meets. And yet his unsuspicious *naïveté*, his untarnished sincerity and simplicity, are combined with penetrating intuition, so that he can read other people's minds like a book.

The general receives him, and he is just as frank and simple with the general as he has been with the servant. He is entirely without means, and has nothing in the world save his little bundle. The general inquires whether his handwriting is good, and resolves to get him some secretarial work; he gives him 25 roubles, and arranges that the prince shall live in his secretary's house. The general makes the prince stay for luncheon, and introduces him to his family. The general's wife is a charming, rather childish person, and she has three daughters, Alexandra, Adelaide and Aglaia. The prince astonishes them very much by his simplicity. They cannot quite understand at first whether he is a child or a knave, but his simplicity conquers them. After they have talked of various matters, his life in Switzerland, the experiences of a man condemned to death, which had been related to him and which I have already quoted, an execution which he had witnessed, one of the girls asks him if he was ever in love.

'No,' he says, 'I have never been in love . . . I was happy otherwise.'

'How was that?' they ask.

Then he relates the following: 'Where I was living they were all children, and I spent all my time with the children, and only with them. They were the children of the village; they all went to school. I never taught them, there was a schoolmaster for that. . . . I perhaps did teach them too, in a way, for I was more with them, and all the four years that I spent there went in this way. I had need of nothing else. I told them everything, I kept nothing secret from them. Their fathers and relations were angry with me because at last the children could not do without me, and always came round me in crowds, and the schoolmaster in the end became my greatest enemy. I made many enemies there, all on account of the children. And what were they afraid of? You can tell a child everything—everything. I have always been struck by the thought of how ignorant grown-up people are of children, how ignorant even fathers and mothers are of their own children. You should conceal nothing from children under the pretext that they are small, and that it is too soon for them to know. That is a sad, an unhappy thought. And how well children themselves understand that their fathers are thinking they are too small and do not understand anything—when they really understand everything. Grown-up people do not understand that a child even in the most difficult matter can give extremely important advice. Heavens! when one of these lovely little birds looks up at you, confiding and happy, it is a shame to deceive it. I call them birds because there is nothing better than birds in the world. To go on with my story, the people in the village were most angry with me because of one thing: the schoolmaster simply envied me. At first he shook his head, and wondered how the children understood everything I told them, and almost nothing of what he told them. Then he began to laugh at me when I said to him that we could neither of us teach them anything, but that they could teach us. And how could he envy me and slander me when he himself lived with children? Children heal the soul.'

Into the character of the hero of this book Dostoievsky has put all the sweetness of his nature, all his sympathy with the unfortunate, all his pity for the sick, all his understanding and love of children. The character of Prince Mwishkin reflects all that is best in Dostoievsky. He is a portrait not of what Dostoievsky was, but of what the author would like to have been. It must not for a moment be thought that he imagined that he fulfilled this ideal: he was well aware of his faults: of the sudden outbursts and the seething deeps of his passionate nature; his capacity for rage, hatred, jealousy and envy; none the less Dostoievsky could not possibly have created the character of Prince Mwishkin, the Idiot, had he not been made of much the same substance himself.

All through Dostoievsky's books, whenever children are mentioned or appear, the pages breathe a kind of freshness and fragrance like that of lilies-of-the-valley. Whatever he says about children or whatever he makes them say, has the rare accent of truth. The smile of children lights up the dark pages of his books, like spring flowers growing at the edge of a dark abyss.

In strong contrast to the character of the prince is the merchant Rogozhin. He is the incarnation of the second type, that of the obdurate spirit, which I have already said dominates Dostoievsky's novels. He is, perhaps, less proud than Raskolnikov, but he is far stronger, more passionate and more vehement. His imperious and unfettered nature is handicapped by no weakness of nerves, no sapping self-analysis. He is undisciplined and centrifugal. He is not 'sicklied o'er with the pale cast of thought', but it is his passions and not his ideas which are too great for the vessel that contains them. Rogozhin loves Nastasia, a *hetaira*, who has likewise unbridled passions and impulses. He loves her with all the strength of his violent and undisciplined nature, and he is tormented by jealousy because she does not love him, although she cannot help submitting to the influence of his imperious personality. The jealous poison in him takes so complete a possession of his body and soul that he ultimately kills Nastasia almost immediately after she has married him and given herself to him, because he feels that she is never his own, least of all at the moment when she abandons herself to him for ever. So great is his passion, that this woman, even while hating him, cannot resist going to him against her will, knowing well that he will kill her.

The description of the night that follows this murder, when Rogozhin talks all night with the prince in front of the bed where Nastasia is lying dead, is by its absence of melodrama and its simplicity perhaps the most icily terrible piece of writing that Dostoievsky ever penned. The reason why Nastasia does not love Rogozhin is that she loves Prince Mwishkin, the Idiot, and so does the third daughter of the general, Aglaia, although he gives them nothing but pity, and never makes love to them. And here we come to the root-idea and the kernel of the book, which is the influence which the Idiot exercises on everybody with whom he comes in contact. Dostoievsky places him in a nest of rascals, scoundrels and villains, a world of usurers, liars and thieves, interested, worldly, ambitious and shady. He not only passes unscathed through all this den of evil, but the most deadly weapons of the wicked, their astuteness, their cunning and their fraud, are utterly powerless against his very simplicity, and there is not one of these people, however crusted with worldliness, however sordid or bad, who can evade his magical influence. The women at first laugh at him; but in the end, as I have already said, he becomes a cardinal factor in the life of both Nastasia the unbridled and passionate woman, and Aglaia the innocent and intelligent girl: so much so that they end by joining in a battle of wild jealousy over him, although he himself is naïvely unconscious of the cause of their dispute.

This book, more than any other, reveals to us the methods and the art of Dostoievsky. This method and this art are not unlike those of Charlotte Brontë. The setting of the picture, the accessories, are fantastic, sometimes to the verge of impossibility, and this no more matters than the fantastic setting of *Jane Eyre* matters. All we see and all we feel is the white flame of light that burns throughout the book. We no more care whether a man like General Epanchin could or could not have existed, or whether the circumstances of his life are possible or impossible, than we care whether the friends of Mr Rochester are possible or impossible. Such things seem utterly trivial in this book, where at every moment we are allowed to look deep down into the very depths of human nature, to look as it were on the spirit of man and woman naked and unashamed. For though the setting may be fantastic if not impossible, though we may never have seen such people in our lives, they are truer than life in a way: we seem to see right inside every one of these characters as though they had been stripped of everything which was false and artificial about them, as though they were left with nothing but their bared souls, as they will be at the Day of Judgment.

With regard to the artistic construction of the book, the method is the same as that of most of Dostoievsky's books. In nearly all his works the book begins just before a catastrophe and occupies the space of a few days. And yet the book is very long. It is entirely taken up by conversation and explanation of the conversation. There are no descriptions of nature; everything is in a dialogue. Directly one character speaks we hear the tone of his voice. There are no 'stage directions'. We are not told that so and so is such and such a person, we feel it and recognize it from the very first word he says. On the other hand, there is a great deal of analysis, but it is never of an unnecessary kind. Dostoievsky never nudges our elbow, never points out to us things which we know already, but he illuminates with a strong searchlight the deeps of the sombre and tortuous souls of his characters, by showing us what they are themselves thinking, but not what he thinks of them. His analysis resembles the Greek Chorus, and his books resemble Greek tragedies in the making, rich ore mingled with dark dross, granite and marble, the stuff out of which Æschylus could have hewn another *Agamemnon*, or Shakespeare have written another *King Lear*.

The Idiot may not be the most artistic of all his books, in the sense that it is not centralized and is often diffuse, which is not the case with *Crime and Punishment*, but it is perhaps the most characteristic, the most personal, for none but Dostoievsky could have invented and caused to live such a character as Prince Mwishkin, and made him positively radiate goodness and love.

VII

THE POSSESSED

The Possessed, or *Devils*, which is the literal translation of the Russian title, is perhaps inferior to Dostoievsky's other work as a whole, but in one sense it is the most interesting book which he ever wrote. There are two reasons for this: in the first place, his qualities and his defects as a writer are seen in this book intensified, under a magnifying glass as it were, at their extremes, so that it both gives you an idea of the furthest range of his powers, and shows you most clearly the limitations of his genius. Stevenson points out somewhere that this is the case with Victor Hugo's least successful novels. In the second place, the book was far in advance of its time. In it Dostoievsky shows that he possessed 'a prophetic soul'.

The book deals with the Nihilists who played a prominent part in the sixties. The explanation of the title is to be found in a quotation from the 8th chapter of St Luke's Gospel.

'And there was there an herd of many swine feeding on the mountain; and they besought Him that He would suffer them to enter into them. And He suffered them. Then went the devils out of the man and entered into the swine: and the herd ran violently down a steep place into the lake and were choked. When they that fed them saw what was done, they fled, and went and told it in the city and in the country.

'Then they went out to see what was done; and came to Jesus, and found the man out of whom the devils were departed, sitting at the feet of Jesus, clothed, and in his right mind; and they were afraid. They also which saw it, told them by what means he that was possessed of the devils, was healed.'

The book, as I have said, undoubtedly reveals Dostoievsky's powers at their highest pitch, in the sense that nowhere in the whole range of his work do we find such isolated scenes of power; scenes which are, so to speak, white hot with the fire of his soul; and characters in which he has concentrated the whole dæmonic force of his personality, and the whole blinding strength of his insight. On the other hand, it shows us, as I added, more clearly than any other of his books, the nature and the extent of his limitations. It is almost too full of characters and incidents; the incidents are crowded together in an incredibly short space of time, the whole action of the book, which is a remarkably long one, occupying only the space of a

few days, while to the description of one morning enough space
is allotted to make a bulky English novel. Again, the narrative
is somewhat disconnected. You can sometimes scarcely see the
wood for the trees. Of course, these objections are in a sense
hypercritical, because, as far as my experience goes, anyone
who takes up this book finds it impossible to put it down until
he has read it to the very end, so enthralling is the mere interest
of the story, so powerful the grip of the characters. I therefore
only suggest these criticisms for those who wish to form an
idea of the net result of Dostoievsky's artistic scope and
achievement.

With regard to the further point, the 'prophetic soul' which
speaks in this book is perhaps that which is its most remarkable quality. The book was some thirty years ahead of its time:
ahead of its time in the same way that Wagner's music was
ahead of its time—and this was not only on account of the
characters and the state of things which it divined and fore-
shadowed, but also on account of the ideas and the flashes of
philosophy which abound in its pages. When the book was
published, it was treated as a gross caricature, and even a few
years ago when Professor Brückner first published his *History
of Russian Literature*, he talked of this book as being a satire
not of Nihilism itself, but of the hangers-on, the camp-fol-
lowers which accompany every army. 'Dostoievsky,' he says,
'did not paint the heroes but the Falstaffs, the silly adepts, the
half and wholly crazed adherents of Nihilism. He was indeed
fully within his rights. Of course there were such Nihilists,
particularly between 1862 and 1869, but there were not only
such: even Nechaev, the prototype of Petrushka, impressed
us by a steel-like energy and a hatred for the upper classes
which we wholly miss in the wind-bag and intriguer Petrushka.'

There is a certain amount of truth in this criticism. It is true
that Dostoievsky certainly painted the Falstaffs and the half-
crazy adherents of Nihilism. But I am convinced that the reason he did not paint the heroes was that he did not believe in
their existence: he did not believe that the heroes of Nihilism
were heroes; this is plain not only from this book, but from

every line which he wrote about the people who played a part in the revolutionary movement in Russia; and so far from the leading personage in his book being merely a wind-bag, I would say that one is almost more impressed by the steel-like energy of the character, as drawn in this book, than by the sayings and doings of his prototype—or rather his prototypes in real life. The amazing thing is that even if a few years ago real life had not furnished examples of revolutionaries as extreme both in their energy and in their craziness as Dostoievsky paints them, real life has done so in the last four years. Therefore, Dostoievsky not only saw with prophetic divination that should circumstances in Russia ever lead to a general upheaval, such characters might arise and exercise an influence, but his prophetic insight has actually been justified by the facts.

As soon as such circumstances arose, as they did after the Japanese War of 1904, characters such as Dostoievsky depicted immediately came to the front and played a leading part. When M. de Vogüé published his book, *La Roman Russe*, in speaking of *The Possessed*, he said that he had assisted at several of the trials of Anarchists in 1871, and he added that many of the men who came up for trial, and many of the crimes of which they were accused, were identical reproductions of the men and the crimes imagined by the novelist. If this was true when applied to the revolutionaries of 1871, it is a great deal truer applied to those of 1904–1909. That Dostoievsky believed that this would happen, I think there can be no doubt. Witness the following passage:

'Chigalev,' says the leading character of *The Possessed*, speaking of one of his revolutionary disciples, a man with long ears, 'is a man of genius: a genius in the manner of Fourier, but bolder and cleverer. He has invented "equality". In his system, every member of society has an eye on every one else. To tell tales is a duty. The individual belongs to the community and the community belongs to the individual. All are slaves and equal in their bondage. Calumny and assassination can be used in extreme cases, but the most important thing is equality. The first necessity is to lower the level of culture science and talent.

A high scientific level is only accessible to superior intellects, and we don't want superior intellects. Men gifted with high capacities have always seized upon power and become despots. Highly gifted men cannot help being despots, and have always done more harm than good. They must be exiled or executed. Cicero's tongue must be cut out, Copernicus' eyes must be blinded, Shakespeare must be stoned. That is Chigalevism. Slaves must be equal. Without despotism, up to the present time, neither liberty nor equality has existed, but in a herd, equality should reign supreme—and that is Chigalevism. . . . I am all for Chigalevism. Down with instruction and science! There is enough of it, as it is, to last thousands of years, but we must organize obedience: it is the only thing which is wanting in the world. The desire for culture is an aristocratic desire. As soon as you admit the idea of the family or of love, you will have the desire for personal property. We will annihilate this desire: we will let loose drunkenness, slander, tale-telling, and unheard-of debauchery. We will strangle every genius in his cradle. We will reduce everything to the same denomination, complete equality. "We have learnt a trade, and we are honest men: we need nothing else." Such was the answer which some English workman made the other day. The indispensable alone is indispensable. Such will thenceforth be the watchword of the world, but we must have upheavals. We will see to that, we the governing class. The slaves must have leaders. Complete obedience, absolute impersonality, but once every thirty years Chigalev will bring about an upheaval, and men will begin to devour each other: always up to a given point, so that we may not be bored. Boredom is an aristocratic sensation, and in Chigalevism there will be no desires. We will reserve for ourselves desire and suffering, and for the slaves there will be Chigalevism. . . . We will begin by fermenting disorder; we will reach the people itself. Do you know that we are already terribly strong? those who belong to us are not only the men who murder and set fire, who commit injuries after the approved fashion, and who bite: these people are only in the way. I do not understand anything unless there be discipline. I myself am a scoundrel, but I am not a Socialist. Ha, ha! listen! I have counted them all: the teacher who laughs with the children whom he teaches, at their God and at their cradle, belongs to us; the barrister who defends a well-educated assassin by proving that he is more educated than his victims, and that in order to get money he was obliged to kill, belongs to us; the schoolboy who in order to experience a sharp sensation kills a peasant, belongs to us; the juries who systematically acquit all criminals, belong to us; the judge who at the tribunal is afraid of not showing himself to be sufficiently liberal, belongs to us; among the administrators, among the men of letters, a great number belong to us, and they do not know it themselves. On the other hand, the obedience of schoolboys and fools has reached its zenith. Everywhere you see an immeasurable vanity, and bestial, unheard-of appetites. Do you know how much we owe to the theories in vogue at present alone? When I left Russia, Littré's thesis, which likens crime to madness, was the rage. I return, and crime is already no longer considered even as madness: it is considered as common sense itself, almost a duty, at least a noble protest. "Why should not an enlightened man kill if he has need of money?" Such is the argument you hear. But that is nothing. The Russian God has ceded his place to drink. The people are drunk, the mothers are drunk, the children are drunk, the churches are empty. Oh, let this generation grow: it is a pity we cannot wait. They would be drunk still. Ah, what a pity that we have no proletariat! But it will come, it will come. The moment is drawing near.'

In this declaration of revolutionary faith, Dostoievsky has concentrated the whole of an ideal on which thousands of ignorant men in Russia have acted during the last three years. All of the so-called Hooliganism which came about in Russia after the war, which although it has greatly diminished has by no means yet been exterminated by a wholesale system of military court-martials, proceeds from this, and its adepts are conscious or unconscious disciples of this creed. For the proletariat which Dostoievsky foresaw is now a living fact, and a great part of it has been saturated with such ideas. Not all of it, of course. I do not for a moment mean to say that every ordinary Russian social-democrat fosters such ideas; but what

I do mean to say is that these ideas exist, and that a great number of men have acted on a similar creed which they have only half digested, and have sunk into ruin, ruining others in doing so, and have ended by being hanged.

Thus the book, *Devils*, which, when it appeared in 1871, was thought a piece of gross exaggeration, and which had not been out long before events began to show that it was less exaggerated than it appeared at first sight—has in the last three years, and even in this year of grace, received further justification by events such as the role that Father Gapon played in the revolutionary movement, and the revelations which have been lately made with regard to Azev and similar characters. Any one who finds difficulty in believing a story such as that which came to light through the Azev revelations, had better read *The Possessed*. It will throw an illuminating light on the motives that cause such men to act as they do, and the circumstances that produce such men.

The main idea of the book is to show that the whole strength of what were then the Nihilists and what are now the Revolutionaries—let us say the Maximalists—lies, not in lofty dogmas and theories held by a vast and splendidly organized community, but simply in the strength of character of one or two men, and in the peculiar weakness of the common herd. I say the peculiar weakness with intention. It does not follow that the common herd, to which the majority of the revolutionary disciples belong, is necessarily altogether weak, but that though the men of whom it is composed may be strong and clever in a thousand ways, they have one peculiar weakness, which is, indeed, a common weakness of the Russian character. But before going into this question, it is advisable first to say that what Dostoievsky shows in his book, *The Possessed*, is that these Nihilists are almost entirely devoid of ideas; the organizations round which so many legends gather, consist in reality of only a few local clubs—in this particular case, of one local club. All the talk of central committees, executive committees, and so forth, existed only in the imagination of the leaders. On the other hand, the character of those few men who were the leaders and who dominated their disciples, was as strong as steel and as cold as ice. And what Dostoievsky shows is how this peculiar strength of the leaders exercised itself on the peculiar weakness of the disciples. Let us now turn to the peculiar nature of this weakness. Dostoievsky explains it at the very beginning of the book. In describing one of the characters, Chatov, who is an unwilling disciple of the Nihilist leaders, he says:

'He is one of those Russian Idealists whom any strong idea strikes all of a sudden, and on the spot annihilates his will, sometimes for ever. They are never able to react against the idea. They believe in it passionately, and the rest of their life passes as though they were writhing under a stone which was crushing them.'

The leading figure of the book is one Peter Verkhovensky, a political agitator. He is unscrupulous, ingenious, and plausible in the highest degree, as clever as a fiend, a complete egotist, boundlessly ambitious, untroubled by conscience, and as hard as steel. His prototype was Nachaef, an actual Nihilist. The ambition of this man is to create disorder, and disorder once created, to seize the authority which must ultimately arise out of any disorder. His means of effecting this is as ingenious as Chichikov's method of disposing of 'dead souls' in Gogol's masterpiece. By imagining a central committee, of which he is the representative, he organizes a small local committee, consisting of five men called 'the Fiver'; and he persuades his dupes that a network of similar small committees exists all over Russia. He aims at getting the local committee entirely into his hands, and making the members of it absolute slaves to his will. His ultimate aim is to create similar committees all over the country, persuading people in every new place that the network is ready everywhere else, and that they are all working in complete harmony and in absolute obedience to a central committee, which is somewhere abroad, and which in reality does not exist. This once accomplished, his idea is to create disorder among the peasants or the masses, and in the general upheaval to seize the power. It is possible that I am defining his aim too closely, since in the book one only sees his work, so far as one local committee is concerned. But it is clear from his character that he has some big idea at the back of his head. He is not merely dabbling with excitement in a small local sphere, for all the other characters in the book, however much they hate him, are agreed about one thing; that in his cold and self-seeking character there lies an element of sheer enthusiasm. The manner in which he creates disciples out of his immediate surroundings, and obtains an unbounded influence over them, is by playing on the peculiar weakness which I have already quoted as being the characteristic of Chigalevism. He plays on the one-sidedness of the Russian character; he plays on the fact that directly one single idea takes possession of the brain of a certain kind of Russian idealist, as in the case of Chatov, or Raskolnikov, for instance, he is no longer able to control it. Peter works on this. He also works on the vanity of his disciples, and on their fear of not being thought advanced enough.

'The principal strength,' he says on one occasion, 'the element which binds everything, is the fear of public opinion, the fear of having an opinion of one's own. It is with just such people that success is possible. I tell you they would throw themselves into the fire if I told them to do so, if I ordered it. I would only have to say that they were bad Liberals. I have been blamed for having deceived my associates here in speaking of a central committee and of "innumerable ramifications". But where is the deception? The central committee is you and me. As to the ramifications, I can have as many as you wish.'

But as Peter's plans advance, this cement, consisting of vanity and the fear of public opinion, is not sufficient for him; he wants a stronger bond to bind his disciples together, and to keep them under his own immediate and exclusive control; and such a bond must be one of blood. He therefore persuades his committee that one of their members, Chatov, to whom I have already alluded, is a spy. This is easy, because Chatov is a member of the organization against his will. He became involved in the business when he was abroad, in Switzerland; and on the first possible occasion he says he will have nothing to do with any Nihilist propaganda, since he is absolutely opposed to it, being a convinced Slavophil and a hater of all acts of violence. Peter lays a trap for him. At a meeting of the committee he asks every one of those present whether, should they be aware that a political assassination were about to take place, they would denounce the man who was to perform it. With one exception all answer no, that they would denounce an ordinary assassin, but that political assassination is not murder. When the question is put to Chatov he refuses to answer. Peter tells the others that this is the proof that he is a spy, and that he must be made away with. His object is that they should kill Chatov, and thenceforth be bound to him by fear of each other and of him. He has a further plan for attributing the guilt of Chatov's murder to another man. He has come across an engineer named Kirilov. This man is also possessed by one idea, in the same manner as Raskolnikov and Chatov, only that, unlike them, his character is strong. His idea is practically that enunciated many years later by Nietzsche, that of the Superman. Kirilov is a maniac: the single idea which in his case has taken possession of him is that of suicide. There are two prejudices, he reasons, which prevent man committing suicide. One of them is insignificant, the other very serious, but the insignificant reason is not without considerable importance: it is the fear of pain. In exposing his idea he argues that were a stone the size of a six-storied house to be suspended over a man, he would know that the fall of the stone would cause him no pain, yet he would instinctively dread its fall, as causing extreme pain. As long as that stone remained suspended over him, he would be in terror lest it should cause him pain by its fall, and no one, not even the most scientific of men, could escape this impression. Complete liberty will come about only when it will be immaterial to man whether he lives or not: that is the aim.

The second cause and the most serious one that prevents men from committing suicide, is the idea of another world. For the sake of clearness I will here quote Kirilov's conversation on this subject with the narrator of the story, which is told in the first person:

'. . . That is to say, punishment?' says his interlocutor.

'No, that is nothing—simply the idea of another world.'

'Are there not atheists who already disbelieve in another world?'

Kirilov was silent.

'You perhaps judge by yourself.'

'Every man can judge only by himself,' said Kirilov, blushing. 'Complete liberty will come about when it will be entirely immaterial to man whether he lives or whether he dies: that is the aim of everything.'

'The aim? Then nobody will be able or will wish to live.'

'Nobody,' he answered.

'Man fears death, and therefore loves life,' I remarked. 'That is how I understand the matter, and thus has Nature ordained.'

'That is a base idea, and therein lies the whole imposture. Life is suffering, life is fear, and man is unhappy. Everything now is in pain and terror. Man loves life now, because he loves pain and terror. Thus has he been made. Man gives his life now for pain and fear, and therein lies the whole imposture. Man is not at present what he ought to be. A new man will rise, happy and proud, to whom it will be immaterial whether he lives or dies. That will be the new man. He who vanquishes pain and fear, he will be God, and the other gods will no longer exist.'

'Then, according to you, the other God does exist?'

'He exists without existing. In the stone there is no pain, but in the fear of the stone there is pain. God is the pain which arises from the fear of death. He who vanquishes the pain and the fear, he will be God. Then there will be a new life, a new man, everything new. Then history will be divided into two parts. From the gorilla to the destruction of God, and from the destruction of God to . . .'

'To the gorilla . . .?'

'To the physical transformation of man and of the world. Man will be God, and will be transformed physically.'

'How do you think man will be transformed physically?'

'The transformation will take place in the world, in thought, sentiments, and actions.'

'If it will be immaterial to men whether they live or die,

then men will all kill each other. That is perhaps the form the
transformation will take?'

'That is immaterial. The imposture will be destroyed. He
who desires to attain complete freedom must not be afraid of
killing himself. He who dares to kill himself, has discovered
where the error lies. There is no greater liberty than this: this
is the end of all things, and you cannot go further. He who
dares to kill himself is God. It is at present in everyone's power
to bring this about: that God shall be no more, and that nothing shall exist any more. But nobody has yet done this.'

'There have been millions of suicides.'

'But they have never been inspired with this idea. They
have always killed themselves out of fear, and never in order to
kill fear. He who will kill himself simply in order to kill fear,
he will be God.'

In this last sentence we have the whole idea and philosophy
of Kirilov. He had made up his mind to kill himself, in order to
prove that he was not afraid of death, and he was possessed by
that idea, and by that idea alone. In another place he says that
man is unhappy because he does not know that he is happy:
simply for this reason: that is all. 'He who knows that he is
happy will become happy at once, immediately.' And further
on he says: 'Men are not good, simply because they do not
know they are good. When they realize this, they will no longer
commit crimes. They must learn that they are good, and instantly they will become good, one and all of them. He who
will teach men that they are good, will end the world.' The
man to whom he is talking objects that He who taught men
that they were good was crucified.

'The man will come,' Kirilov replies, 'and his name will be
the Man-God.'

'The God-Man?' says his interlocutor.

'No, the Man-God—there is a difference.'

Here we have his idea of the Superman.[1]

As soon as Peter discovers Kirilov's obsession, he extracts
from him a promise that, as he has determined to commit

---

[1] It is characteristic that Dostoievsky puts the idea of the 'Superman' into the
mouth of a monomaniac.

suicide, and that as it is quite indifferent to him how and when he does it, he shall do it when it is useful to him, Peter. Kirilov consents to this, although he feels himself in no way bound to Peter, and although he sees through him entirely and completely, and would hate him were his contempt not too great for hatred. But Peter's most ambitious plans do not consist merely in binding five men to him by an indissoluble bond of blood: that is only the means to an end. The end, as I have already said, is vaguely to get power; and besides the five men whom he intends to make his slaves for life, Peter has another and far more important trump card. This trump card consists of a man, Nicholas Stavrogin, who is the hero of the book. He is the only son of a widow with a landed estate, and after being brought up by Peter's father, an old, harmless and kindly Radical, he is sent to school at the age of sixteen, and later on goes into the army, receiving a commission in one of the most brilliant of the Guards regiments in St Petersburg. No sooner does he get to St Petersburg, than he distinguishes himself by savage eccentricities. He is what the Russians call a *skandalist*. He is a good-looking young man of Herculean strength, and quiet, pleasant manners, who every now and then gives way to the wildest caprices, the most extravagant and astounding whims, when he seems to lose all control over himself. For a time he leads the kind of life led by Prince Harry with Falstaff, and his extravagances are the subject of much talk. He drives over people in his carriage, and publicly insults a lady of high position. Finally, he takes part in two duels. In both cases he is the aggressor. One of his adversaries is killed, and the other severely wounded. On account of this he is court-martialled, degraded to the ranks, and has to serve as a common soldier in an infantry regiment. But in 1863 he has an opportunity of distinguishing himself, and after a time his military rank is given back to him. It is then that he returns to the provincial town, where the whole of the events told in the book take place, and plays a part in Peter's organisation. Peter regards him, as I have said, as his trump card, because of the strength of his character. He is one of those people who represent the extreme Lucifer quality of the Russian nature. He is proud and inflexible, without any trace of weakness. There is nothing in the world he is afraid of, and there is nothing he will not do if he wishes to do it. He will commit the wildest follies, the most outrageous extravagances, but as it were *deliberately*, and not as if he were carried away by the impetuosity of his temperament. On the contrary, he seems throughout to be as cold as ice, and eternally unruffled and cool; and he is capable when he chooses of showing a self-control as astonishing and remarkable as his outbursts of violence. Peter knows very well that he cannot hope to influence such a man. Stavrogin sees through Peter and despises him. At the same time, Peter hopes to entangle him in his scheme, as he entangles the others, and thinks that, this once done, a man with Stavrogin's character cannot help being his principal asset. It is on this very character, however, that the whole of Peter's schemes break down. Stavrogin has married a lame, half-witted girl; the marriage is kept secret, and he loves and is loved by an extremely beautiful girl called Lisa. Peter conceives the idea of getting a tramp, an ex-convict who is capable of everything, to murder Stavrogin's wife and the drunken brother with whom she lives, and to set fire to a part of the town and the house where the two are living. He hopes that Stavrogin will marry Lisa, and then not be able to withdraw from his organization for fear of being held responsible for the murder of his wife.

Stavrogin sees through the whole scheme. He announces his marriage publicly; but this act, instead of alienating Lisa from him, increases her passion. Nevertheless Stavrogin's wife and her brother are murdered, and a large quarter of the town is burned. When Lisa asks Stavrogin if he is in any way connected with this murder, he replies that he was opposed to it, but that he had guessed that they would be murdered, and that he had taken no steps to prevent it. Lisa herself is killed, almost by accident, on the scene of the murder of Stavrogin's wife. She is killed by an excited man in the crowd, who holds her responsible for the deed, and thinks that she has come to gloat over her victims. After this Stavrogin washes his hands of the whole business, and leaves the town. It is then that Peter carries out the rest of his plans. Chatov is murdered, and Peter calls upon Kirilov to fulfil his promise and commit suicide. He wishes him, before committing the act, to write a paper in which he shall state that he has disseminated revolutionary pamphlets and proclamations, and that he has employed the ex-convict who committed the murders. He is also to add that he has killed Chatov on account of his betrayal. But Kirilov has not known until this moment that Chatov is dead, and he refuses to say a word about him. Then begins a duel between these two men in the night, which is the most exciting chapter in the book, and perhaps one of the most exciting and terrifying things ever written. Peter is in terror lest Kirilov should fail him, and Kirilov is determined not to be a party to Peter's baseness. Peter plays upon his vanity, and by subtle taunts excites to a frenzy the man's monomania, till at last he consents to sign the paper. Then snatching a revolver he goes into the next room. Peter waits, not knowing what is going to happen. Ten minutes pass, and Peter, consumed by anxiety, takes a candle and opens the door of the room in which Kirilov has shut himself. He opens the door, and somebody flies at him like a wild beast. He shuts the door with all his might, and remains listening. He hears nothing, and as he is now convinced that Kirilov will not commit suicide, he makes up his mind to kill Kirilov himself, now that he has got the paper. He knows that in a quarter of an hour his candle will be entirely consumed; he sees there is nothing else to be done but to kill Kirilov, but at the same time he does not wish to do it.

At last he takes the revolver in his right hand and the candle in his left hand, and with his left hand manages to open the door. The room is apparently empty. At first he thinks that Kirilov has fled; then he becomes aware that against the wall, between a window and a cupboard, Kirilov is standing, stiff and motionless as a ghost. He rushes toward him. Kirilov remains motionless, but his eye is fixed on Peter, and a sardonic smile is on his lips, as though he had guessed what was in Peter's mind. Peter, losing all self-control, flies at Kirilov, who knocks the candle out of Peter's hand, and bites his little finger nearly in two. Peter beats him on the head with the butt of his revolver, and escapes from the room. As he escapes, he hears terrifying screams of 'At once! at once! at once!' Peter is running for his life, and is already in the vestibule of the house, when he hears a revolver shot. Then he goes back and finds that Kirilov has killed himself.

This is practically the end of the book. Peter gets away to St Petersburg, and all his machinations are discovered. The corpse of Chatov is found; the declaration in Kirilov's handwriting at first misleads the police, but the whole truth soon comes out, since nearly all the conspirators confess, each being overcome with remorse. Peter escapes and goes abroad. Nicholas Stavrogin returns to his home from St Petersburg; he is not inculpated in any way in the plots, since the conspirators bear witness that he had nothing to do with them. But he hangs himself nevertheless.

As I have said before, the chief characters of this book, Stavrogin, Peter, Chatov, and Kirilov, who seemed such gross exaggerations when the book was published, would surprise nobody who has had any experience of contemporary Russia. Indeed, Peter is less an imitation of Nechaev than a prototype of Azev. As to Kirilov, there are dozens of such men, possessed by one idea and one idea only, in Russia. Stavrogin also is a type which occurs throughout Russian history. Stavrogin has something of Peter the Great in him, Peter the Great run to seed, and of such there are also many in Russia today.

VIII

THE BROTHERS KARAMAZOV

The subject of *The Brothers Karamazov*[1] had occupied Dostoievsky's mind ever since 1870, but he did not begin to write it until 1879, and when he died in 1881, only half the book was finished; in fact, he never even reached what he intended to be the real subject of the book. The subject was to be the life of a great sinner, Alosha Karamazov. But when Dostoievsky died,

[1] The French translation of this book is an abridgement. It is quite incomplete.

F

he had only written the prelude, in itself an extremely long book; and in this prelude he told the story of the bringing up of his hero, his surroundings and his early life, and in so doing he tells us all that is important about his hero's brothers and father. The story of Alosha's two brothers, and of their relations to their father, is in itself so rich in incident and ideas that it occupies the whole book, and Dostoievsky died before he had reached the development of Alosha himself.

The father is a cynical sensualist, utterly wanting in balance, vain, loquacious, and foolish. His eldest son, Mitya, inherits his father's sensuality, but at the same time he has the energy and strength of his mother, his father's first wife; Mitya is full of energy and strength. His nature does not know discipline; and since his passions have neither curb nor limit, they drive him to catastrophe. His nature is a mixture of fire and dross, and the dross has to be purged by intense suffering. Like Raskolnikov, Mitya has to expiate a crime. Circumstantial evidence seems to indicate that he has killed his father. Everything points to it, so much so that when one reads the book without knowing the story beforehand, one's mind shifts from doubt to certainty, and from certainty to doubt, just as though one were following some absorbing criminal story in real life. After a long series of legal proceedings, cross-examinations, and a trial in which the lawyers perform miracles of forensic art, Mitya is finally condemned. I will not spoil the reader's pleasure by saying whether Mitya is guilty or not, because there is something more than idle curiosity excited by this problem as one reads the book. The question seems to test to the utmost one's power of judging character, so abundant and so intensely vivid are the psychological data which the author gives us. Moreover, the question as to whether Mitya did or did not kill his father is in reality only a side-issue in the book; the main subjects of which are, firstly, the character of the hero, which is made to rise before us in its entirety, although we do not get as far as the vicissitudes through which it is to pass. Secondly, the root-idea of the book is an attack upon materialism, and the character of Alosha forms a part of this attack. Materialism is represented in the second of the brothers, Ivan Karamazov, and a great part of the book is devoted to the tragedy and the crisis of Ivan's life.

Ivan's mind is, as he says himself, Euclidean and quite material. It is impossible, he says, to love men when they are near to you. You can only love them at a distance. Men are hateful, and there is sufficient proof of this in the sufferings which children alone have to endure upon earth. At the same time, his logical mind finds nothing to wonder at in the universal sufferings of mankind. Men, he says, are themselves guilty: they were given Paradise, they wished for freedom, and they stole fire from heaven, knowing that they would thereby become unhappy; therefore they are not to be pitied. He only knows that suffering exists, that no one is guilty, that one thing follows from another perfectly simply, that everything proceeds from something else, and that everything works out as in an equation. But this is not enough for him: it is not enough for him to recognize that one thing proceeds simply and directly from another. He wants something else; he must needs have compensation and retribution, otherwise he would destroy himself; and he does not want to obtain this compensation somewhere and some time, in infinity, but here and now, on earth, so that he should see it himself. He has not suffered, merely in order that his very self should supply, by its evil deeds and its passions, the manure out of which some far-off future harmony may arise. He wishes to see with his own eyes how the lion shall lie down with the lamb. The great stumbling-block to him is the question of children: the sufferings of children. If all men have to suffer, in order that by their suffering they may build an eternal harmony, what have children got to do with this? It is inexplicable that they should suffer, and that it should be necessary for them to attain to an eternal harmony by their sufferings. Why should *they* fall into the material earth, and make manure for some future harmony? He understands that there can be solidarity in sin between men; he understands the idea of solidarity and retaliation, but he cannot understand the idea of solidarity with children in sin. The mocker will say, he adds, that the child will grow up and have time to sin; but he is not yet grown up. He understands, he says, what the universal vibration of joy must be, when every-thing in heaven and on earth joins in one shout of praise, and every living thing cries aloud, 'Thou art just, O Lord, for Thou hast revealed Thy ways.' And when the mother shall embrace the man who tormented and tore her child to bits—when mother, child, and tormentor shall all join in the cry, 'Lord, Thou art just!' then naturally the full revelation will be accomplished and everything will be made plain. Perhaps, he says, he would join in the Hosanna himself, were that moment to come, but he does not wish to do so; while there is yet time, he wishes to guard himself against so doing, and therefore he entirely renounces any idea of the higher harmony. He does not consider it worth the smallest tear of one suffering child; it is not worth it, because he considers that such tears are irreparable, and that no compensation can be made for them; and if they are not compensated for, how can there be an eternal harmony? But for a child's tears, he says, there is no compensation, for retribution—that is to say, the punishment of those who caused the suffering—is not compensation. Finally, he does not think that the mother has the right to for-give the man who caused her children to suffer; she may for-give him for her own sufferings, but she has not the right to forgive him the sufferings of her children. And without such forgiveness there can be no harmony. It is for love of mankind that he does not desire this harmony: he prefers to remain with his irreparable wrong, for which no compensation can be made. He prefers to remain with his unavenged and un-avengeable injuries and his tireless indignation. Even if he is not right, they have put too high a price, he says, on this eternal harmony. 'We cannot afford to pay so much for it; we cannot afford to pay so much for the ticket of admission into it. Therefore I give it back. And if I am an honest man, I am obliged to give it back as soon as possible. This I do. It is not because I do not acknowledge God, only I must respectfully return Him the ticket.'

The result of Ivan's philosophy is logical egotism and materialism. But his whole theory is upset, owing to its being pushed to its logical conclusion by a half-brother of the

Karamazovs, a lackey, Smerdyakov, who puts into practice the theories of Ivan, and commits first a crime and then suicide. This and a severe illness combine to shatter Ivan's theories. His physical being may recover, but one sees that his epicurean theories of life cannot subsist.

In sharp contrast to the two elder brothers is the third brother, Alosha, the hero of the book. He is one of the finest and most sympathetic characters that Dostoievsky created. He has the simplicity of 'The Idiot,' without his naïveté, and without the abnormality arising from epilepsy. He is a normal man, perfectly sane and sensible. He is the very incarnation of 'sweet reasonableness'. He is *Ivan Durak*, Ivan the Fool, but without being a fool. Alosha, Dostoievsky says, was in no way a fanatic; he was not even what most people call a mystic, but simply a lover of human beings; he loved humanity; all his life he believed in men, and yet nobody would have taken him for a fool or for a simple creature. There was something in him which convinced you that he did not wish to be a judge of men, that he did not wish to claim or exercise the right of judging others. One remarkable fact about his character, which is equally true of Dostoievsky's own character, was that Alosha with this wide tolerance never put on blinkers, or shut his eyes to the wickedness of man, or to the ugliness of life. No one could astonish or frighten him, even when he was quite a child. Everyone loved him wherever he went. Nor did he ever win the love of people by calculation, or cunning, or by the craft of pleasing. But he possessed in himself the gift of making people love him. It was innate in him; it acted immediately and directly, and with perfect naturalness. The basis of his character was that he was a *Realist*. When he was in the monastery where he spent a part of his youth, he believed in miracles; but Dostoievsky says, 'Miracles never trouble a Realist; it is not miracles which incline a Realist to believe. A true Realist, if he is not a believer, will always find in himself sufficient strength and sufficient capacity to disbelieve even in a miracle. And if a miracle appears before him as an undeniable fact, he will sooner disbelieve in his senses than admit the fact of the miracle. If, on the other hand, he admits it, he will admit it as a

natural fact, which up to the present he was unaware of. The
Realist does not believe in God because he believes in miracles,
but he believes in miracles because he believes in God. If a
Realist believes in God, his realism will necessarily lead him to
admit the existence of miracles also.'

Alosha's religion, therefore, was based on common sense,
and admitted of no compromise. As soon as, after having
thought about the matter, he becomes convinced that God and
the immortality of the soul exist, he immediately says to himself quite naturally: 'I wish to live for the future life, and to
admit of no half-way house.' And just in the same way, had he
been convinced that God and the immortality of the soul do
not exist, he would have become an atheist and a socialist. For
Dostoievsky says that Socialism is not only a social problem,
but an *atheistic* problem. It is the problem of the incarnation of
atheism, the problem of a Tower of Babel to be made without
God, not in order to reach Heaven from earth, but to bring
Heaven down to earth.

Alosha wishes to spend his whole life in the monastery,
and to give himself up entirely to religion, but he is not allowed
to do so. In the monastery, Alosha finds a spiritual father,
Zosima. This character, which is drawn with power and
vividness, strikes us as being a blend of saintliness, solid sense,
and warm humanity. He is an old man, and he dies in the convent; but before he dies, he sees Alosha, and tells him that he
must leave the convent for ever; he must go out into the
world, and live in the world, and suffer. 'You will have many
adversaries,' he says to him, 'but even your enemies will love
you. Life will bring you many misfortunes, but you will be
happy on account of them, and you will bless life and cause
others to bless it. That is the most important thing of all."
Alosha is to go into the world and submit to many trials, for he
is a Karamazov too, and the microbe of lust which rages in the
blood of that family is in him also. He is to put into practice
Father Zosima's precepts: 'Be no man's judge; humble love is
a terrible power which effects more than violence. Only active
love can bring out faith. Love men and do not be afraid of their
sins: love man in his sin; love all the creatures of God, and

pray God to make you cheerful. Be cheerful as children and as the birds.' These are the precepts which Alosha is to carry out in the face of many trials. How he does so we never see, for the book ends before his trials begin, and all we see is the strength of his influence, the effect of the sweetness of his character in relation to the trials of his two brothers, Mitya and Ivan.

That Dostoievsky should have died before finishing this monumental work which would have been his masterpiece, is a great calamity. Nevertheless the book is not incomplete in itself: it is a large piece of life, and it contains the whole of Dostoievsky's philosophy and ideas. Moreover, considered merely as a novel, as a book to be read from the point of view of being entertained, and excited about what is going to happen next, it is of enthralling interest. This book, therefore, can be recommended to a hermit who wishes to ponder over something deep, in a cell or on a desert island, to a philosopher who wishes to sharpen his thoughts against a hard whetstone, to a man who is unhappy and wishes to find some healing balm, or to a man who is going on a railway journey and wishes for an exciting story to while away the time.

IX

This study of Dostoievsky, or rather this suggestion for a study of his work, cannot help being sketchy and incomplete. I have not only not dealt with his shorter stories, such as *White Nights, The Friend of the Family, The Gambler* and *The Double*, but I have not even mentioned two longer novels, *The Hobbledehoy* and *Despised and Rejected*. The last named, though it suffers from being somethat melodramatic in parts, contains as strong a note of pathos as is to be found in any of Dostoievsky's books; and an incident of this book has been singled out by Robert Louis Stevenson as being—together with the moment when Mark Antony takes off his helmet, and the scene when Kent has pity on the dying Lear—one of the most greatly moving episodes in the whole of literature. The reason why I have not dwelt on these minor works is that to the

English reader, unacquainted with Dostoievsky, an exact and minute analysis of his works can only be tedious. I have only dealt with the very broadest outline of the case, so as to enable the reader to make up his mind whether he wishes to become acquainted with Dostoievsky's work at all. My object has been merely to open the door, and not to act as a guide and to show him over every part of the house. If I have inspired him with a wish to enter the house, I have succeeded in my task. Should he wish for better-informed guides and fuller guide-books, he will find them in plenty; but guides and guide-books are utterly useless to people who do not wish to visit the country of which they treat. And my sole object has been to give in the broadest manner possible a rough sketch of the nature of the country, so as to enable the traveller to make up his mind whether he thinks it worth while or not to buy a ticket and to set forth on a voyage of exploration. Should such an one decide that the ex-exploration is to him attractive and worth his while, I should advise him to begin with *The Letters from a Dead House,* and to go on with *The Idiot, Crime and Punishment,* and *The Brothers Karamazov*; and to read *The Possessed* last of all. If he understands and appreciates *The Letters from a Dead House,* he will be able to understand and appreciate the character of Dostoievsky and the main ideas which lie at the root of all his books. If he is able to understand and appreciate *The Idiot,* he will be able to understand and appreciate the whole of Dostoi-evsky's writings. But should he begin with *Crime and Punish-ment,* or *The Possessed,* it is possible that he might be put off, and relinquish the attempt; just as it is possible that a man who took up Shakepeare's plays for the first time and began with *King Lear,* might make up his mind not to persevere, but to choose some more cheerful author. And by so doing he would probably lose a great deal, since a man who is repelled by *King Lear* might very well be able to appreciate not only *The Mer-chant of Venice,* but *Henry IV* and the *Winter's Tale.* If one were asked to sum up briefly what was Dostoievsky's message to his generation and to the world in general, one could do so in two words: love and pity. The love which is in Dostoievsky's work is so great, so bountiful, so overflowing, that it is impossible to find a parallel to it, either in ancient or in modern literature. It is human, but more than human, that is to say, divine. Supposing the Gospel of St John were to be annihilated and lost to us for ever, although nothing could replace it, Dostoievsky's work would go nearer to replacing it than any other books written by any other man. It is the love which faces everything and which shrinks from nothing. It is the love which that saint felt who sought out the starving and freezing beggar, and warmed and embraced him, although he was covered with sores, and who was rewarded by the beggar turning into His Lord and lifting him up into the infinite spaces of Heaven.

Dostoievsky tells us that the most complete of his characters, Alosha, is a Realist, and that was what Dostoievsky was himself. He was a Realist in the true sense of the word, and he was exactly the contrary of those people who when they wrote particularly filthy novels in which they singled out and dwelt at length on certain revolting details of life, called themselves Realists. He saw things as they really are; he never shut his eyes or averted his gaze from anything which was either cruel, hateful, ugly, bitter, diseased or obscene; but the more he looked at the ugly things, the more firmly he became convinced of the goodness that is in and behind everything: To put it briefly, the more clearly he realized mortal misery and sin, the more firmly he believed in God. Therefore, as I have more than once said in this study, although he sounds the lowest depths of human gloom, mortal despair, and suffering, his books are a cry of triumph, a clarion peal, a hosanna to the idea of goodness and to the glory of God. There is a great gulf between Dostoievsky and such novelists as make of their art a clinical laboratory, in which the vices and the sores, and only the vices and and the sores, are dissected and observed, not under a microscope, but under a magnifying-glass, so that a totally distorted and exaggerated impression of life is the result. And this all the more remarkable, because a large part of his most important characters are abnormal: monomaniacs, murderers, or epileptics. But it is dealing with such characters that the secret of Dostoievsky's greatness is revealed. For in contradistinction to many writers who show us what is insane in the sanest men, who search for and find a spot of disease in the healthiest body, a blemish in the fairest flower, a flaw in the brightest ruby, Dostoievsky seeks and finds the sanity of the insane, a healthy spot in the sorest soul, a gleam of gold in the darkest mine, a pearl in the filthiest refuse heap, a spring in the most arid desert. In depicting humanity at its lowest depth of misery and the human soul at its highest pitch of anguish, he is making a great act of faith, and an act of charity, and conferring a huge benefit on mankind. For in depicting the extremest pain of abnormal sufferers, he persuades us of the good that exists even in such men, and of the goodness that is in suffering itself; and by taking us in the darkest of dungeons, he gives us a glimpse such as no one else has given us of infinite light and love.

On the other hand, Dostoievsky is equally far removed from such writers (of which we have plenty in England) who throw a cloak over all evil things, and put on blinkers, and who, because the existence of evil is distasteful to them, refuse to admit and face it. Such an attitude is the direct outcome of either conscious or unconscious hypocrisy. Dostoievsky has not a grain of hypocrisy in his nature, and therefore such an attitude is impossible to him.

Dostoievsky is a Realist, and he sees things as they are all through life, from the most important matters down to the most trivial. He is free from cant, either moral or political, and absolutely free from all prejudice of caste or class. It is impossible for him to think that because a man is a revolutionary he must therefore be a braver man than his fellows, or because a man is a Conservative he must therefore be a more cruel man than his fellows, just as it is impossible for him to think the contrary, and to believe that because a man is a Conservative he cannot help being honest or because a man is a Radical he must inevitably be a scoundrel. He judges men and things as they are, quite apart from the labels which they choose to give to their political opinions. That is why nobody who is by nature a doctrinaire[1] can appreciate or enjoy the works of

---

[1] By a doctrinaire I mean not a man who has strong principles and convictions; but a man who deliberately shuts his eyes to those facts which contradict his theory, and will pursue it to the end even when by so doing the practice resulting is the contrary of his aim.

Dostoievsky, since any one who bases his conduct upon theory cannot help at all costs being rudely shocked at every moment by Dostoievsky's creed, which is based on reality and on reality alone. Dostoievsky sees and embraces everything as it really is. The existence of evil, of ugliness and of suffering, inspires him with only one thing, and this is pity; and his pity is like that which King Lear felt on the Heath when he said:

> *'Poor naked wretches, wheresoe'er you are,*
> *That bide the pelting of this pitiless storm,*
> *How shall your houseless heads and unfed sides,*
> *Your loop'd and window'd raggedness, defend you*
> *From seasons such as these? O, I have ta'en*
> *Too little care of this! Take physic, pomp;*
> *Expose theyself to feel what wretches feel,*
> *That thou may'st shake the superflux to them,*
> *And show the heavens more just.'*

Dostoievsky has a right to say such things, because throughout his life he not only exposed himself, but was exposed, to feel what wretches feel; because he might have said as King Lear said to Cordelia:

> *'I am bound*
> *Upon a wheel of fire that mine own tears*
> *Do scald like molten lead.'*

He knew what wretches feel, by experience and not by theory, and all his life he was bound upon a 'wheel of fire'.

With regard to Dostoievsky's political opinions, he synthesized and expressed them all in the speech which he made in June 1880, at Moscow, in memory of Pushkin. 'There was never,' he said, 'a poet who possessed such universal receptivity as Pushkin. It was not only that he was receptive, but this receptivity was so extraordinarily deep, that he was able to embrace and absorb in his soul the spirit of foreign nations. No other poet has ever possessed such a gift; only Pushkin; and Pushkin is in this sense a unique and a prophetic apparition, since it is owing to this gift, and by means of it, that the strength of Pushkin – that in him which is national and Russian

—found expression. . . . For what is the strength of the Russian national spirit other than an aspiration towards a universal spirit, which shall embrace the whole world and the whole of mankind? And because Pushkin expressed the national strength he anticipated and foretold its future meaning. Because of this he was a prophet. For what did Peter the Great's reforms mean to us? I am not only speaking of what they were to bring about in the future, but of what they were when they were carried out. These reforms were not merely a matter of adopting European dress, habits, instruction and science. . . . But the men who adopted them aspired towards the union and the fraternity of the world. We in no hostile fashion, as would seem to have been the case, but in all friendliness and love, received into our spirit the genius of foreign nations, of all foreign nations, without any distinction of race, and we were able by instinct and at the first glance to distinguish, to eliminate contradictions, to reconcile differences; and by this we expressed our readiness and our inclination, we who had only just been united together and had found expression, to bring about a universal union of all the great Aryan race. The significance of the Russian race is without doubt European and universal. To be a real Russian and to be wholly Russian means only this: to be a brother of all men, to be universally human. All this is called Slavophilism; and what we call "Westernism" is only a great, although an historical and inevitable misunderstanding. To the true Russian, Europe and the affairs of the great Aryan race, are as dear as the affairs of Russia herself and of his native country, because our affairs are the affairs of the whole world, and they are not to be obtained by the sword, but by the strength of fraternity and by our brotherly effort towards the universal union of mankind. . . . And in the long-run I am convinced that we, that is to say, not we, but the future generations of the Russian people, shall every one of us, from the first to the last, understand that to be a real Russian must signify simply this: to strive towards bringing about a solution and an end to European conflicts; to show to Europe a way of escape from its anguish in the Russian soul, which is universal and all-embracing; to instil into her a brotherly love for all men's brothers, and in the end perhaps to utter the great and final word of universal harmony, the fraternal and lasting concord of all peoples according to the gospel of Christ.'

So much for the characteristics of Dostoievsky's moral and political ideals. There remains a third aspect of the man to be dealt with: his significance as a writer, as an artist, and as a maker of books; his place in Russian literature, and in the literature of the world. This is, I think, not very difficult to define. Dostoievsky, in spite of the universality of his nature, in spite of his large sympathy and his gift of understanding and assimilation, was debarred, owing to the violence and the want of balance of his temperament, which was largely the result of disease, from seeing life steadily and seeing it whole. The greatest fault of his genius, his character, and his work, is a want of proportion. His work is often shapeless, and the incidents in his books are sometimes fantastic and extravagant to the verge of insanity. Nevertheless his vision, and his power of expressing that vision, make up for what they lose in serenity and breadth, by their intensity, their depth and their penetration. He could not look upon the whole world with the calm of Sophocles and of Shakespeare; he could not paint a large and luminous panorama of life unmarred by any trace of exaggeration, as Tolstoy did. On the other hand, he realized and perceived certain heights and depths of the human soul which were beyond the range of Tolstoy, and almost beyond that of Shakespeare. His position with regard to Tolstoy, Fielding, and other great novelists is like that of Marlowe with regard to Shakespeare. Marlowe's plays compared with those of Shakespeare are like a series of tumultuous fugues, on the same theme, played on an organ which possesses but a few tremendous stops, compared with the interpretation of music, infinitely various in mood, by stringed instruments played in perfect concord, and rendering the finest and most subtle gradations and shades of musical phrase and intention. But every now and then the organ fugue, with its thunderous bass notes and soaring treble, attains to a pitch of intensity which no delicacy of blended strings can rival: So, every now and then, Marlowe, in the scenes, for instance, when Helena appears to Faustus, when Zenocrate speaks her passion, when Faustus counts the minutes to midnight, awaiting in an agony of terror the coming of Mephistopheles, or when Edward II is face to face with his executioners, reaches a pitch of soaring rapture, of tragic intensity which is not to be found even in Shakespeare. So it is with Dostoievsky. His genius soars higher and dives deeper than that of any other novelist, Russian or European. And what it thus gains in intensity it loses in serenity, balance and steadiness. Therefore, though Dostoievsky as a man possesses qualities of universality, he is not a universal artist such as Shakespeare, or even as Tolstoy, although he has one eminently Shakespearian gift, and that is the faculty for discerning the 'soul of goodness in things evil'. Yet, as a writer, he reached and expressed the ultimate extreme of the soul's rapture, anguish and despair, and spoke the most precious words of pity which have been heard in the world since the Gospels were written. In this man were mingled the love of St John, and the passion and the fury of a fiend; but the goodness in him was triumphant over the evil. He was a martyr; but bound though he was on a fiery wheel, he maintained that life was good, and he never ceased to cry 'Hosanna to the Lord: for He is just!' For this reason Dostoievsky is something more than a Russian writer: he is a brother to all mankind, especially to those who are desolate, afflicted and oppressed. He had 'great allies':

> '*His friends were exaltations, agonies,*
> *And love, and man's unconquerable mind.*'

CHAPTER VII

The Plays of Anton Tchekov

ANTON TCHEKOV IS chiefly known in Russia as a writer of short stories.[1] He is a kind of Russian Guy de Maupassant, without the bitter strength of the French writer, and without the quality which the French call 'cynisme', which does not mean cynicism, but ribaldry.

Tchekov's stories deal for the greater part with the middle classes, the minor landed gentry, the minor officials, and the professional classes. Tolstoy is reported to have said that Tchekov was a photographer, a very talented photographer, it is true, but still only a photographer. But Tchekov has one quality which is difficult to find among photographers, and that is humour. His stories are frequently deliciously droll. They are also often full of pathos, and they invariably possess the peculiarly Russian quality of simplicity and unaffectedness. He never underlines his effects, he never nudges the reader's elbow. Yet there is a certain amount of truth in Tolstoy's criticism. Tchekov does not paint with the great sweeping brush of a Velasquez, his stories have not the great broad colouring of Maupassant, they are like mezzotints; and in some ways they resemble the new triumphs of the latest developments of artistic photography in subtle effects of light and shade, in delicate tones and half-tones, in elusive play of atmosphere.

Apart from its artistic merits or defects, Tchekov's work is historically important and interesting. Tchekov represents the extreme period of stagnation in Russian life and literature. This epoch succeeded to a period of comparative activity following after the Russo-Turkish war. For in Russian history one will find that every war has been followed by a movement, a

---

[1] Two volumes of selections from his stories have been admirably translated by Mr Long.

renascence in ideas, in political aspirations, and in literature. Tchekov's work represents the reaction of flatness subsequent to a transitory ebullition of activity; it deals with the very class of men which naturally hankers for political activity, but which in Tchekov's time was as naturally debarred from it.

The result was that the aspirations of these people beat their grey wings ineffectually in a vacuum. The middle class being highly educated, and, if anything, over-educated, aspiring towards political freedom, and finding its aspirations to be futile, did one of two things. It either moped, or it made the best of it. The moping sometimes expressed itself in political assassination; making the best of it meant, as a general rule, dismissing the matter from the mind, and playing vindt. Half the middle class in Russia, a man once said to me, has run to seed in playing vindt. But what else was there to do?

Tchekov, more than any other writer, has depicted for us the attitude of mind, the nature and the feelings of the whole of this generation, just as Tourgeniev depicted the preceding generation; the aspirations and the life of the men who lived in the sixties, during the tumultuous epoch which culminated in the liberation of the serfs. And nowhere can the quality of this frame of mind, and the perfume, as it were, of this period be better felt and apprehended than in the plays of Anton Tchekov; for in his plays we get not only what is most original in his work as an artist, but the quintessence of the atmosphere, the attitude of mind, and the shadow of what the *Zeitgeist* brought to the men of his generation.

Before analysing the dramatic work of Tchekov, it is necessary to say a few words about the Russian stage in general. The main fact about the Russian stage that differentiates it from ours, and from that of any other European country, is the absence of the modern French tradition. The tradition of the 'well-made' French play, invented by Scribe, does not, and never has existed in Russia.

Secondly, reformers and demolishers of this tradition do not exist either, for they have nothing to reform or demolish. In Russia it was never necessary for naturalistic schools to rise with a great flourish of trumpets, and to proclaim that they were about to destroy the conventions and artificiality of the stage, and to give to the public, instead of childish senti- mentalities and impossible Chinese puzzles of intrigue, slices of real life. Had anybody behaved thus in Russia he would simply have been beating his hands against a door which was wide open. For the Russian drama, like the Russian novel, has, without making any fuss about it, never done but one thing—to depict life as clearly as it saw it, and as simply as it could.

That is why there has never been a naturalist school in Russia. The Russians are born realists; they do not have to label themselves realists, because realism is the very air which they breathe, and the very blood in their veins. What was labelled realism and naturalism in other countries simply appeared to them to be a straining after effect. Even Ibsen, whose great glory was that, having learnt all the tricks of the stagecraft of Scribe and his followers, he demolished the whole system, and made Comedies and Tragedies just as skilfully out of the tremendous issues of real life—even Ibsen had no great influence in Russia, because what interests Russian dramatists is not so much the crashing catastrophes of life as life itself, ordinary everyday life, just as we all see it. 'I go to the theatre,' a Russian once said, 'to see what I see every day.' And here we have the fundamental difference between the drama of Russia and that of any other country.

Dramatists of other countries, be they English, or French, or German, or Norwegian, whether they belong to the school of Ibsen, or to that which found its temple in the Théâtre Antoine at Paris, had one thing in common; they were either reacting or fighting against something—as in the case of the Norwegian dramatists—or bent on proving a thesis—as in the case of Alexandre Dumas *fils*, the Théâtre Antoine school, or Mr Shaw—; that is to say, they were all actuated by some definite purpose; the stage was to them a kind of pulpit.

On the English stage this was especially noticeable, and what the English public has specially delighted in during the last fifteen years has been a sermon on the stage, with a dash of impropriety in it. Now the Russian stage has never gone in for sermons or theses: like the Russian novel, it has been a looking-glass for the use of the public, and not a pulpit for the use of the playwright. This fact is never more strikingly illustrated than when the translation of a foreign play is performed in Russia. For instance, when Mr Bernard Shaw's play, *Mrs Warren's Profession*, was performed last December at the Imperial State-paid Theatre at St Petersburg, the attitude of the public and of the critics was interesting in the extreme. In the first place, that the play should be produced at the Imperial State-paid Theatre is an interesting illustration of the difference of the attitude of the two countries towards the stage. In England, public per-formance of this play is forbidden; in America it was hounded off the stage by an outraged and indignant populace; in St Petersburg it is produced at what, in Russia, is considered the temple of respectability, the home of tradition, the citadel of conservatism. In the audience were a quantity of young, un-married girls. The play was beautifully acted, and well re-ceived[1] but it never occurred to anyone that it was either daring or dangerous or startling; it was merely judged as a story of English life, a picture of English manners. Some people thought it was interesting, others that it was un-interesting, but almost all were agreed in considering it to be too stagey for the Russian taste; and as for considering it an epoch-making work, that is to say, in the region of thought and ideas, the very idea was scoffed at.

These opinions were reflected in the Press. In one of the newspapers, the leading Liberal organ, edited by Professor Milioukov, the theatrical critic said that Mr Bernard Shaw was the typical middle-class Englishman, and satirized the faults and follies of his class, but that he himself belonged to the class that he satirized, and shared its limitations. 'The play,' they said, 'is a typical middle-class English play, and it suffers from the faults inherent to this class of English work: false senti-ment and melodrama.'

Another newspaper, the *Russ*, wrote as follows: 'Bernard Shaw is thought to be an *enfant terrible* in England. In Russia we take him as a writer, and as a writer only, who is not absolutely

[1] It proved a success.

devoid of advanced ideas. In our opinion, his play belongs neither to the extreme right nor to the extreme left of dramatic literature; it is an expression of the ideas of moderation which belong to the centre, and the proof of this is the production of it at our State-paid Theatre, which in our eyes is the home and shelter of what is retrograde and respectable.'[1]

Such was the opinion of the newspaper critic on Mr Bernard Shaw's play. It represented more or less the opinion of the man in the street. For nearly all European dramatic art, with the exception of certain German and Norwegian work, strikes the Russian public as stagey and artificial. If a Russian had written *Mrs Warren's Profession*, he would never have introduced the scene between Crofts and Vivy which occurs at the end of Act III., because such a scene, to a Russian, savours of melodrama. On the other hand, he would have had no hesitation in putting on the stage (at the Imperial State-paid Theatre) the interior, with all its details, of one of the continental hotels from which Mrs Warren derived her income. But, as I have already said, what interests the Russian dramatist most keenly is not the huge catastrophes that stand out in lurid pre-eminence, but the incidents, sometimes important, sometimes trivial, and sometimes ludicrous, which happen to every human being every day of his life. And nowhere is this so clearly visible as in the work of Tchekov; for although the plays of Tchekov—which have not yet been discovered in England, and which will soon be old-fashioned in Russia—are not a reflection of the actual state of mind of the Russian people, yet as far as their artistic aim is concerned, they are more intensely typical, and more successful in the achievement of their aim than the work of any other Russian dramatist.[2]

Tchekov has written in all eleven plays, out of which six are farces in one act, and five are serious dramas. The farces,

[1] The dramatic critics of these newspapers are not the Mr William Archers, the Mr Walkleys, not the Faguets or the Lemaîtres of Russia, if any such exist. I have never come across anything of interest in their articles; on the other hand, they are perhaps more representative of public opinion.

[2] Since this was written Mr Shaw's genius has had greater justice done to it in Russia. His *Cæsar and Cleopatra* has proved highly successful. It was produced at the State Theatre of Moscow in the autumn of 1909 and is still running as I write. Several intelligent articles were written on it in the Moscow press.

though sometimes very funny, are not important; it is in his serious dramatic work that Tchekov really found himself, and gave to the world something new and entirely original. The originality of Tchekov's plays is not that they are realistic. Other dramatists — many Frenchmen, for instance — have written interesting and dramatic plays dealing with poignant situations, happening to real people in real life. Tchekov's discovery is this, that real life, as we see it every day, can be made just as interesting on the stage as the catastrophes or the difficulties which are more or less exceptional, but which are chosen by dramatists as their material because they are dramatic. Tchekov discovered that it is not necessary for real life to be dramatic in order to be interesting. Or rather that ordinary everyday life is as dramatic on the stage, if by dramatic one means interesting, as extraordinary life. He perceived that things which happen to us every day, which interest us, and affect us keenly, but which we would never dream of thinking or of calling dramatic when they occur, may be made as interesting on the stage as the most far-fetched situations, or the most terrific crises. For instance, it may affect us keenly to leave for ever a house where we have lived for many years. It may touch us to the quick to see certain friends off at the railway station. But we do not call these things dramatic. They are not dramatic, but they are human.

Tchekov has realized this, and has put them on the stage. He has managed to send over the footlights certain feelings, moods, and sensations, which we experience constantly, and out of which our life is built. He has managed to make the departure of certain people from a certain place, and the staying on of certain others in the same place, as interesting behind the footlights as the tragic histories of Œdipus or Othello, and a great deal more interesting than the complicated struggles and problems in which the characters of a certain school of modern dramatists are enmeshed. Life as a whole never presents itself to us as a definite mathematical problem, which needs immediate solution, but is rather composed of a thousand nothings, which together make something vitally important. Tchekov has understood this, and given us glimp-

ses of these nothings, and made whole plays out of these
nothings.

At first sight one is tempted to say that there is no action in
the plays of Tchekov. But on closer study one realizes that the
action is there, but it is not the kind usually sought after and
employed by men who write for the stage. Tchekov is, of
course, not the first dramatic writer who has realized that the
action which consisted in violent things happening to violent
people is not a whit more interesting, perhaps a great deal less
interesting, than the changes and the vicissitudes which happen
spiritually in the soul of man. Molière knew this, for *Le
Misanthrope* is a play in which nothing in the ordinary sense
happens. Rostand's *L'Aiglon* is a play where nothing in the
ordinary sense happens.[1] But in these plays in the extraordinary sense everything happens. A violent drama occurs in
the soul of the Misanthrope, and likewise in that of the Duke
of Reichstadt. So it is in Tchekov's plays. He shows us the
changes, the revolutions, the vicissitudes, the tragedies, the
comedies, the struggles, the conflicts, the catastrophes, that
happen in the souls of men, but he goes a step further than
other dramatists in the way in which he shows us these things.
He shows us these things as we ourselves perceive or guess
them in real life, without the help of poetic soliloquies or mono-
logues, without the help of a Greek chorus or a worldly
raisonneur, and without the aid of startling events which strip
people of their masks. He shows us bits of the everyday life of
human beings as we see it, and his pictures of ordinary human
beings, rooted in certain circumstances, and engaged in certain
avocations, reveal to us further glimpses of the life that is going
on inside these people. The older dramatists, even when they
deal exclusively with the inner life of man, without the aid of
any outside action, allow their creations to take off their masks
and lay bare their very inmost souls to us.

Tchekov's characters never, of their own accord, take off
their masks for the benefit of the audience, but they retain them
in exactly the same degree as people retain them in real life;

[1] Not to mention many modern French comedies, such as those of Lemaître,
Capus, etc.

that is to say, we sometimes guess by a word, a phrase, a gesture, the humming of a tune, or the smelling of a flower, what is going on behind the mask; at other times we see the mask momentarily torn off by an outbreak of inward passion, but never by any pressure of an outside and artificial machinery, never owing to the necessity of a situation, the demands of a plot, or the exigencies of a problem; in fact, never by any forces which are not those of life itself. In Tchekov's plays, as in real life, to use Meredith's phrase, 'Passions spin the plot'; he shows us the delicate webs that reach from soul to soul across the trivial incidents of every day.

I will now analyse in detail two of the plays of Tchekov. The first is a drama called *Chaika*. 'Chaika' means 'Sea-gull'. It was the first serious play of Tchekov that was performed: and it is interesting to note that when it was first produced at the Imperial Theatre at St Petersburg it met with no success, the reason being, no doubt, that the actors did not quite enter into the spirit of the play. As soon as it was played at Moscow it was triumphantly successful.

The first act takes place in the park in the estate belonging to Peter Nikolaievitch Sorin, the brother of a celebrated actress, Irina Nikolaievna, whose stage name is Arkadina. Preparations have been made in the park for some private theatricals. A small stage has been erected. The play about to be represented has been written by Constantine, the actress's son, who is a young man, twenty-five years old. The chief part is to be played by a young girl, Ina, the daughter of a neighbouring land-owner. These two young people are in love with each other. Irina is a successful actress of the more or less conventional type. She has talent and brains. 'She sobs over a book,' one of the characters says of her, 'and knows all Russian poetry by heart; she looks after the sick like an angel, but you must not mention Eleanora Duse in her presence, you must praise her only, and write about her and her wonderful acting in *La Dame aux Camélias*. In the country she is bored, and we all become her enemies, we are all guilty. She is superstitious and avaricious.' Constantine, her son, is full of ideals with regard to the reform of the stage; he finds the old forms conventional and tedious, he is longing to pour new wine into the old skins, or rather to invent new skins.

There is also staying in the house a well-known writer, about forty years old, named Trigorin. 'He is talented and writes well,' one of the other characters says of him, 'but after reading Tolstoy you cannot read him at all.' The remaining characters are a middle-aged doctor, named Dorn; the agent of the estate, a retired officer, his wife and daughter, and a schoolmaster. The characters all assemble to witness Constantine's play; they sit down in front of the small extemporized stage, which has a curtain but no back cloth, since this is provided by nature in the shape of a distant lake enclosed by trees. The sun has set, and it is twilight. Constantine begs his guests to lend their attention. The curtain is raised, revealing a view of the lake with the moon shining above the horizon, and reflected in the water. Ina is discovered seated on a large rock dressed all in white. She begins to speak a kind of prose poem, an address of the Spirit of the Universe to the dead world on which there is supposed to be no longer any living creature.

Arkadina (the actress) presently interrupts the monologue by saying softly to her neighbour, 'This is decadent stuff.' The author, in a tone of imploring reproach, says, 'Mamma!' The monologue continues, the Spirit of the World speaks of his obstinate struggle with the devil, the origin of material force. There is a pause. Far off on the lake two red dots appear. 'Here,' says the Spirit of the World, 'is my mighty adversary, the devil. I see his terrible glowing eyes.' Arkadina once more interrupts, and the following dialogue ensues:

Arkadina: It smells of sulphur; is that necessary?
Constantine: Yes.
Arkadina (laughing): Yes, that is an effect.
Constantine: Mamma!
Ina (continuing to recite): He is lonely without man.
Paulin (the wife of the agent): (*To the doctor*): You have taken off your hat. Put it on again, you will catch cold.
Arkadina: The doctor has taken off his hat to the devil, the father of the material universe.

Constantine (*losing his temper*): The play's over. Enough!
Curtain!

Arkadina: Why are you angry?

Constantine: Enough! Pull down the curtain! (*The curtain
is let down.*) I am sorry I forgot, it is only certain chosen
people that may write plays and act. I infringed the mono-
poly, I . . . (*He tries to say something, but waves his arms and goes
out.*)

Arkadina: What is the matter with you?

Sorin (*her brother*): My dear, you should be more gentle
with the *amour propre* of the young.

Arkadina: What did I say to him?

Sorin: You offended him.

Arkadina: He said himself it was a joke, and I took his
play as a joke.

Sorin: All the same . . .

Arkadina: Now it appears he has written a masterpiece!
A masterpiece, if you please! So he arranged this play, and
made a smell of sulphur, not as a joke, but as a manifesto! He
wished to teach us how to write and how to act. One gets
tired of this in the long-run – these insinuations against me,
these everlasting pin-pricks, they are enough to tire any one.
He is a capricious and conceited boy!

Sorin: He wished to give you pleasure.

Arkadina: Really? Then why did he not choose some
ordinary play, and why did he force us to listen to this
decadent rubbish? If it is a joke I do not mind listening to
rubbish, but he has the pretension to invent new forms, and
tries to inaugurate a new era in art; and I do not think the
form is new, it is simply bad.

Presently Ina appears; they compliment her on her performance. Arkadina tells her she ought to go on to the stage, to
which she answers that that is her dream. She is introduced to
Trigorin the author: this makes her shy. She has read his works,
she is overcome at seeing the celebrity face to face. 'Wasn't it
an odd play?' she asks Trigorin. 'I did not understand it,' he
answers, 'but I looked on with pleasure—your acting was so

sincere, and the scenery was beautiful.' Ina says she must go home, and they all go into the house except the doctor. Constantine appears again, and the doctor tells him that he liked the play, and congratulates him. The young man is deeply touched. He is in a state of great nervous excitement. As soon as he learns that Ina has gone he says he must go after her at once. The doctor is left alone. Masha, the daughter of the agent, enters and makes him a confession: 'I don't love my father,' she says, 'but I have confidence in you. Help me.' 'What is the matter?' he asks. 'I am suffering,' she answers, 'and nobody knows my suffering. I love Constantine.' 'How nervous these people are,' says the doctor, 'nerves, all nerves! and what a quantity of love. Oh, enchanted lake! But what can I do for you, my child, what, what?' and the curtain comes down.

The second act is in the garden of the same estate. It is a hot noon. Arkadina has decided to travel to Moscow. The agent comes and tells her that all the workmen are busy harvesting, and that there are no horses to take her to the station. She tells him to hire horses in the village, or else she will walk. 'In that case,' the agent replies, 'I give notice, and you can get a new agent.' She goes out in a passion. Presently Constantine appears bearing a dead sea-gull; he lays it at Ina's feet.

Ina: What does this mean?

Constantine: I shot this sea-gull today to my shame. I throw it at your feet.

Ina: What is the matter with you?

Constantine: I shall soon shoot myself in the same way.

Ina: I do not recognize you.

Constantine: Yes, some time after I have ceased to recognize you. You have changed towards me, your look is cold, my presence makes you uncomfortable.

Ina: During these last days you have become irritable, and speak in an unintelligible way, in symbols. I suppose this sea-gull is a symbol. Forgive me, I am too simple to understand you.

Constantine: It all began on that evening when my play was such a failure. Women cannot forgive failure. I burnt it all to the last page. Oh, if you only knew how unhappy I am! Your coldness is terrifying, incredible! It is just as if I awoke, and suddenly saw that this lake was dry, or had disappeared under the earth. You have just said you were too simple to understand me. Oh, what is there to understand? My play was a failure, you despise my work, you already consider that I am a thing of no account, like so many others! How well I understand that, how well I understand! It is as if there were a nail in my brain; may it be cursed, together with the *amour propre* which is sucking my blood, sucking it like a snake! (*He sees Trigorin, who enters reading a book.*) Here comes the real genius. He walks towards us like a Hamlet, and with a book too. 'Words, words, words.' This sun is not yet come to you and you are already smiling, your looks have melted in its rays. I will not be in your way. (*He goes out rapidly.*)

There follows a conversation between Trigorin and Ina, during which she says she would like to know what it feels like to be a famous author. She talks of his interesting life.

Trigorin: What is there so very wonderful about it? Like a monomaniac who, for instance, is always thinking day and night of the moon, I am pursued by one thought which I cannot get rid of, I must write, I must write, I must . . . I have scarcely finished a story, when for some reason or another I must write a second, and then a third, and then a fourth. I write uninterruptedly, I cannot do otherwise. What is there so wonderful and splendid in this, I ask you? Oh, it is a cruel life! Look, I get excited with you, and all the time I am remembering that an unfinished story is waiting for me. I see a cloud which is like a pianoforte, and I at once think that I must remember to say somewhere in the story that there is a cloud like a pianoforte.

Ina: But does not your inspiration and the process of creation give you great and happy moments?

Trigorin: Yes, when I write it is pleasant, and it is nice to correct proofs; but as soon as the thing is published, I cannot bear it, and I already see that it is not at all what I meant, that it is a mistake, that I should not have written it at all, and I am vexed and horribly depressed. The public reads it, and says: 'Yes, pretty, full of talent, very nice, but how different from Tolstoy!' or, 'Yes, a fine thing, but how far behind *Fathers and Sons*; Tourgeniev is better.' And so, until I die, it will always be 'pretty and full of talent', never anything more; and when I die my friends as they pass my grave will say: 'Here lies Trigorin, he was a good writer, but he did not write as well as Tourgeniev.'

Ina tells him that whatever he may appear to himself, to others he appears great and wonderful. For the joy of being a writer or an artist, she says, she would bear the hate of her friends, want, disappointment; she would live in an attic and eat dry crusts. 'I would suffer from my own imperfections, but in return I should demand fame, real noisy fame.' Here the voice of Arkadina is heard calling Trigorin. He observes the sea-gull; she tells him that Constantine killed it. Trigorin makes a note in his notebook. 'What are you writing?' she says. 'An idea has occurred to me,' he answers, 'an idea for a short story: On the banks of a lake a young girl lives from her infancy onwards. She loves the lake like a sea-gull, she is happy and free like a sea-gull; but unexpectedly a man comes and sees her, and out of mere idleness kills her, just like this sea-gull.' Here Arkadina again calls out that they are not going to Moscow after all. This is the end of the second act.

At the third act, Arkadina is about to leave the country for Moscow. Things have come to a crisis. Ina has fallen in love with the author, and Constantine's jealousy and grief have reached such a point that he has tried to kill himself and failed, and now he has challenged Trigorin to a duel. The latter has taken no notice of this, and is about to leave for Moscow with Arkadina. Ina begs him before he goes to say good-bye to her. Arkadina discusses with her brother her son's strange and violent behaviour. He points out that the youth's position is intolerable. He is a clever boy, full of talent, and he is obliged to live in the country without any money, without a situation. He is ashamed of this, and afraid of his idleness. In any case, he tells his sister, she ought to give him some money, he has not even got an overcoat; to which she answers that she has not got any money. She is an artist, and needs every penny for her own expenses. Her brother scoffs at this, and she gets annoyed. A scene follows between the mother and the son, which begins by an exchange of loving and tender words, and which finishes in a violent quarrel. The mother is putting a new bandage on his head, on the place where he had shot himself. 'During the last few days,' says Constantine, 'I have loved you as tenderly as when I was a child; but why do you submit to the influence of that man?'—meaning Trigorin. And out of this the quarrel arises. Constantine says, 'You wish me to consider him a genius. His works make me sick.' To which his mother answers, 'That is jealousy. People who have no talent and who are pretentious, have nothing better to do than to abuse those who have real talent.' Here Constantine flies into a passion, tears the bandage off his head, and cries out, 'You people only admit and recognize what you do yourselves. You trample and stifle everything else!' Then his rage dies out, he cries and asks forgiveness, and says, 'If you only knew, I have lost everything. She no longer loves me; I can no longer write; all my hopes are dead!' They are once more reconciled. Only Constantine begs that he may be allowed to keep out of Trigorin's sight. Trigorin comes to Arkadina, and proposes that they should remain in the country. Arkadina says that she knows why he wishes to remain; he is in love with Ina. He admits this, and asks to be set free.

Up to this point in the play there had not been a syllable to tell us what were the relations between Arkadina and Trigorin, and yet the spectator who sees this play guesses from the first that he is her lover. She refuses to let him go, and by a somewhat histrionic declaration of love cleverly mixed with flattery and common sense she easily brings him round, and he is like wax in her fingers. He settles to go. They leave for Moscow; but before they leave, Trigorin has a short interview with Ina, in which she tells him that she has decided to leave her home to go on the stage, and to follow him to Moscow. Trigorin gives her his address in Moscow. Outside—the whole of this act takes place in the dining-room—we hear the noise and bustle of people going away. Arkadina is already in the carriage. Trigorin and Ina say good-bye to each other, he gives her a long kiss.

Between the third and fourth acts two years elapse. We are once more in the home of Arkadina's brother. Constantine has become a celebrated writer. Ina has gone on the stage and proved a failure. She went to Moscow; Trigorin loved her for a while, and then ceased to love her. A child was born. He returned to his former love, and in his weakness, played a double game on both sides. She is now in the town, but her father will not receive her. Arkadina arrives with Trigorin. She has been summoned from town because her brother is ill. Everything is going on as it was two years ago. Arkadina, the agent, and the doctor sit down to a game of Lotto before dinner. Arkadina tells of her trimphs in the provincial theatres, of the ovations she received, of the dresses she wore. The doctor asks her if she is proud of her son being an author. ' Just fancy,' she replies ' I have not yet read his books, I have never had time!' They go in to supper. Constantine says he is not hungry, and is left alone. Somebody knocks at the glass door opening into the garden. Constantine opens it; it is Ina. Ina tells her story; and now she has got an engagement in some small provincial town, and is starting on the following day. Constantine declares vehemently that he loves her as much as ever. He cursed her, he hated her, he tore up her letters and photographs, but every moment he was forced to admit to himself that he was bound to her for ever. He could never cease to love her. He begs her either to remain, or to let him follow her. She takes up her hat, she must go. She says she is a wandering sea-gull, and that she is very tired. From the dining-room are heard the voices of Arkadina and Trigorin. She listens, rushes to the door, and looks through the keyhole. 'He is here, too,' she says, 'do not tell him anything. I love him, I love him more than ever.' She goes out through the garden. Constantine tears up all his MSS. and goes into the next room. Arkadina and the others come out of the dining-room, and sit down once more to the card-table to play Lotto. The agent brings to Trigorin the stuffed

sea-gull which Constantine had shot two years ago, and which
had been the starting-point of Trigorin's love episode with Ina.
He has forgotten all about it; he does not even remember that
the sea-gull episode ever took place. A noise like a pistol shot is
heard outside. 'What is that?' says Arkadina in fright. 'It is
nothing,' replies the doctor, 'one of my medicine bottles has
probably burst.' He goes into the next room, and returns half a
minute later. 'It was as I thought,' he says, 'my ether bottle has
burst.' 'It frightened me,' says Arkadina, 'it reminded me of
how . . .' The doctor turns over the leaves of the newspaper.
He then says to Trigorin, 'Two months ago there was an
article in this Review written from America. I wanted to ask
you . . .' He takes Trigorin aside, and then whispers to him,
'Take Irina Nikolaievna away as soon as possible. The fact of
the matter is that Constantine has shot himself.'

Of all the plays of Tchekov, *Chaika* is the one which most
resembles ordinary plays, or the plays of ordinary dramatists.
It has, no doubt, many of Tchekov's special characteristics,
but it does not show them developed to their full extent. Besides which, the subject is more dramatic than that of his other
plays: there is a conflict in it—the conflict between the son and
the mother, between the older and the younger generation,
the older generation represented by Trigorin and the actress,
the younger generation by Constantine. The character of the
actress is drawn with great subtlety. Her real love for her son is
made just as plain as her absolute inability to appreciate his
talent and his cleverness. She is a mixture of kindness, common
sense, avarice, and vanity. Equally subtle is the character of
the author, with his utter want of wit; his absorption in the
writing of short stories; his fundamental weakness; his egoism,
which prevents him recognizing the existence of any work
but his own, but which has no tinge of ill-nature or malice in
it. When he returns in the last act, he compliments Constantine on his success, and brings him a Review in which
there is a story by the young man. Constantine subsequently
notices that in the Review the only pages which are cut contain
a story by Trigorin himself.

If *Chaika* is the most dramatically effective of Tchekov's

plays, the most characteristic is perhaps *The Cherry Garden*. It is notably characteristic in the symbolical and historical sense, for it depicts for us the causes and significance of the decline of the well-born, landed gentry in Russia.

A slightly Bohemian lady belonging to this class, Ranievskaia—I will call her Madame Ranievskaia for the sake of convenience, since her Christian name 'Love' has no equivalent, as a name, in English—is returning to her country estate with her brother Leonidas after an absence of five years. She has spent this time abroad in Nice and Paris. Her affairs and those of her brother are in a hopeless state. They are heavily in debt. This country place has been the home of her childhood, and it possesses a magnificent cherry orchard. It is in the south of Russia.

In the first act we see her return to the home of her childhood—she and her brother, her daughter, seventeen years old, and her adopted daughter. It is the month of May. The cherry orchard is in full blossom; we see it through the windows of the old nursery, which is the scene of the first act. The train arrives at dawn, before sunrise. A neighbour is there to meet them, a rich merchant called Lopachin. They arrive with their governess and their servant, and they have been met at the station by another neighbouring landowner. And here we see a thing I have never seen on the stage before: a rendering of the exact atmosphere that hangs about such an event as (*a*) the arrival of people from a journey, and (*b*) the return of a family to its home from which it has long been absent. We see at a glance that Madame Ranievskaia and her brother are in all practical matters like children. They are hopelessly casual and vague. They take everything lightly and carelessly, like birds; they are convinced that something will turn up to extricate them from their difficulties.

The merchant, who is a nice, plain, careful, practical, but rather vulgar kind of person, is a millionaire, and, what is more, he is the son of a peasant; he was born in the village, and his father was a serf. He puts the practical situation very clearly before them. The estate is hopelessly overloaded with debt, and unless these debts are paid within six months, the estate will be sold by auction. But there is, he points out, a solution to the matter. 'As you already know,' he says to them, 'your cherry orchard will be sold to pay your debts. The auction is fixed for the 22nd of August, but do not be alarmed, there is a way out of the difficulty. . . . This is my plan. Your estate is only fifteen miles from the town, the railway is quite close, and if your cherry orchard and the land by the river is cut up into villa holdings, and let for villas, you will get at the least 25,000 roubles (£2,500) a year.' To which the brother replies, 'What nonsense!' 'You will get,' the merchant repeats, 'at the very least twenty-five roubles a year a desiatin,'—a desiatin is about two acres and a half: much the same as the French hectare—'and by the autumn, if you make the announcement now, you will not have a single particle of land left. In a word, I congratulate you; you are saved. The site is splendid, only, of course, it wants several improvements. For instance, all these old buildings must be destroyed, and this house, which is no use at all, the old orchard must be cut down.'

Madame Ranievskaia: Cut down? My dear friend, forgive me, you do not understand anything at all! If in the whole district there is anything interesting not, to say remarkable, it is this orchard.

Lopachin: The orchard is remarkable simply on account of its size.

Leonidas: The orchard is mentioned in the Encyclopaedia.

Lopachin: If we do not think of a way out of the matter and come to some plan, on the 22nd of August the cherry orchard and the whole property will be sold by auction. Make up your minds; there is no other way out, I promise you.

But it is no good his saying anything. They merely reply, 'What nonsense!' They regard the matter of splitting up their old home into villas as a sheer impossibility. And this is the whole subject of the play. The merchant continues during the second act to insist on the only practical solution of their difficulties, and they likewise persist in saying this solution is madness, that it is absolutely impossible. They cannot bring themselves to think of their old home being turned into a collection of villas; they keep on saying that something will turn up, an old aunt will die and leave them a legacy, or something of that kind will happen.

In the third act, the day of the auction has arrived, there is a dance going on in the house. The impression is one of almost intolerable human sadness, because we know that nothing has turned up, we know that the whole estate will be sold. The whole picture is one of the ending of a world. At the dance there are only the people in the village, the stationmaster, the post-office officials, and so forth. The servant they have brought from abroad gives notice. An old servant, who belongs to the house, and is in the last stage of senile decay, wanders about murmuring of old times and past brilliance. The guests dance quadrilles through all the rooms. Leonidas has gone to the auction, and Madame Ranievskaia sits waiting in hopeless suspense for the news of the result. At last he comes back, pale and tired, and too depressed to speak. The merchant also comes triumphantly into the room; he is slightly intoxicated, and with a triumphant voice he announces that he has bought the cherry garden.

In the last act, we see them leave their house for ever, all the furniture has been packed up, all the things which for them are so full of little associations; the pictures are off the walls, the bare trees of the cherry garden—for it is now autumn—are already being cut down, and they are starting to begin a new life and to leave their old home for ever. The old house, so charming, so full of old-world dignity and simplicity, will be pulled down, and make place for neat, surburban little villas to be inhabited by the new class which has arisen in Russia. Formerly there were only gentlemen and peasants, now there is the self-made man, who, being infinitely more practical, pushes out the useless and unpractical gentleman to make way for himself. The pathos and naturalness of this last act are extraordinary. Every incident that we know so well in these moments of departure is noted and rendered. The old servant, who belongs to the house, is supposed to be in the hospital, and is not there to say good-bye to them; but when they are all gone, he appears and closes the shutters, saying, 'It is all closed, they are gone, they forgot me; it doesn't matter, I will sit here. Leonidas Andreevitch probably forgot his cloak, and only went in his light overcoat, I wasn't there to see.' And he lies motionless in the darkened, shuttered room, while from outside comes the sound of the felling of the cherry orchard.

Of course, it is quite impossible in a short analysis to give any idea of the real nature of this play, which is a tissue of small details, every one of which tells. Every character in it is living; Leonidas, the brother, who makes foolish speeches and is constantly regretting them afterwards; the plain and practical merchant; the good-natured neighbour who borrows money and ultimately pays it back; the governess; the clerk in the estate office; the servants, the young student who is in love with the daughter—we learn to know all these people as well as we know our own friends and relations, and they reveal themselves as people do in real life by means of a lifelike representation of the conversation of human beings. The play is historical and symbolical, because it shows us why the landed gentry in Russia has ceased to have any importance, and how these amiable, unpractical, casual people must necessarily go under, when they are faced with a strong energetic class of rich, self-made men who are the sons of peasants. Technically the play is extraordinarily interesting; there is no conflict of wills in it, nothing which one could properly call action or drama, and yet it never ceases to be interesting; and the reason of this is that the conversation, the casual remarks of the characters, which seem to be about nothing, and to be put there anyhow, have always a definite purpose. Every casual remark serves to build up the architectonic edifice which is the play. The structure is built, so to speak, in air; it is a thing of atmosphere, but it is built nevertheless with extreme care, and the result when interpreted, as it is interpreted at Moscow by the actors of the artistic theatre, is a stage triumph.

The three other most important plays of Tchekov are *Ivanoff*, *Three Sisters*, and *Uncle Vania*—the latter play has been well translated into German.

Three Sisters is the most melancholy of all Tchekov's plays.

It represents the intense monotony of provincial life, the grey life which is suddenly relieved by a passing flash, and then rendered doubly grey by the disappearance of that flash. The action takes place in a provincial town. A regiment of artillery is in garrison there. One of the three sisters, Masha, has married a schoolmaster; the two others, Irina and Olga, are living in the house of their brother, who is a budding professor. Their father is dead. Olga teaches in a provincial school all day, and gives private lessons in the evening. Irina is employed in the telegraph office. They have both only one dream and longing, and that is to get away from the provincial corner in which they live, and to settle in Moscow. They only stay on Masha's account. Masha's husband is a kind and well-meaning, but excessively tedious schoolmaster, who is continually reciting Latin tags. When Masha married him she was only eighteen, and thought he was the cleverest man in the world. She subsequently discovered that he was the kindest, but not the cleverest man in the world. The only thing which relieves the tedium of this provincial life is the garrison.

When the play begins, we hear that a new commander has been appointed to the battery, a man of forty called Vershinin. He is married, has two children, but his wife is half crazy. The remaining officers in the battery are Baron Tuzenbach, a lieutenant; Soleny, a major; and two other lieutenants. Tuzenbach is in love with Irina, and wishes to marry her; she is willing to marry him, but she is not in the least in love with him, and tells him so. Masha falls passionately in love with Vershinin. The major, Soleny, is jealous of Tuzenbach. Then suddenly while these things are going on, the battery is transferred from the town to the other end of Russia. On the morning it leaves the town, Soleny challenges the Baron to a duel, and kills him. The play ends with the three sisters being left alone. Vershinin says a passionate good-bye to Masha, who is in floods of tears, and does not disguise her grief from her husband. He, in the most pathetic way conceivable, tries to console her, while the cheerful music of the band is heard gradually getting fainter and fainter in the distance. Irina has been told of the death of the Baron, and the sad thing about this is that she does not really care. The three sisters are left to go on working, to continue their humdrum existence in the little provincial town, to teach the children in the school; the only thing which brought some relief to their monotonous existence, and to one of the sisters the passion of her life, is taken away from them, and the departure is made manifest to them by the strains of the cheerful military band.

I have never seen anything on the stage so poignantly melancholy as this last scene. In this play, as well as in others, Tchekov, by the way he presents you certain fragments of people's lives, manages to open a window on the whole of their life. In this play of *Three Sisters* we get four glimpses. A birthday party in the first act; an ordinary evening in the second act; in the third act a night of excitement owing to a fire in the town, and it is on this night that the love affair of Vershinin and Masha culminates in a crisis; and in the fourth act the departure of the regiment. Yet these four fragments give us an insight, and open a window on to the whole life of these people, and, in fact, on to the lives of many thousand people who have led this life in Russia.

Tchekov's plays are as interesting to read as the work of any first-rate novelist. But in reading them, it is impossible to guess how effective they are on the stage, the delicate succession of subtle shades and half-tones, of hints, of which they are composed, the evocation of certain moods and feelings which it is impossible to define—all this one would think would disappear in the glare of the footlights, but the result is exactly the reverse. Tchekov's plays are a thousand times more interesting to see on the stage than they are to read. A thousand effects which the reader does not suspect make themselves felt on the boards. The reason of this is that Tchekov's plays realize Goethe's definition of what plays should be. 'Everything in a play,' Goethe said, 'should be symbolical, and should lead to something else.' By symbolical, of course, he meant morally symbolical—he did not mean that the play should be full of enigmatic puzzles, but that every event in it should have a meaning and cast a shadow larger than itself.

The atmosphere of Tchekov's plays is laden with gloom, but

it is a darkness of the last hour before the dawn begins. His note is not in the least a note of despair: it is a note of invincible trust in the coming day. The burden of his work is this—life is difficult, there is nothing to be done but to work and to continue to work as cheerfully as one can; and his triumph as a playwright is that for the first time he has shown in prose—for the great poets have done little else—behind the footlights, what it is that makes life difficult. Life is too tremendous, too cheerful, and too sad a thing to be condensed into an abstract problem of lines and alphabetical symbols; and those who in writing for the stage attempt to do this, achieve a result which is both artificial and tedious. Tchekov disregarded all theories and all rules which people have hitherto laid down as the indispensable qualities of stage writing; he put on the stage the things which interested him because they were human and true; things great or infinitesimally small; as great as love and as small as a discussion as to what are the best *hors d'œuvres*; and they interest us for the same reason.

CHAPTER VIII

Russian Poetry: Introduction to the Oxford Book of Russian Verse

I

FOR ALL STUDENTS of literature—and especially for the foreign student—Russian literature and, of Russian literature, Russian poetry in particular, begins with the nineteenth century. The seeds of it were sown centuries earlier and are as obscure as the origins of Russian history and Russian civilization. These origins are still a matter of dispute among historians; and the most plausible theories advanced by certain brilliant writers of history are said by other equally brilliant critics to be highly conjectural. There are, it is true, certain facts and certain factors that stand out like landmarks and monuments of the past in writing as well as in stone.

The course of Russian literature, just as the course of Russian history, was interrupted by a series of startling events which again and again put back the clock of its normal progress.

The first centre of Russian culture was the city of Kiev on the Dnieper. Kiev was the mother of Russian letters; Moscow and St Petersburg were the heirs of Kiev. In the eleventh century Kiev was one of the most enlightened cities of Europe. Her rulers were at this time related to the Kings of France, England, Hungary, and Norway. The Russian manuscripts of the eleventh century are as good as the finest manuscripts of western European countries of the same period. Kiev was the centre of wealth, learning, and art. Byzantine artists went thither, and Kiev sent her own painters to the West. There was no barrier during this epoch between the East and the West. Nothing could have been more promising than such a beginning. It was followed by a series of disasters which retarded the growth of civilization and culture. First of all came the schism of the Eastern and Western Churches, which started in the ninth century and was never truly remediable after the excommunication of Cerularius in 1054, although attempts were made to heal it. It was caused by the rivalry between the Greeks and the Latins—a rivalry which ever since then has continued to exist between Rome and the East. The Slavs were the accidental victims of this racial quarrel. The schism erected a barrier between Russia and western Europe. Later, in the thirteenth century, another and a still more crushing and retarding blow was dealt to Russian civilization and Russian culture—The Tartar invasion, which was followed by the Tartar yoke. The Russians remained under the yoke of the Tartars from 1240 to 1480. Because of the Tartar yoke, from the fourteenth until the beginning of the nineteenth century Russian literature has nothing to give to the outside world. Kiev was destroyed by the Tartars in 1240. After this the south was abandoned; Poland was separated from the east; the eastern principalities were gradually drawn towards Moscow, and by the fourteenth century Moscow had taken the place of Kiev and had become the kernel of Russian culture. From the fourteenth until the beginning of the nineteenth century, Russian literature, instead of developing in a series of splendid and various phases of production, such as the Middle Ages in Italy, the Renaissance in France and England, the *Grand Siècle* in France, and the Georgian epoch in England, had nothing to present to western Europe. There were no literary Middle Ages in Russia, no Renaissance. Russia was debarred on one side from the living culture of the West and was cut off from the antique traditions of Rome and Greece on the other. There was, it is true, a popular poetry, but it was a flower which grew by the wayside and nobody took any notice of it until the nineteenth century.

In the twelfth century the beginnings of a new literature and of a national poetry are visible in the story of the 'Raid of Prince Igor', a prose epic which is not only one of the most remarkable memorials to the ancient written language of Russia but, by virtue of its originality, its historical subject-matter, and its picturesque vividness, colour, and detail, has a place in the literary history of Europe. After the Tartar invasion, the history of Russian literature is the story of the destruction of the barrier and the wall which had shut off Russia from western Europe. This destruction came about gradually. It began when a link was forged between Moscow and the Byzantine Emperors and Italian architects and other foreigners poured into Moscow. This was followed by the establishment of the first printing press in Moscow during the reign of Ivan the Terrible, and by a slight infection of Polish manners and Latin culture which followed the brief reign of that enigmatic and romantic figure, the 'False Dimitrius', who claimed to be a son of Ivan the Terrible. Kiev rose again from its ruins and became the centre of learning. Schools were founded in Moscow, and in 1665 Latin was taught by Simeon Polotsky, who wrote syllabic verse. In the latter half of the seventeenth century, another influence besides that of Kiev and Poland was felt: another breach was made in the wall. German officers, soldiers, capitalists, and artisans settled in the German suburb of Moscow and brought with them the technical crafts and the letters of western Europe. It was here that the Russian stage and the Russian ballet were born. Peter the Great made still wider breaches in the wall between Russia and western Europe, but the 'Peter the Great' of Russian literature and of the Russian language was Michael Lomonosov (1711–1765), who was mathematician, chemist, astronomer, political economist, historian, electrician, geologist, grammarian, as well as a poet. He scraped the crust of foreign barbarism from his native language, and by his example still more than by his precept he displayed the Russian language in its native purity, and left it as an instrument ready attuned for a great player. Thanks to Lomonosov and to Prince Kantemir (1708–1744), who wrote the first Russian literary verse, the literary wall between Russia and French and German culture was finally broken down. Prince Kantemir wrote in the French manner. His style was modelled on that of Boileau. During Catherine the Second's reign, French influence was felt in Russia. Poets began to spring up, especially writers of odes, and the best of these was Derzhavin (1743–1816), a master of the French classical manner, in whose work the elements of real poetical beauty entitle him to be called the first Russian poet. It is with an example of his verse that this book begins. But it was not until the nineteenth century and the advent of Krylov that a poet of national importance was born.

II

Peter the Great, in a speech he made at a banquet after the Peace of Nystadt, said that historians placed the seat of all sciences in Greece, whence, being expelled by fate, they migrated to Italy and later to the rest of Europe, but owing to the perverseness of the ancient Russians they went no farther than Poland in their trend eastwards. He compared the transmigration of science to the circulation of the blood in the human body, and he prophesied that art and science and culture would travel one day from England, France, and Germany to Russia, and finally perhaps to Greece, their earliest home. The prophecy has in some ways been fulfilled, but the interesting point about Russian poetry and Russian music is this: thanks either to chance or to the logical march of history, the characteristics of both these arts are Greek, in spite of any other influences either from the west, the east, or the north.

In the songs of the Russian peasants the Greek modes are or (until the European war) were still in use: the Doric, the hypo-Dorian, the Lydian, the hypo-Phrygian. 'La musique, telle qu'elle était pratiquée en Russie au Moyen Age', writes M. Soubier in his *History of Russian Music*, 'tenait à la tradition des religions et des mœurs païennes.' In the secular as well as in the ecclesiastical music of Russia there is an element of influence which is purely Hellenic.

When national poetry blossomed in Russia at the beginning of the nineteenth century, it revealed certain qualities and characteristics of its own which are different from what we find in the verse of other European nations, but in some respects singularly like the qualities which are peculiar to the verse of ancient Greece. In writing on the nature of Greek beauty Professor Gilbert Murray, in *The Legacy of Greece*, says: 'It is not a beauty of ornament; it is a beauty of structure, a beauty of rightness and simplicity. . . . Greek poetry is statuesque in the sense that it depends greatly on its organic structure; it is not in the least so in the sense of being cold or colourless or stiff. But Greek poetry on the whole has a bareness and severity which disappoints a modern reader, accustomed as he is to lavish ornament and exaggeration at every turn. It has the same simplicity and straightforwardness as Greek sculpture. The poet has something to say and he says it as well and truly as he can in the suitable style, and if you are not interested, you are not.'

And in the same volume Mr R. W. Livingstone says: 'If a reader new to the classics opened Thucydides, his first impression would probably be one of jejuneness, of baldness. If, fresh from Shelley or Tennyson, he came across the epigram of Simonides on the Spartan dead at Thermopylae,

$$\vec{\omega} \; \xi\epsilon\hat{\iota}\nu', \; \dot{a}\gamma\gamma\epsilon\lambda\lambda\epsilon\iota\nu \; \varLambda a\kappa\epsilon\delta a\iota\mu o\nu\acute{\iota}o\iota\varsigma \; \overset{"}{o}\tau\iota \; \tau\hat{\eta}\delta\epsilon$$
$$\kappa\epsilon\acute{\iota}\mu\epsilon\theta a, \; \tau o\hat{\iota}\varsigma \; \kappa\epsilon\acute{\iota}\nu\omega\nu \; \dot{\rho}\acute{\eta}\mu a\sigma\iota \; \pi\epsilon\iota\theta\acute{o}\mu\epsilon\nu o\iota,$$

he might see little in it but a prosaic want of colour. This exceeding simplicity or economy is a stumbling-block to those who are accustomed to the expansive modern manner. Yet such a reader would have been making the acquaintance of some of the finest things in Greek literature, which is always at its best when most simple, and he would have been face to face with a characteristic quality of it.'

Almost exactly the same thing could be said of the student who, fresh from the western European languages, approaches Russian verse for the first time, and in writing on the salient characteristics of Russian poetry, fourteen years ago, in a book called *Landmarks in Russian Literature*, I made the same point about Russian poetry as the two scholars I have quoted make about the poetry of the Greeks. I can but quote what I wrote then, as this broad summary of the main qualities of Russian poetry has been approved by Russian critics, and indeed translated into Russian:

'It is in Russian poetry that the quality of Russian realism is perhaps most clearly made manifest. Any reader familiar with German literature will, I think, agree that if we compare French or English poetry with German poetry, and French and English Romanticism with German Romanticism, we are conscious, in approaching the work of the Germans, of entering into a more sober and more quiet dominion; we leave behind the exuberance of England; 'the purple patches of a Shakespeare, the glowing richness of a Keats, the soaring fancies of a Shelley, the wizard horizons of a Coleridge. We leave behind the splendid sword-play and gleaming decision of the French: the clarions of Corneille, the harps and flutes of Racine, the great many-piped organ of Victor Hugo, the stormy pageants of Musset, the gorgeous lyricism of Flaubert, the jewelled dreams of Gautier, and all the colour and the pomp of the Parnassians. We leave all these things behind, to step into a world of quiet skies, rustling leaves, peaceful meadows, and calm woods, where the birds twitter cheerfully and are answered by the plaintive notes of pipe or reed, or interrupted by the homely melody, sometimes cheerful and sometimes sad, of the wandering fiddler.

'In this country it is true, we have visions and vistas of distant hills and great brooding waters, of starlit nights and magical twilights; in this country, it is also true that we hear the echoes of magic horns, the footfall of the fairies, the tinkling hammers of the sedulous Kobolds, and the champing and the neighing of the steeds of Chivalry. But there is nothing wildly fantastic, nor portentous, unbridled or extreme. When the Germans have wished to express such things, they have done so in their music; they certainly have not done so in their poetry. What they have done in their poetry, and what they have done better than any one else, is to express in the simplest of all words the simplest of all thoughts and feelings. They have spoken of first love, of spring and the flowers, the smiles and tears of children, the dreams of youth and the musings of old age—with a simplicity, a homeliness no writers of any other country have ever excelled. And when they deal with the supernatural, with ghosts, fairies, legends, deeds of prowess or

phantom lovers, there is a quaint homeliness about the recital
of such things, as though they were being told by the fireside in
a cottage, or being sung on the village green to the accompaniment of a hurdy-gurdy. To many Germans the phantasy of
a Shelley or of a Victor Hugo is alien and unpalatable. They
feel as though they were listening to men who are talking too
loud and too wildly, and they merely wish to get away or to
stop their ears. Again, poets like Keats or Gautier often give
them the impression that they are listening to sensuous and
meaningless echoes.

'Now Russian poetry is a step farther on in the same direction. The reader who enters the kingdom of Russian poetry,
after having visited those of France and England, experiences
what he feels in entering the German region, but still more so.
The region of Russian poetry is still more earthly. Even the
mysticism of certain German Romantic writers is alien to it.
The German poetic country is quiet and sober, it is true; but
in its German forests you hear, as I have said, the noise of those
hoofs which are bearing riders to the unknown country. You
have, too, in German literature, allegory and pantheistic
dreams which are foreign to the Russian poetic temperament,
and for this reason unreflected in Russian poetry.

'The Russian poetical temperament and, its expression,
Russian poetry, does not only closely cling to the solid earth,
but it is based on and saturated with sound common sense,
with a curious matter-of-fact quality. And this common sense,
which the greatest Russian poet, Pushkin, is so thoroughly impregnated with, is as foreign to German *Schwärmerei* as it is to
French rhetoric, or the imaginative exuberance of England. In
the Russian poetry of the early part of the nineteenth century,
in spite of the enthusiasm kindled in certain Russian poets by
the romantic scenery of the Caucasus, there is very little feeling
for nature. Nature, in the poetry of Pushkin, is more or less
conventional: almost the only flower mentioned is the rose,
almost the only bird the nightingale. And although certain
Russian poets adopted the paraphernalia and the machinery of
Romanticism (largely owing to the influence of Byron), their
true nature, their fundamental sense, keeps on breaking out.

Moreover, there is an element in Russian Romanticism of passive obedience, of submission to authority, which arises partly from the passive quality in all Russians, and partly from the atmosphere of the age and the political order of the beginning of the nineteenth century. Thus it is that no Russian Romantic poet would have ever tried to reach the dim pinnacles of Shelley's speculative cities, and no Russian Romantic poet would have uttered a wild cry of revolt such as Musset's 'Rolla'. But what the Russian poets did, and what they did in a manner which gives them a unique place in the history of the world's literature, was to extract poetry from the daily life they saw around them, and to express it in forms of incomparable beauty. Russian poetry, like the Russian temperament, is plastic. Plasticity, adaptability, comprehensiveness, are the great qualities of Pushkin. His verse is 'simple, sensuous, and impassioned'; there is nothing indistinct about it, no vague outline and no blurred detail; it is perfectly balanced, and it is this sense of balance and proportion blent with a rooted common sense, which reminds the reader of Greek art when he reads Pushkin, and gives us the impression that the poet is a classic, however much he may have employed the stock-in-trade of Romanticism.

'Meredith says somewhere that the poetry of mortals is their daily prose. It is precisely this kind of poetry, the poetry arising from the incidents of everyday life, which the Russian poets have been successful in transmuting into verse. There is a quality of matter-of-factness in Russian poetry which is unmatched; the same quality exists in Russian folklore and fairy tales; even Russian ghosts, and certainly the Russian devil, have an element of matter-of-factness about them; and the most Romantic of all Russian poets, Lermontov, has certain qualities which remind one more of Thackeray than of Byron or Shelley, who undoubtedly influenced him.'

The passage which I have just quoted is, I repeat, a generalization, and, like all generalizations, it lays stress on one side to the exclusion of others, and it requires modification and qualification; but roughly, broadly, I am told by those Russians whose literary judgement I respect and believe in, that it is true.

It is certainly true of the great poets who heralded the dawn of the new age at the beginning of the nineteenth century in Russia.

III

Krilov's first Fables appeared in 1806, and he went on writing fables till he died in 1844. His earliest fables were translations from La Fontaine. Their success encouraged him to translate others from the French or to adapt from Aesop or other sources, but as time went on he invented fables of his own. At his death he left two hundred fables, of which one hundred and forty are original. His translations are often as successful as his original work, and they are re-creations rather than translations. Krilov was a satirist with a fund of the shrewdest sense—*le gros bon sens*; but, like La Fontaine, he was not only a poet but a poet of nature. His imagery, the machinery of his verse, is conventional; he uses zephyrs, nymphs, gods, and demi-gods, but he breathes a new life into these outworn forms. In speaking of a cornflower he will recall Aristophanes; in his fable of the eagle and the spider he will give you a vista as from an aeroplane, an airscape; and he can evoke the nightingale's song no less magically than Keats. He is a master of the *Volkston* and his fables abound in native proverbial turns of speech, and many of the phrases he himself coined have become part of the Russian language.

Compared with La Fontaine he is a more careless and a less spontaneously finished artist; at times he seems heavy beside the French fabulist, slovenly and even clumsy, but the two poets have many qualities in common, and chiefly that of being popular. Pushkin said Krilov was 'le plus populaire de nos poètes'.

Up to the beginning of the nineteenth century a superstition had reigned in the Russian literary world that the literature of France was the only literature that counted. This superstition was exploded by Zhukovsky (1783–1852). He opened the door on the kingdoms of German and English poetry. He translated Gray's *Elegy* twice—the second version, written after a visit to Stoke Poges, will be found in this book—and the ballads and lyrics of Bürger, Uhland, Hebbel, Schiller, and Goethe. It is no exaggeration to say he is the first and best translator in European literature; he re-created and made his own what he touched, and being a master of technique and a 'lord of language' second only in Russian poetry to Pushkin, he finished the work of attuning the instrument of Russian verse, and made it ready for a poet of genius to take and play upon it and to master its whole gamut.

The moment demanded a man, and the man came. His name was Pushkin. He was born in 1799 at Moscow, of ancient lineage, with a streak of Abyssinian blood on his mother's side. Of all Russian writers both of verse and prose Pushkin is the one whom the Russians admire most. V. Soloviev said he would give the whole of the works of Tolstoy for an unpublished poem of Pushkin. Tourgeniev said there were four lines of the 'Conversation between the Bookseller and the Poet'[1] he would gladly have burnt all his work to have written. Some of his prose works (and his prose has the same excellence and the same qualities as his verse—for his verse is, as a Frenchman said of some one else, 'beau comme de la prose') have been admirably translated by Prosper Mérimée, but his verse is little known outside Russia, because it is untranslatable.

Dr Johnson said we learn foreign languages and dead languages because of their poetry, which we cannot taste without reading them in the original, and it is worth while learning Russian simply for the sake of reading Pushkin.

The fundamental moral characteristic of his genius, of the substance and groundwork of his genius, was his power of understanding. There was nothing which he could not understand. Dostoievsky called him πανάνθρωπος, and it is this capacity for understanding everything and everybody, for

[1] Там, там, где тень, где лист чудесный,
Где льются вечные струи,
Я находил огонь небесный,
Сгорая жаждою любви.

being able to assimilate anything, however alien, that makes him so profoundly Russian. So much for his substance, '*pour le fond*'.

As to his form, his qualities as an artist can be summed up in one word, he is classic. Classic in the same way that the Greeks are classic.

To quote Professor Murray once more, he had something to say and he said it as well and as truly as he could in the suitable style. Suitable, yes, but that is *meiosis*; it is a huge understatement of the case. Supremely appropriate and inevitable would be the more accurate description, and never, as the aesthetic Lady says in Gilbert's *Patience*, 'supremely all-but'. His themes were often romantic, but romanticism to Pushkin was only a means to an end; a mask through which he could try the pitch of his voice and cast aside as soon as he was sure that he had attained it.

Pushkin is remarkable because he combines gifts that are rarely met with in conjunction: the common sense, the reality, the detachment, and the finish of a Miss Austen; the swiftness and masculinity of a Byron; and the form, the lofty form, easy withal and perfectly natural, of a Racine; reaching at times, and should it be necessary, the sublimity of a Milton. When he wants to, Pushkin can 'build lofty rhyme' with the greatest. He is, in a word, the Mozart of poetry: he can be as light as Figaro and as tremendous as the chords of the *Commendatore* or the message of the *Requiem*; and to translate his poems into another language is as hopeless a task as it would be to try to transmute the melodies of Mozart into another medium, into colour or stone. It is for this reason that Pushkin, perhaps more than all other Russian poets, is akin to the Greeks. Pushkin lisped in numbers like Pope; fame came to him as easily as the power of writing verse. His genius met with immediate recognition from his contemporaries, and the new accent which can be heard so distinctly in his early work was instantly acclaimed. When the first of his poems which sought the suffrages of the general public, namely, 'Ruslan and Ludmila', was published in 1820, it was received with enthusiasm by the public, and Pushkin's reputation was definitely sealed. But the

poem itself, although Pushkin borrowed the subject from
Russian folklore, was still an offspring of French influence.
When the second edition was published eight years later,
Pushkin added a prologue to it in his finest manner, which will
be found in this book. In 1820 Pushkin was banished to the
south of Russia. His exile lasted six years, two years of which
were spent on his own estate. This temporary banishment
ripened and matured his genius and provided him with new
subject-matter. He learnt Italian and English, and came under
the influence of André Chénier and Byron. The influence of
Byron is discernible in a long poem, 'The Prisoner of the
Caucasus'. Byron helped Pushkin to emancipate himself from
the influence of France and opened his eyes to a new world, but
the methods of the two poets are radically different, and
Pushkin cannot be said ever to have imitated Byron. Pushkin
derived his inspiration from his own country, which he discovered during his banishment to it. It was during this period
that he wrote some of his finest lyrics, notably the 'Conversation between the Bookseller and the Poet'; also a longer poem
called 'The Gipsies', and his dramatic chronicle, 'Boris
Godunov'. Byron's influence was followed by that of Shakespeare. It was Shakespeare's influence that led Pushkin to try
the historical drama. In 'Boris Godunov' both the tragic and
the poetical scenes and those that depict common life are vivid,
and the characters live, but Pushkin, like Goethe, lacked the
gift of stage architectonics and the optics which are necessary
for successful stage-craft. So his play, though a dramatic poem
of the highest order, is not an acting drama. It was published in
1831 and passed almost unnoticed. In 1828 Pushkin wrote his
'Poltava', of which the subject is Mazeppa and which in reality
is the epic of Peter the Great. In 1831 he finished the eighth
and last canto of his 'Evgenie Oniegin'. This is his best-
known and perhaps his most characteristic work, for, with the
publication of 'Oniegin', Pushkin conquered a new kingdom;
so far he had written the best Russian verse and the best
Russian prose; in writing 'Oniegin' he created the Russian
novel. 'Oniegin' is a story of contemporary life told in verse, a
novel in verse, the first Russian novel and the best. It has the

ease of Byron's 'Don Juan', the reality of Fielding and Miss Austen, and nevertheless, when the situation demands it, it rises and takes on radiance and expresses poetry and passion. It contains one of the great confessions of love in poetry, a performance without parallel because only a Russian could have written it, and of Russians only Pushkin. It has the perspicuity of a crystal sphere, a liquid spontaneity, as of a blackbird's song. Pushkin in his 'Oniegin' succeeded in doing what Shelley urged Byron to do, in creating, that is to say, something new, and in accordance with the spirit of the age. 'Oniegin' has been compared to Byron's 'Don Juan', but the only resemblance between the two poems is that they both deal with contemporary life, and in both poems there are rapid transitions from the grave to the gay and from the lively to the severe, and the author frequently breaks off the narrative to make digressions. 'Oniegin' is an organic whole with a well-constructed plot: a beginning, a middle, and an end, so that it makes an admirable libretto for an opera. In the workmanship, the standard of 'Oniegin' is higher than that of 'Don Juan', for, although Pushkin is just as spontaneous a writer as Byron, he is at the same time an impeccable artist and cannot drop a stitch, strike a false note, or blur an outline. Later on, Pushkin sought the province of Russian folklore and wrote some admirable fairy tales which are as homely as those of Grimm. But throughout his whole career he continued to pour out a stream of lyrics and occasional pieces, many of which are among the most beautiful of his poems. The width of his range is astonishing. Pushkin will sometimes write lines which gave the grace of a Greek epigram, at other times he will write a poem as bitter and as passionate as the most packed of Shakespeare's sonnets, or he will write you an ode blazing with indignant patriotism, or a description of a winter's drive, or an autumn morning, or a lofty prayer, a playful or a tender love poem, a finished Horatian ode, or a lyric as galloping as any of those of Byron. He understood the hearts of all men, and because he understood the hearts of men, of whatever nation and of whatever race, he understood the Russian heart better than any of his countrymen. He loved his people for what they were, and as they were; and he told the story of the soul of his people in the cadence of his words and the lilt of his songs. In his verse you can hear the *troika* circling, blind and bewildered in the blizzard; you can feel the shadow of Peter the Great; you can peer into the crystal of the heart of the Russian woman; you can hear his old nurse crooning the fairy tales that were told when Rurik came over the sea. You can watch in the silence of the night the sleepless soul gazing at the blurred and blotched scroll, the smeared chronicle of its past deeds, powerless with all the tears in the world to wash away the written characters, and you can read in eight short lines an expression of the inexpressible: the declaration of love of all the unhappy lovers in the world. But perhaps the greatest of his short poems is 'The Prophet', and even a rough prose translation gives some idea of the imaginative splendour of the poem, although of course none of the infinite range and suggestion of its sonorous music, none of its perfectly planned and magnificently close utterance. I print this translation here simply in the hope of stimulating in some reader the desire to learn Russian so as to read this poem in the original.

THE PROPHET

'My spirit was weary and I was athirst, and in the dark wilderness I went astray. And a seraph with six wings appeared to me at the crossing of the ways: And he touched my eyelids and his fingers were as soft as sleep: and my prophetic eyes were awakened like those of a startled eagle. And the angel touched my ears and he filled them with noise and with sound: and I heard the Heavens shuddering, and the flight of the angels in the height, and the moving of the beasts under the waters, and the noise of the growing vine in the valley. He bent down over me and he looked upon my lips; and he tore out my sinful tongue, and he took away all idle things and all evil with his right hand, and his right hand was dabbled with blood; and he set there in its stead, between my perished lips, the tongue of a wise serpent. And he clove my breast asunder with a sword, and he plucked out my trembling heart and in my stricken breast he set a live coal of fire. Like a corpse in the desert I lay. Then the voice of God called out and said unto me: "Prophet, arise, and take heed, and hear. Be filled with My Will and go forth over the sea and over the land, and set light with My Word to the hearts of the people."'

Pushkin is Russia's national poet. He emancipated the Russian language from the bondage of the conventional. He is above all things a lyrical poet and a realistic poet. He revealed to the Russians the beauty and charm of their own country, the goodness of their own people, and the beauty of their own folklore. He was a great artist, and fundamentally a classical artist, although he handled romantic themes in a romantic manner at the beginning of his career. He was gifted with divine ease, and, since his expression is inseparable from his thought, his work is, as I have already said, untranslatable. To appreciate Pushkin it is necessary to learn Russian.

Pushkin died comparatively young at the age of thirty-eight in 1837. As Schiller says:

> ' *Nimmer, das glaubt mir,*
> *Erscheinen die Götter—*
> *Nimmer allein.*'

Pushkin's successor was Lermontov, who was born at Moscow in 1814. After a brief, troubled, and unsatisfactory career, in which temporary periods of exile to the Caucasus were the brightest and most profitable events, he was killed in a duel which was fought over a trivial incident in 1841. Lermontov achieved fame through his 'Ode on the Death of Pushkin', in which he struck strong and bitter chords: a note which he was to strike several times, notably in the poem called 'A Thought' and in another which has for subject the transfer of Napoleon's body to Paris. But it is not in such poems that you will find Lermontov at his most characteristic. Lermontov is a romantic poet. He sought out his own path and remained in it. He chose certain themes in his youth and he clung to them. His most widely known poem is 'The Demon', which tells of the love of a demon for a woman. The subject is as romantic as any that might have been chosen by Byron or Moore, but Lermontov's poem is as fresh today as when it was written. The poem contains magnificent descriptions of the Caucasus. He wrote other romantic tales in which he made experiments with his brush and his colours until, in 'Mtsyry' (the Novice), he produced a finished picture. In this tale of a Circassian orphan Lermontov reaches the high-water mark of his descriptive powers. The pages and the lines glow like jewels. Although Lermontov was a romantic—and he felt Byron's influence more deeply than Pushkin—his treatment of romantic themes is that of a realist. Like Pushkin, he is a lyric poet, and profoundly original, subjective, and self-centred. His descriptions—and here Shelley's influence is said to be discernible—however magnificent, are always concrete and sharp; he can be the most unadorned, truthful, and vivid of all Russian poets at times. In fact, he succeeds in writing a poem or presenting a situation without any exaggeration, emphasis, imagery, or metaphor, in the very language of everyday conversation, and at the same time achieving poetry of the highest, most 'inevitable' order. This was Wordsworth's ideal, but whereas Wordsworth constantly relapses into 'poetic diction', Lermontov never does. For instance, Lermontov would never call a spade a 'tool of honour', he would simply call it a spade, and if he wrote a poem about a spade it would be poetical, in spite of the fact, perhaps because of it. Lermontov, again, could never have expressed himself in diction equivalent to a line of Wordsworth's, such as

'Whence comes', said I, 'this piteous moan?'

or addressed a child as follows,

'My child, in Durham do you *dwell*?'

Lermontov would have used the Russian equivalent for *live* instead of *dwell*, and yet he would have achieved poetry. His diction is far more like that of everyday life than that of Wordsworth, and yet his verse is never prosaic.

The best examples of Lermontov's gifts at their finest are,

of his long poems, the 'Song of Tsar Ivan Vasilievich the *Oprichnik* (bodyguardsman) and the Merchant Kalashnikov'; and among his shorter poems, 'The Testament', where a wounded officer gives his last instructions to a friend who is going home on leave, or his account of the battle of Borodino as told by a veteran. His short lyrics, many of which are included in *The Oxford Book of Russian Verse*, every Russian child used to know by heart. A prose translation of 'The Testament' will give an idea of the way in which Lermontov handles a subject:

THE TESTAMENT

'I want to be alone with you, my friend, just for a moment. They say I have not long to live and you will soon be going home on leave. Well, look . . . but why? There is not a soul over there who will be greatly troubled about my fate.

'And yet, if some one were to ask you, whoever it might be, tell them a bullet hit me in the chest and say that I died honourably "for king and country", that our doctors are fools and that I send my best love to the old country.

'My father and my mother you will scarcely find alive, and to tell the truth it would be a pity to make them unhappy, but if one of them should still be living, say that I am bad at writing, that they sent us to the front and that they need not wait for me.

'We had a neighbour . . . as you will remember, I and she—how long ago it is—we said good-bye! She will not ask after me. But no matter, tell her everything, do not spare her empty heart, let her have her cry, tears cost her nothing.'

Lermontov only left behind him one poet: the greatest of Russian folk-poets, Koltsov. There followed in Russian literature an epoch of prose: Gogol, the Westerners and Herzen; and the Slavophils. Among the latter was a poet, the patriot Khomyakov.

Then came the age of the great novelists, Tourgeniev, Gon-
charov, Saltikov (the satirist), Tolstoy, Dostoievsky, and
Leskov. The neglect of verse in Russia lasted right until the
end of the 'seventies, but after a wave of political crisis which
reached its climax with the assassination of Alexander II, reaction and stagnation set in, the poets were rediscovered, and
many who had been quietly singing from the 'sixties onward
were appreciated once more. Among these the most important
is Tyutchev, whose work was unnoticed (except by men of
genius such as Tolstoy and Tourgeniev) until 1854, and met with
no appreciation until a great deal later. He went on living until
1873 and was the greatest poet of his day, which happened to
be the Parnassian period, for in Russia, as in the rest of Europe,
there was a Parnassian period which corresponded to the
epochs of Parnassian poetry in England and France. I am
using the word 'Parnassian' and 'Parnassus' in the widest
sense of the words. In the sense I am using it, it would include
Tennyson (although he wrote political poems and on current
subjects) as well as Rossetti and Swinburne: Verlaine as well
as Leconte de Lisle (Verlaine began by being a Parnassian),
and Sully Prudhomme (although he wrote a great many
didactic poems) as well as Heredia. Tyutchev, for instance,
although his work was first noticed in this period, was not a
Parnassian. He preceded the epoch and might be said to have
affinities with the German Romantic School. He also wrote a
great many political poems. But in the poems of the remaining
writers of the 'fifties and 'sixties, even the works of those who
are most unlike French or English poets, there is a note that
in an undefinable way reminds one of the contemporary verse
of the period of all other European countries, and which is
post-Romantic and 'Parnassian' in quality. It may be objected
that the word *Parnassian* is here a misnomer, and that it is absurd to include in one and the same category poets as widely
different as Sully Prudhomme and Verlaine, Tennyson and
Browning and Swinburne. But it might be remembered that
time throws a startling light on the past, and that under its
mellowing and dissolving influence books and works of art
which at one time seemed so strangely dissimilar, suddenly

seem to belong unmistakably to one given period and become strangely alike. People once cut their throats over the difference between the music of Gluck and Piccini; to our ears it is now difficult to perceive any difference between the 'date' of their respective work; and the time will perhaps come when it will be difficult to detect much difference between the lyrics of Byron, Shelley, and Wordsworth, or even—I admit that this at present seems wildly improbable—between those of writers who appèared to their contemporaries as startlingly different as Browning, Tennyson, and Patmore. However this may be, in Russia there was a Parnassian epoch, and the Russian Parnassians varied perhaps less from one another than those of France and England. The Olympian calm and the serene slopes of the Russian Parnassus were disturbed by a stern and disturbing visitor in the shape of Nekrasov (1821–1877)—a poet of the first rank. Nekrasov sang the life of the people, the peasants' life, with power and with authority and without any idealization. He is not unlike the English poet Crabbe, and, like Crabbe, he has a keen and marvellous eye for landscape, a gift of unsentimental pathos, an uncompromising brush and palette, and a strong transparent sincerity. He reaches at times to imaginative sublimity in his descriptions, especially in his poem called 'The Red-nosed Frost', where King Frost comes to a peasant woman who is at work in the wintry forest and freezes her to death. The passage will be found in this volume.

The best-known of the Parnassians proper are Maikov (1821–1897), Fet (1820–1892), and Polonsky (1820–1898). All three of these began to write in the 'forties: they all three paid great attention to form. All three were typical Parnassians. They had no didactic message and they remained aloof from political and social questions. Of the three, Maikov is the most concrete. He was drawn towards classical themes; Italy and old ballads fascinated him. His verse is plastic and coloured. He paints Russian landscape and evokes reminiscences of childhood in fresh and vivid colours. Fet, on the other hand, lives in another world, he is farther removed from reality. His muse is elusive. His delicate lyrics express the intangible: overtones, echoes, flickering shades, half-tints. His verse is iridescent like a shell with an orient tint, and soft and delicate as a petal of blossom. 'Men che di rose e più che di viole.' He has something in common with the French poet Albert Samain, and something which sometimes reminds one of Verlaine. Indeed his verse observes the canon and fulfils the standard of Verlaine's *Ars poetica*:

> '*Pas la Couleur, rien que la nuance!*
> *Oh! la nuance seule fiance*
> *Le rêve au rêve et la flûte au cor!*'

Polonsky is nearer to the earth; he has a wide range of subjects and his lyrics have sometimes a dramatic quality. His verse is above all things musical and reflects the charm of his personality. Of these three poets he is perhaps, considering the whole of his production, the most remarkable. But in the Parnassian group there is another lyrical poet who is more important than these: Count Alexis Tolstoy (1817–1875). He wrote a noble trilogy of historical plays on the subject of Ivan the Terrible and many beautiful lyrics, Tennysonian in their tenderness but entirely Russian in their 'touch', accent, and naturalness. One of the most characteristic examples of his nature poems and a matchless rendering of Russian landscape is No. 132 in *The Oxford Book of Russian Verse*.

> По гребле неровной и тряской,
> Вдоль мокрых рыбачьих сетей.

> *Through the slush and the ruts of the roadway—*
> *By the side of the dam of the stream;*
> *Where the wet fishing-nets are drying,*
> *The carriage jogs on, and I muse.*

> *I muse and I look at the roadway,*
> *At the damp and the dull grey weather,*
> *At the shelving bank of the lake,*
> *And the far-off smoke of the villages.*

By the dam, with a cheerless face,
Is walking a tattered old Jew.
From the lake, with a splashing of foam,
The waters rush through the weir.

A little boy plays on a pipe,
He has made it out of a reed.
The startled wild-ducks have flown,
And call as they sweep from the lake.

Near the old tumbling-down mill
Some labourers sit on the grass.
An old worn horse in a cart
Is lazily dragging some sacks.

And I know it all, oh! so well,
Though I never have been here before,
The roof there, far away yonder,
And the boy, and the wood, and the weir.

And the mournful voice of the mill,
And the crumbling barn in the field—
I have been here and seen it before,
And forgotten it all long ago.

This very same horse plodded on,
It was dragging the very same sacks;
And under the mouldering mill
The labourers sat on the grass.

And the Jew, with his beard, walked by,
And the weir made just such a noise.
All this has happened before,
Only, I cannot tell when.

But the poem in which he rises to greatest heights is
'Tropar', an imitation of the ἰδιόμελα of St John Damascene,
which is a part of the funeral service of the Eastern Church
blent with other motifs from the same service. Here is a prose
translation of it:

HYMN

'What joy does this life possess that is not mingled with earthly sorrow? What hope is not in vain and where among mortals is there one who is happy? Of all the fruits of our labour and toil there is nothing which shall endure nor anything of any value. Where is the earthly glory that shall remain and pass not away? All things are but ashes, phantom, shadow, and smoke. Everything shall vanish as the dust of a whirlwind; and face to face with death we are unarmed and without defence; the right hand of the mighty is feeble and the commands of kings are as nothing. Receive, O Lord, Thy departed Servant into Thy happy dwelling-place!

'Death, like a furious knight-at-arms encountered me, and like a robber he laid me low; the grave opened its jaws and took away from me all that was alive. Save yourselves, kinsmen and children. I call to you from the grave. Be saved, my brothers, my friends, so that you behold not the flames of hell! Life is a kingdom of vanity, and as we breathe the corruption of death, we wither away like flowers. Why do we toss about in vain? Our thrones are nothing but graves and our palaces but ruins. Receive, O Lord, Thy departed Servant into Thy happy dwelling-place!

'Amidst the heap of rotting bones, who is king or servant or judge or warrior? Who shall deserve the Kingdom of God, and who shall be the outcast and the evil-doer? O brothers, where is the gold and the silver, where are the hosts of servants? Among the forgotten graves who is the rich man and who is the poor man? All is but ashes and smoke, and dust and mould, phantom and shadow and dream; only with Thee in Heaven, O Lord, is there refuge and salvation; all that was once flesh shall disappear and our pomps shall fall in decay. Receive, O Lord, Thy departed Servant into Thy happy dwelling-place!

'And Thou who dost intercede on behalf of us all, Thou the defender of the oppressed; to Thee, most blessed among women, we cry on behalf of our brother who lies here. Pray to Thy Divine Son, pray, O most Immaculate, for him:

that having lived out his life upon earth, he may leave his
sorrow behind him. All things are but ashes, dust and smoke
and shadow. O friends, put not your faith in a phantom!
When, on some sudden day, the corruption of death shall
breathe upon us, we shall perish like wheat, mown down by
the sickle in the cornfields. Receive, O Lord, Thy departed
Servant into Thy happy dwelling-place!

'I follow I know not what path; half in hope and half in
fear I go; my sight is dimmed, my heart has grown chill, my
hearing is faint, my eyelids are closed; I am lying voiceless
and I cannot move, I cannot hear the wailing of the brethren,
and the blue smoke from the censer brings to me no fragrance; yet, until I sleep the eternal sleep, my love shall not
die, and in the name of that love I implore you, O my
brothers, that each one of you may thus call upon God:
"Lord, on that day, when the trumpet shall sound the end of
the world, receive Thy departed Servant into Thy happy
dwelling-place!"'

In the 'eighties, Nadson (1862–1887), who died at the age
of twenty-four of consumption, left behind him a legacy of
verse which enjoyed an almost incredible popularity. His verse
is at times magically musical, but ultra-morbid, super-delicate,
and, to the taste of a later day, mawkish. After Nadson came
the so-called 'Decadent' School, in which the influence of
Shelley, Verlaine, the French Symbolists, and Edgar Allan Poe
made itself felt. This school produced two remarkable poets:
Valery Bryusov and Alexander Blok. The latter, who died in
Russia during the Russian Revolution, started as an exquisite
and ended as a great poet, as will be seen from the extracts quoted
in *The Oxford Book of Russian Verse*. His most famous poem,
and the masterpiece of modern Russian poetry, 'The Twelve',
which is a vision of Bolshevism and amazingly impressive—
especially if one hears it read out—was too long for quotation
in that volume, but it will be seen from a poem called «На поле
Куликовом» (No. 158) how poignant a note he is able to strike.

In spite of the War and the Revolution, perhaps because of
them, Russian poetry has continued and is continuing to

flourish, but as this book was compiled at the beginning of the War, and I have since then had no access to modern Russian literature, I have not attempted, with one exception, to deal with Russian poetry of the present day. Those who wish to get an idea of contemporary Russian verse cannot do better than consult Prince Dmitri Sviatopolk-Mirsky's anthology,[1] *Russkaia Lyrika*, published in Paris, where, among other interesting things, he will become acquainted with the work of a remarkable poetess, Anna Akhmatova.

IV

I have said that Russian poetry resembles Greek poetry in its absence of ornament, its beauty of structure, of rightness and simplicity. Lomonosov, in speaking of the Russian language, said that it possessed the vivacity of French, the strength of German, the softness of Italian, the richness and concision of Greek and Latin. The Russian language in the hands of an artist such as Pushkin reminds one constantly of Greek art. Pushkin's eight lines (No. 33 in the anthology) could only have been written either in Russian or in Greek:

> Я вас любил; любовь еще, быть-может,
> В душе моей угасла не совсем;
> Но пусть она вас больше не тревожит;
> Я не хочу печалить вас ничем.
> Я вас любил безмолвно, безнадежно,
> То робостью, то ревностью томим;
> Я вас любил так искренно, так нежно,
> Как дай вам Бог любимой быть другим.

'I loved you and it may be that my love within my soul has not yet altogether died away; howbeit, it will not trouble you any more, I do not wish to sadden you in any way. I loved you in silence and without hope, worn out now with jealousy and now with shamefastedness; I loved you so truly and so tenderly as may God grant you may be loved by some other one.'

[1] Paris, 'Presse Franco-Russe', 1924. 216, Bd. Raspail.

Pushkin, moreover, at times has the simplicity and the power of evoking a whole picture in one line without ornament or epithet, such as we find only in Homer. For instance, in a speech from his tale, 'The Miserly Knight', there is a line which in Russian is:

И море, где бежали корабли.

(I morye gdye bezhali korabli.)

The literal translation is 'and the sea where the ships were scudding'. The Russian line evokes without a single epithet a whole picture. Swinburne praises Tennyson for what he calls a triumph of evocation and accurate observation in the line:

'and white ships flying on the yellow sea',

but in Tennyson's line there are two epithets. Pushkin achieves a still more vivid picture without mentioning a colour or a shade, by the perfect lilt and appropriateness of his words and his rhythm, and by the movement and accent of the particular verb employed. Although the other Russian poets do not attain to Pushkin's matchless standard, nevertheless in all Russian poetry from Derzhavin down to the poets of the present day, we find the same unique quality of naturalness and sincerity; the same love of realism, that is to say, of reality, the same absence of unnecessary ornament. All these qualities can be said to be Greek in their essentials, but Russian poetry has, in its subject-matter, qualities which are widely different from anything that is to be found in Greek literature, qualities which, in fact, were unknown to the ancients and which only came to the world with Christianity. Russian poetry expresses the Russian soul. The method of expression may be Greek, but the quality expressed is essentially Russian and widely different from anything Greek in its essentials. What it expresses is a spiritual flame, a fraternal sympathy, a great-hearted wisdom—pity, love, an all-embracing charity:

'Infinite passion and the pain
Of finite hearts that yearn.'

Index